Star Trek

The Human Frontier

Michèle Barrett and Duncan Barrett

Routledge
New York

Published in North America in 2001 by
Routledge
29 West 35th Street
New York, NY 10001
www.routledge-ny.com

By arrangement with Polity Press

ISBN 0–415–92981–4
ISBN 0–415–92982–2 (pbk)

Typeset in $10\frac{1}{2}$ on 12 pt Sabon
by Best-set Typesetter Ltd., Hong Kong

Printed in Great Britain by TJ International, Padstow, Cornwall

This book is printed on acid-free paper.

Star Trek

Contents

Preface and Acknowledgements

Beyond the rim of the Starlight
My love is wand'ring in starflight

I know he'll find in star-clustered reaches
Love, strange love a star-woman teaches

I know his journey ends never
His Star Trek will go on forever

But tell him that while he sails his starry sea
Remember, remember me

The original words to the *Star Trek* theme music, these gems were inspired by the need to reduce the royalties owed to Alexander Courage, which fell to only 50 per cent if Gene Roddenberry could claim himself as lyricist (even if such lyrics were never used). It is tempting to read meaning into this little episode: to see it as demonstrating the financial constraints under which Roddenberry struggled to put on his utopian view of a progressive future would be a kind interpretation. On the other hand, Alexander Courage, whose 'Bright Galactic Beguine' is the basis of all *Star Trek* music, was from the outset a victim of dubious business practice. The contradiction is one that has run through *Star Trek* from that day to this: a profoundly progressive and intelligent dream of an egalitarian future, but one that is now part of an immense financial empire that owns and controls what is known in the trade as 'The Franchise'.

This book is about neither the corporate and institutional basis of *Star Trek*, nor the social culture of its famously enthusiastic fans. Background research in these areas has been undertaken (including a trip to the '*Star Trek* Experience' in Las Vegas) but these considerations inform our analysis rather than being the main focus of it. The story of the lyrics is more interesting for what it tells us about how Roddenberry conceived of his idea of space travel. The 'starry sea' applies to space a metaphor of the sea, one so common that it has become 'naturalized' or 'dead'; we no longer even notice it. Maritime exploration and the technological superiority of the ships in which modern western powers 'discovered' and colonized 'new worlds' are themes played on and replayed in *Star Trek*'s imagination of space. For this reason, we have devoted a lengthy first part of this book to an account of this 'nautical metaphor' in the world of *Star Trek*, along with a discussion of the influence of traditional maritime literature on the program. Melville, Conrad, Forester and Verne all feature in our analysis.

The central section of the book examines what is the central preoccupation of *Star Trek*: what does it mean to be human? Although this question has long been out of bounds in critical theory, *Star Trek* and the rest of the population appear to find it extremely interesting. This is the context in which we consider the arguments about colonialism and race in *Star Trek*. The 'discoverers' of the modern globe were exercised about the 'human' status of the peoples they encountered; in *Star Trek* the debate is prosecuted through a vast range of differing life forms, including cybernetic and holographic entities. Questions about humanity and human nature are consistently, even relentlessly, the focus of the varying forms of *Star Trek* from the 1960s to the present. Much attention has been paid to the boyishly cavalier *Original Series* and its high-minded successor *The Next Generation*. The two more recent series of *Star Trek*, however, have developed a radical alternative to the scientific rationalism that was taken for granted in these earlier series. In charting the development of this 'temporal rift' we look at the introduction of religion into *Star Trek*, at the challenge to rationalism presented through mental instability, and at the radically destabilized identities found in *Deep Space Nine* and *Voyager*. These developments mark a very significant distance from the values of *TNG*, whose faith in science and technology, in rationalism and democracy, are characteristic of what we call 'modern' societies. In this sense, the two new series are 'post-modern' in substance and content, as well as in their more obvious visual style, self-referentiality and representational conventions. This analysis forms the basis of Part Three of this book.

The support of many people has been substantial in the writing of this book and we should like to thank them for their contributions, their enthusiasm and their friendship: in publishing the book, John Thompson, Gill Motley, Sue Leigh and Ingrid Grimes at Polity and Bill Germano at Routledge in the United States; Ros Brunt, Dave Machin and Cora Kaplan for their advice on the first draft manuscript, and David Glover for his assistance with this; Alison and David Eldred for their terrific cover; Martin Humphries at the Ronald Grant Archive for his generosity and helpfulness; and Andrew Whittuck for the photography of the authors. From our family, we would like to thank Linda and Johanna King for introducing us to *Star Trek*; Helen Hudson for help with copy-editing; Michael and Kelly Barrett for assisting with our research in the United States; Gilly Furse for her help with American book-shopping. Thanks to François Evans for musical material. Our friends also deserve thanks for their interest, enthusiasm and support – in particular Mary McIntosh, Stuart Hall, Roberta Hamilton and Edward Eldred.

Illustrations

Plates 1–4 and the illustrations on pp. 36, 50, 58, 65, 86, 113, 151, 181, 185, and 194 are reproduced by courtesy of Paramount Pictures, and supplied by the Ronald Grant Archive; those on pp. 3, 4, 56 and 205 are reproduced by courtesy of NASA.

1   *Star Trek* (1966–9) and the films I–VI. From left: Spock, Hikaru Sulu, Pavel Chekov, James Ki
    Montgomery Scott, Leonard McCoy, Uhura

2   *Star Trek: The Next Generation* (1987–94) and the films *Star Trek: Generations*, *Star Trek: First Contact* and *Star Trek: Insurrection*. Back row: Guinan, Beverly Crusher, Worf, Deanna Troi, Wesley Crusher; front row: Geordi LaForge, Jean-Luc Picard, William Riker, Data

3 *Star Trek: Deep Space Nine* (1992–9). Back row: Worf, Julian Bashir,
Odo; middle row: Miles O'Brien, Quark, Kira Nerys; front row: Jadzia Dax,
Benjamin Sisko, Jake Sisko

4 *Star Trek: Voyager* (1995–). Back row: Harry Kim, the Doctor, Tuvok, Neelix; middle row: Chakotay, Tom Paris; front row: Seven of Nine, Kathryn Janeway, B'Elanna Torres

For I dipt in to the future, far as human eye could see,
Saw the Vision of the world, and all the wonder that would be:

Saw the heavens fill with commerce, argosies of magic sails,
Pilots of the purple twilight, drooping down with costly bales;

Heard the heavens fill with shouting, and there rain'd a ghastly dew
From the nations' airy navies grappling in the central blue;

Far along the world-wide whisper of the south-wind rushing warm,
With the standards of the peoples plunging thro' the thunder storm;

Till the war-drum throbb'd no longer, and the battle-flags were furl'd
In the Parliament of man, the Federation of the world.

from *Locksley Hall* (1842)
Alfred, Lord Tennyson.

Introduction: Earthrise

Star Trek is a set of elaborately interwoven stories about space travel; for many people this fictional universe has acquired the status of a modern myth. Paradoxically, although this fiction appears to be about looking outside ourselves – attempting to go beyond human boundaries – it is more concerned with looking back at the earth, at ourselves, than it is in going elsewhere. This voyage out is, also, a voyage in.

Space travel, at the beginning of the twenty-first century, is at a curious moment. On the one hand, it has become almost domesticated. It is estimated that by 2017 you will be able to check into an orbiting space hotel, a hybrid between a theme park and a cruise ship, for your annual holiday. Already, bookings are being taken for commercial space flights of a modest kind.[1] So the idea itself of space travel is one that is becoming more of a reality for those with the money to contemplate joining in. On the other hand, it has lost much of its earlier excitement. The stalling of the space programmes of the 1960s and 1970s, and their jumpy restarting after the end of the Cold War, has left a sense of *ennui* and *déjà vu*. The search for life beyond our planet is not looking very encouraging so far, although the SETI project has proved surprisingly popular worldwide.[2] Exo-biologists sound implausibly excited about the remote possibility that a tiny microbe might once have existed somewhere; the distances for us to get any further are so vast as to lead to a feeling of defeat. Space has become more tame to us now – more realistic and less romantic than it was before. *Star Trek*, on the other hand, offers us a continuing drama that has lost none of its pace, however much it has moved and changed – as we shall argue that it has – with the times.

One image that best evokes the meaning of both space travel and the imaginative world of *Star Trek* is the photograph of the earth as seen from space. This was identified in a television series as one of the 'pictures that changed the world' and, indeed, it has changed the way in which we view the earth. The first version of the picture was taken, more or less accidentally, from the 1968 Apollo 8 flight to the moon. William Anders, taking photographs of the surface of the moon for scientific purposes, suddenly realized that if he turned round he could capture the sight of the earth rising against the lunar landscape. This first image, subsequently entitled *Earthrise Seen for the First Time by Human Eyes*, has had a mesmeric effect. Now, of course, there are many such images – it is a view that we have become used to. There is no doubt, however, that the sight of our planet as seen from outside – from a vantage point that (almost) none of us has experienced – has changed our perception of it. From space, the human factor is missing; we do not see the people, we see the physical landmasses and oceans, the swirling clouds and atmospheric features. This view of the earth reminds people that this is a physical planet for which we are responsible – it typically humbles human grandiosity. Also, the image is silent. It is as if the noise and din of humanity has gone, leaving space for contemplation, for a sense of history and cosmology. Finally, the image allows us to think about humanity, to some extent at least, from outside – an effect that renders it as troubling to some as it has proved exciting for others.

For over three decades this image has retained the power to attract and compel people. At a recent exhibition of lunar photography ('Full Moon: Apollo Mission Photographs of the Lunar Landscape', Hayward Gallery, London, 1999) it was noticeable that, although we were supposed to be engrossed by the photos of the moon, in fact there was always a knot of far more enthusiastic people at the small section devoted to *Earthrise* and other images of the earth. So popular are these that NASA has set up a website to make this 'national treasure' available to the public. A data set of 'astronaut acquired imagery of Earth' (http://earth.jsc.nasa.gov) enables you to examine specific cities and regions, or to view weather systems and so on. One of the main features of the space hotel will be that it will have a viewing deck from which guests can watch planet earth as they go round.

The image of earth as seen from space is used in significant ways in *Star Trek*. Jean-Luc Picard, the captain of the *Next Generation* series, has an *Earthrise*-style picture on his wall, which is glimpsed

Earthrise

at opportune moments. The image has a particular function in *Star Trek*, exemplified in the 1996 film, *First Contact*. In this film, a young woman from the twenty-first century, displaced on to the twenty-fourth-century *Enterprise*, has cornered the captain with one of his own weapons. How to show her where she is? How to make her understand what is happening? How to explain the reality of space travel? Picard walks her across to the window and makes her look out at earth as seen from space, daring her to jump if she doubts that it is real. It induces wonder, and understanding; it encapsulates the (supposed) reality of travel in time and space. In fact, the move is one that can be used to explain these realities to the representatives of any culture that is not as yet space-literate. Many episodes of *The Next Generation* do exactly the same thing with ('primitive') non-human cultures when they want to make them understand about

Earth from space

space travel: they beam them into the *Enterprise*, walk them over to the window, and point out at their planet, which they always recognize and gasp at. Being able to see your own home world from space is a dominant trope of space travel. It is important not simply because it stands in for the fictional technical accomplishment of space travel; it represents something that is philosophically more complex – the ability to detach human existence from the planet earth.

It was this that severely upset the existentialist philosopher Martin Heidegger. Towards the end of his life he gave an interview to the magazine *Der Spiegel*, on the understanding that it was not to be published until after his death. This was because it concerned the question of his collaboration with the Nazis and he was attempting to reduce his notoriety in his own lifetime. Interestingly, he made a comment relating specifically to the late sixties, when the interview was done, about the new photographs of the earth coming back from the moon. His response was that he found them 'frightening', because the project of men in space was one that reduced humanity to technology. Humanity, in his view, really *belonged* only on the earth. He said that 'everything essential and everything great originated from the fact that man had a home and was rooted in a tradition'.[3] This view is typically a conservative one, that fears the intellectual consequences of displacing the pre-eminence of one's culture. (Heidegger seems to be adopting an intellectual stance equivalent to that of pre-Copernican astronomy.) Space travel, exemplified by the image of the earth as seen from space, has the effect of problematizing the status of humanity. As we shall see, in *Star Trek* this does not mean abandoning a central focus on the question of what humanity means. On the contrary, the issue becomes more and more crucial – we have to travel further and further to find out who we 'really' are.

Space travel is the contemporary equivalent of the exploration that underpinned what we now call 'modern' societies. This exploration was, of course, the foundation of the colonial nature of these modern western societies. But the exploration of the globe, historically paralleling the scientific revolution in understanding the place of the earth in the solar system, was in itself a very important development. When we look at modern and early modern exploration, it is important to emphasize that this was an exploration based on sea-power. Space travel in *Star Trek* is an imaginative transposition of the period of early modern nautical exploration. The extent to which the models, assumptions, techniques, culture, aesthetics and principles of sailing have been written into space travel is surprising. One feature of this book is a 'reading' of *Star Trek* in terms of what we call the 'nautical metaphor'. The naval exploration of the globe was a crucial element in the historical development of what we now call modernity. The exploration of space can be seen to function in an analogous way; whereas the conquest of the seas allowed the western powers to define their superiority through other cultures, so the exploration of space allows for a definition of that which is specifically human. Stuart Hall has expressed this in terms of 'the rest' of the world acting as the 'constitutive outside' of 'the west' – the west was only able to define itself by means of a contrast with its inferiorized others.[4] Space, we may say, functions metaphorically as the 'constitutive outside' of the project to define humanity. That such an enterprise should have trouble – as we shall see – negotiating the dangerous reefs of colonialism is hardly surprising.

In this book we interpret *Star Trek* in a historical, cultural context. Much of its preoccupation lies in the nexus of questions around what we might shorthand as 'modernity' and 'humanism'. This is particularly obvious in the ideas and culture elaborated in the series *Star Trek: The Next Generation*. But, as many readers will know, *Star Trek* is a larger phenomenon. So far, it comprises four major television series: *Star Trek: The Original Series* (TOS), 1966–9, with Captain Kirk and Mr Spock; *Star Trek: The Next Generation* (TNG), 1987–94, starring Patrick Stewart as Jean-Luc Picard; *Star Trek: Deep Space Nine* (DS9), 1992–9, with Avery Brooks as Benjamin

Sisko; and *Star Trek: Voyager* (*Voy*), 1995– , with Kate Mulgrew as Captain Kathryn Janeway. There have been nine *Star Trek* feature films, some more successful than others. There was also an animated TV series. The volume of *Star Trek* peripheral merchandizing is legendary. *Star Trek* is a very large cultural and economic player. However, in the course of its development it has changed considerably. The modern rationalism that reached its peak in *TNG* has been dramatically challenged in the narrative structure and assumptions of the two most recent series. In this book we look first at what can be said to preoccupy *Star Trek* constantly – the question of what it means to be human is one that is relentlessly probed from 1966 to the present. Later we look at what is so different about *DS9* and *Voyager*, and we suggest that these show the characteristic features of a popular form that is 'post-modern' in form and substance.

Part I

The Starry Sea

The original idea for *Star Trek* was pitched as 'wagon train to the stars', and this reference to the western frontier continued to resonate for many years. It was also described as 'Hornblower in space', according to one of the leading scriptwriters,[1] but this nautical forerunner has been paid rather less attention. The mission statement was 'to explore strange new worlds'. The idea was to project on to the backdrop of space a thoroughly modern drive for scientific exploration and a push for the extension of peace and democracy. The original series of *Star Trek*, and perhaps even more so the second series (*TNG*), can be seen to encode the core values of 'modern' culture. 'Modernity' is a description of a particular type of social order whose characteristics can be sketched out as follows.

Modern societies are based on the ideal of democracy rather than the imposition of authority from those who were born to rule. Modern societies respect the rights of the individuals within them. They reject the arbitrary demands of religion, favouring science and reason as the basis of belief. This amounts to a *secular humanism*, that privileges the individual as the centre of action and meaning. The historical development of these societies went hand in hand with the maritime exploration of the Atlantic, Pacific and Indian Oceans, with a division of the spoils of conquest. At a social level, these societies are also characterized by a detailed and sophisticated division of labour (involving highly specialized skills), and by the expansion of the market as the key economic mechanism.

It is impossible to understand the universe of *Star Trek* without seeing it in the context of the American ideals of democracy and individual rights, and a secular faith in science and technology. Gene Roddenberry's conception of the series was based on those values. In fact, the idea of setting the series in space, and 300 years into the future, was explicitly directed at these goals. The inclusion of ethnic minorities, and women, as part of the command structure of the *Enterprise*, was not thought possible for popular TV in the 1960s – but it was thought acceptable if projected far into future time.

At the risk of sounding simplistic, there is much that is good in these values. Individual rights are better than tyranny, secular humanism is better than religious intolerance. In so far as *Star Trek* has been a solid ambassador for these values, we should respect it for that. America's Peace Corps may have been naïve and patronizing in its assumptions, but on any scale of real political evil it would come fairly low down the list. It is perhaps necessary to make this rather elementary point, if only to put in context some of the more alarming judgements of practitioners in the often spiky academic debates about *Star Trek*. The editors of one collection say that 'while pretending to be politically progressive . . . *Star Trek* maintains an oppressive political system'.[2] How a popular entertainment franchise has either the power to reproduce capitalism and colonialism, or the motivation and agency to be pretending to do something else, remains rather lightly addressed.

If we step round these rather heavy-handed responses to the politics of *Star Trek*, we can identify the issues rather differently. On a number of points we might note that the values of 'modernity' have been open to challenge. In the first place, there is the obvious issue of colonialism. In what follows we compare the imaginative exploration of space in *Star Trek* with some of the literature linked to maritime exploration on earth. Nowhere is the offensively racist aspect of the colonial project more troublingly evoked than in the novels of Joseph Conrad (1857–1924), the prime narrator of sea-power fiction. In Conrad, as indeed in *Star Trek*, there is a constant focus on the question of 'what does it mean to be human?' The presence of racism in the literature of exploration and colonization is both pervasive and significant. Later in the book, we shall return to the question of race, and the charge of racism, in *Star Trek*. For the moment, we want simply to signal the need to look at colonialism, if a pun is acceptable, as the 'darker side' of modernity.

If Conrad's work speaks to the debate about colonialism and racism in maritime fiction, there is another writer whose novels of the sea provide a pertinent critical commentary of the modern rationalism of *Star Trek*: Herman Melville (1819–91). This is a connection that *Star Trek* itself has made: the film *First Contact* has a crucial turning point when Picard is forced to realize that his crusade against the Borg has become as irrational and self-destructive as Captain Ahab's against *Moby Dick*. As we shall see, the relentless rationalism of the *TNG* series of *Star Trek* is dramatically rejected in the two most recent series, *DS9* and *Voyager*.

The values of the 'modern' societies that ushered in democracy and individualism were, as many feminists have now pointed out, masculine in character. *Star Trek* is a fascinating laboratory for the examination of changing attitudes to this question. In 1966, Roddenberry's attempt to cast his future wife as the second-in-command of the *Enterprise* foundered on the prejudices of the TV networks: a woman simply could not hold this position. Mrs Majel Barrett Roddenberry was severely demoted and given the role of Nurse Chapel, whose main personality marker was that she had a hopeless crush on Mr Spock. ('She was kind of a loser,' the actress points out.) From this less than auspicious beginning, *Star Trek* has progressed to the point where the current series (*Voyager*) has a female captain. So few prece-

dents for this exist that we can find no reference-points in the literature of modern exploration. Captain Janeway's situation resembles
nothing in eighteenth- or nineteenth-century fiction; certainly none of
the maritime literature brings us any parallels. If anything, what
comes to mind in Janeway's long voyage home is the saga of
Odysseus. Even here, there is only a limited parallel, as several of the
years it took Odysseus to navigate his way back from Troy to Ithaca
were spent in the arms of the seductress Calypso. There is not a lot
of sex on *Voyager*, and certainly almost none for its captain.

A central aspect of modern societies, and one of enormous rele-
vance to the way in which *Star Trek* functions, is what we now call
'time/space compression'. More accurately, *Star Trek* returns us to
the geopolitics of a world system *before* time/space became so compressed. This is why the idea was first pitched as 'Hornblower in
space'. The key point is that a captain of the *Enterprise* has no means
of communicating with his base on earth. He is the ultimate representative, his personal authority and decision-making is final. C. S.
Forester's *Hornblower* novels are enjoying something of a revival at
present: often the scripts of *Star Trek* resemble them in spirit. Gene
Roddenberry has explained that Captain Kirk was partly modelled
on Hornblower.[3]

The values of modernity are examined and challenged, as well as
selectively endorsed, in *Star Trek*. Central to its vision are questions
of democracy and power, of the rights of individuals (and of peoples).
Star Trek's history itself takes us through changing perceptions of
rationalism, of gender, and of the meaning of human identity. The
question of what constitutes human identity and human nature is
perhaps the most persistently asked in all the *Star Trek* series. Before
examining this in detail, we want to open up the parallel between
Star Trek's imaginative exploration of space and the imaginative
literature of the exploration of the sea. This earlier literature offers
a compelling reference-point from which to read the fictionalizing
of space.

The nautical legacy

It is worth emphasizing the scale of *Star Trek*'s borrowing from the
nautical lexicon. *Star Voyage* might have been a better title for the
whole thing. The vehicles are star *ships*, part of a star *fleet*. The senior
officers on board ships are *captains, commanders, lieutenants. Admirals* tend to be solidly at starbases or fleet command. The much-used

'number one', the captain's first officer, is based on the role of the 'first mate'. Meals are eaten in the *mess hall*, casualties are dealt with in a *sick bay*. Prisoners are put in the *brig*. The ship is navigated, using a *conn* and giving orders to a *helm*, from a superstructure known as the *bridge*. To turn around you give the order to *bring us about* (from 'going about': to change tack in a sailing ship). Records and diaries are not kept, but the *captain's log* and personal logs are. Star ships do not park or land, they *dock* and when they need repairs they have them in *drydock*. Space ships have *port* and *starboard*, they have *bows* and *sterns*, they have *fore* and *aft*. *Quarters* is a naval term, as are *vessels* and *torpedoes*, *shore leave* and *battle stations*. On a ship you *hail* an approaching vessel, store your *cargo* and remark the arrival of the *captain on the bridge*. Expressions used in *Star Trek* – such as 'Make it so!' and 'godspeed' are from naval use. (Though Janeway's 'Do it!' is not to be found in the nautical dictionary.) The nautical metaphor in *Star Trek* is so naturalized that it is a technically 'dead' metaphor: we simply do not notice it any more.

Some of *Star Trek*'s vocabulary is slightly adapted from the original. The *captain's yacht* would have been the captain's *barge*; the *away team* is clearly a *landing party*; *shuttles* have the same function as *launches* and so on. Yellow and Red Alert have the warning function of 'clear for action'. It is perhaps worth pointing out that many expressions in common English usage have a sailing provenance – to change tack, clear the decks, or be in the doldrums, for instance. But the usage in *Star Trek* goes far beyond this. The NCC prefixing the various *Enterprise* ships, stands for 'Naval Construction Contract'. The attraction of 'the age of sail' is felt very strongly by some key figures in the various series of *Star Trek*. In 'Explorers', Benjamin Sisko makes a 'solar sailor' to reproduce the experience of sailing from ancient Bajor. Tom Paris is depicted as passionate about sailing, and thwarted by his father from taking it up as a career; the episode 'Thirty Days' concerns his attempt to turn a space shuttle into a submarine. Picard has a model of a sailing ship among the indexical objects in his 'ready room'. Some episodes have nautical titles, such as 'Tacking into the Wind' or 'Rocks and Shoals'.

A trawl through the nautical dictionary[4] is the best way to learn the meaning of many of the technical terms used in *Star Trek*. Some that appear to be invented for the phenomena of space are a revisit of older nautical expressions. The name of the ebullient 'Q' has several histories: one being the 'Q' Ship – a trick used in the 1914–18 War, when a British naval crew would take over and arm a merchant ship in order to decoy German submarines into gun range. The term 'warp' has an even odder history. In *Star Trek*, 'warp drive' is the mechanism that enables all significant space travel – it is the ability to travel faster than the speed of light, by means of bending space/time. In the *Star Trek* reference system,[5] it was invented in the year 2061 by Zefram Cochrane, hence the measurement of warp speed is in units known as Cochranes. A more recent development is the invention of a 'trans-warp drive', which enables warp speeds to go beyond the previous limit of warp 10.[6] Acquainted with this vocabulary, it is surprising to read, in maritime fiction set in the period of the Napoleonic Wars, descriptions of sailing ships 'warping' out of the harbour. 'Warp' in the nautical sense is a means of propulsion that is very slow indeed – to 'warp' is to move a ship by hauling on a cable to which it has been attached; to pull it along by the sheer physical effort of a human crew. Obviously, there is a great deal of present and future technical vocabulary (much of it invented for the purpose) in *Star Trek*; however, the basic principles of its lexicon are not merely nautical, but specifically drawn from the age of exploration and conflict by sailing ship ('the age of fighting sail', as it is often referred to).

The naval historian Peter Padfield, in his book *Maritime Supremacy and the Opening of the Western Mind*, has put forward an argument that might help us to explain why this moment of earth history should be so significant to *Star Trek*. Padfield frames a detailed analysis of key naval battles, from 1588 to 1782, in a general theory about the nature and character of maritime as opposed to land-based powers.[7] He considers the supremacy first of the Dutch, then of the English and, lastly, of the Americans, all of whom developed maritime empires. His interpretation is that maritime culture itself encourages a particularly flexible view of the world. Padfield suggests that while powers that rule on land tend towards centralization and rigidity, those that rule the seas tend towards liberty and enterprise.

Padfield's first case is the earliest of the maritime empires of modern western society: the seventeenth-century Dutch. He argues that the Dutch came to dominate the most lucrative of the world's trades, enabling them to develop a culture famed not only for its wealth, but for its humanist thinkers, arts, and a constitution where power was diffused. In the eighteenth century their pre-eminence gave way to that of the British. On the one hand, maritime supremacy has to be understood in terms of technical improvements – the aim was to develop ships that functioned as floating castles. They had speed, but also a formidable armament that made them invincible to attack. Until superseded by the American clipper design, the square-rigged, three-masted British ships of war were the basis of naval control of the oceans. This went hand in hand with a philosophy of liberty very different from the autocracy – both of the Bourbon monarchy and Napoleon – that held sway on the other side of the channel. London was the centre of trade, but also of humanist philosophy and secular rationalism. Padfield locates philosophy and literature as key centres of this rising freedom of expression, the cultural coeval of maritime success.

The young United States of America – taking over from Britain the baton of the race for maritime supremacy – at length tackled its own most obvious abuse of freedom: slavery. Padfield makes the argument that it was the 'navigating' individuals, the Federalists of the seaport cities, whose concerns with freedom came to be entrenched in the constitution of 1788. 'So the liberalizing inspirations of the great trading cities of the United provinces, transferred to England under William of Orange and spread under the shelter of British trading and naval supremacy to the North American colonies, were inscribed in the constitution of the infant United States of America.'[8] The American belief in 'freedom' was the sovereign value; it went inconsistently hand in hand with the ruthless exploitation of the slave and indigenous populations in parts of the country. Padfield concludes that British naval supremacy sheltered not only the building of the British empire but also the expansion of American colonization westwards by land, and globally through the development of the American merchant marine, 'spreading its sails in every sea'.[9] The parallel with the United Federation of Planets is clear. We have a metaphor of technological supremacy, where space occupies the position of the sea. We have a humanist, secular and democratic impetus, to be admired in comparison with the violence and autocracy with which it frequently conflicts. Michael Adas has examined the relationship between technology and colonial power. The advantage of technology applied strongly to the early maritime explorers: 'sailing ships with superior maneuverability and armament permitted the Europeans to explore, trade, and conquer all around the world'.[10] When they arrived, the 'discoverers' of these strange new worlds used technology to assert their own authority, and the lack of obvious technology among the indigenous peoples led to the inference that they had no interest in controlling the world in which they lived. There is a link between exploration, technological superiority and the definition of human progress – at least, in the view of the colonizers: 'the capacity to master the natural world through scientific investigation and application of machine power was a vital source of optimism regarding the human condition'.[11]

Melville's influence: from the *Pequod* to Picard

We have already mentioned *Star Trek*'s cinematic nod in the direction of Melville. The author of a popular American epic, it is perhaps not surprising that the iconic figure of Herman Melville is significant for *Star Trek*. It turns out that Melville himself explains for us an important phrase in *Star Trek* – the captain's order 'Make it so!'. This is favoured by Captain Jean-Luc Picard of the *TNG* series, and is most frequently used to bring into effect a suggestion made by someone else. 'Make It So!' is a hallmark of the weighty, Shakespearean-trained British actor, Patrick Stewart, who plays Picard. It has proved so successful that it has been taken as the title of a popular manual on how to be a successful leader in business: *Make It So: Leadership Lessons from Star Trek: The Next Generation*.[12] According to Melville, the expression originates in the conventions in which the absolute authority of a ship's captain extends even to ascertaining the time: 'He is lord and master of the sun.' Melville paints an amusing picture in which the sailing-master, whose job is to observe these things, touches his hat and reports 'twelve o'clock' to the officer on deck, who then charges a midshipman to go to the captain and 'humbly inform him of the respectful suggestion of the sailing-master'.

> 'Twelve o'clock reported, sir,' says the middy.
> '*Make* it so,' replies the captain.
> And the bell is struck eight by the messenger-boy, and twelve o'clock it is.[13]

In this instance it might be thought sensible for the captain to take some control of when 12 noon ('eight bells' in the nautical watch system) was deemed to have arrived – in the British Navy it was the signal for the long-awaited daily ration of rum ('Spirits Up!') and in the American Navy it presaged dinner-time for the hands. But the more general point stands: the captain's authority was total. Melville's novel *White-Jacket* is an account of a voyage he made in 1843–4 as an ordinary seaman on the US Navy man-of-war the *United States*. This ship, renamed for literary purposes the *Neversink*, provides the basis for a detailed description of life at sea in this type of vessel, as well as an indictment of the brutality of naval discipline. The book examines the consequences of a system in which despotic power was a structural element. The point is that in these ships, the captain represents not merely the authority of the nation, he actually *is* that authority. These ships were out of touch with any superior authority and therefore, as Melville put it 'a ship is a bit of terra firma cut off from the main; it is a state in itself; and the captain is its king'.[14]

It is important to stress that the model here is one where time and space have not been 'compressed', as yet, through modern systems of transport and – most especially – communication. The out-of-touchness of the main players is crucial. In the *Hornblower* stories, there are frequent examples of the significance of this fact. In one instance, the unfortunate Hornblower overpowers an enemy ship, only to find that in the months he has been at sea a diplomatic change has occurred and the enemy in question is now an ally.[15] One of the early *Star Trek* scriptwriters, David Gerrold, explains how directly they saw the parallel between this earlier period of independent naval authority and the leader of the *Enterprise*:

> The situation of this interstellar society is almost exactly analogous to the Earth of the eighteenth century. . . . Because communications were so slow, an ambassador could be a particularly important individual. He was the arm and authority of his government. He was its voice. He was the man who determined and enacted the policies of his nation with regard to his specific area of authority.

Gerrold continues:

> Likewise, the Captain of the *Enterprise* must be just such an ambassador. . . . Carefully briefed as to Starfleet's goals and policies, it will be his responsibility to interpret them and act in the wide variety of situations he will confront. He is a piece of Starfleet itself.[16]

'A bit of terra firma', 'a piece of Starfleet': when out of range of communications, the captain of a ship has an authority that is sovereign. It is this that underlies the parallel between a sea captain with the oceans to command and a space captain with the galaxy to explore. In the account by Melville in *White-Jacket*, we see the negative consequences of this authority, when taken to the level of despotism within the ship itself. Melville's story deals with the issues of mutiny, and of flogging. On the *Neversink*, these are all part and parcel of the captain's disposition towards arbitrary authoritarianism. The issues relate to each other, as what is at stake is the men's response to a petty and malign order from the captain that, just as they are nearing home, they shave their heads as well as remove the beards they have cultivated for the entire voyage. The ensuing mutiny is suppressed, with the exception of one intransigent old man, who is in the end flogged for his disobedience. The descriptions of flogging ('scourging') in *White-Jacket* focus on three symbolic instances. One case has already been mentioned – the frail old man who on a point of honour refuses to surrender his beard and is given twelve lashes (a very light sentence). He says afterwards ''tis no dishonour when he who would dishonour you, only dishonours himself'.[17]

A second discussion, which Melville says he has 'to painfully nerve myself' to discuss, is the practice by which courts martial could sentence a man to a sentence lesser than death but from which he might well die, such was its brutality: 'flogging through the fleet'. This practice, following the British Navy's example, functioned as a non-capital response to serious charges of disobedience to orders, or to cowardice. It involved the imposition of a huge numbers of lashes – perhaps 500 or 1,000 strokes, or more. It was compulsory for the entire crew of a ship to witness all floggings; the purpose of a flogging through the fleet was to display the spectacle to an even larger audience. The man was first flogged by his own crew-mates, then taken round and flogged on or in the sight of the various ships in the squadron. As Melville points out, this was never done in home waters, for the outrage it would cause if seen by non-naval personnel. (This style of punishment is described by Foucault as 'exemplary public torture'; he argues that it was waning in popularity by this period.[18]) The man so punished, if he survived, would usually be crippled for life.

In these circumstances, it is irrelevant how trivial an order the disobedience involved, or what cause for cowardice there may have been. In one of the last Hornblower novels, a nineteen-year-old cornet player in the band is court-martialled for refusing to play the B flat on his music sheet – he thought it should be a B natural and could not bring himself to play the wrong note. For this disobedience to orders, for which the court was obliged to find him guilty, the available punishments were death or flogging round the fleet. Reinforcing the point made earlier about the absolute nature of the power of a ship's commander, Hornblower has no escape from the decision (according to the Navy, anyway). When asked if the bandsman cannot appeal, he replies, 'In home waters he could. But I am a Commander-in-Chief in a foreign station, and from my decision there is no appeal.'[19]

The third case of flogging dealt with in *White-Jacket* raises the issue of race. The captain capriciously orders the flogging of two men for fighting – he has stitched them up as he often gets them to head-butt each other for his own entertainment. The two men are black.

In this passage the narrative relationship between Melville the liberal and critical author and the character 'White-Jacket' (metonymically named from his jacket) becomes complex, and self-aware:

> Poor mulatto! Thought I, one of an oppressed race, they degrade you like a hound. Thank God! I am a white. Yet I had seen whites also scourged; for, black or white, all my shipmates were liable to that. Still, there is something in us, somehow, that, in the most degraded condition, we snatch at a chance to deceive ourselves into a fancied superiority to others, whom we suppose lower in the scale than ourselves.[20]

Very soon after this, however, 'White-Jacket' is himself 'arraigned at the mast' for a misdemeanour he was unaware of having committed. He escapes the flogging the captain had ordered. Do we see here a recognition of 'fancied superiority' as everyday racist attitudes, or an outcome that draws attention to the structural privilege of the white sailor? The whole episode serves to racialize the degrading practice of flogging, but in a complex and troubling way.

It has been suggested that what is going on here is a displacement of one anxiety on to another – that the ostensible source of concern may be flogging, but the deeper and less tractable problem is that of slavery. Flogging is being regarded as dehumanizing: it amounts to treating men as animals. Slavery is precisely defined by its refusal of human rights and freedoms. Tony Tanner points out that Melville's attack on flogging comes just at the point that flogging in the American Navy was being abolished anyway – the argument had been won. But the issue of slavery, and whether it should be abolished, was far from consensual: it was growing a bigger source of conflict every year. On this issue, Melville shows the ambivalence and contradiction of even a progressive liberal of this period. As Tanner puts it, 'this is not to suggest that within Melville's rightly famous democratic and humane heart there lingered traces of a toxic racism, but rather that this work of 1849 contains within it some of the crucial tensions, ambivalences, and contradictions that were to tear the nation to pieces little more than a decade later'.[21]

Star Trek offers a mode of discipline that has been devised in explicit opposition to the history of the extreme brutality of the British and American navies. Punishment in Starfleet is very humane, the equivalent of being sent to your room for some quiet reflection on the error of your ways. The occasion when Tom Paris is put in solitary confinement for thirty days is very unusual in terms of disciplinary protocols.[22] Serious infractions are dealt with by demotion of rank and/or court martial. The naval tradition of flogging has not been entirely forgotten though. The conditions on board *Voyager* provide the nearest equivalent to the discipline problems of a man-of-war on a long voyage. With no end in sight to their journey, the balance between morale and discipline is hard to strike. At one point Captain Janeway (suffering from alien-induced stress, it turns out), rounds on Tuvok as head of security and tells him he must beef up discipline and 'straighten out' all his section commanders. His laconic reply of 'Shall I flog them as well?' is enough to make her realize she needs a vacation.[23]

Melville's *White-Jacket* is fascinating in terms of the nautical theme that links *Star Trek* to the historical literature of American maritime supremacy. The *Neversink* and the *Enterprise* – in spite of fundamental differences of tone and values – have some things in common. What does the image of a ship call forth? As Paul Gilroy has put it, a ship is a 'living, micro-cultural, micro-political system in motion'.[24] These two ships share their isolation, their systems of rank, a 'multicultural' crew, and an existence that the compression of time and space has made alien to us on earth in the twenty-first century. They differ, quite obviously, in many key aspects of their social and political values. As we shall see, the issues of race, of colonialism and of slavery, haunt the world of *Star Trek* – in some respects comparably to the representation of these evils in the maritime literature of the nineteenth century. The *Neversink* offers a critical evocation of naval life in all its brutality. It raises, as does *Star Trek*, some basic questions about the definition of humanity and human rights. But it is Melville's *Moby Dick* (1851), a canonical text of American fiction and culture, that takes us to the more complicated issue of the character of rationalism in what we call 'modern' society.

In this book we trace the rise of the representation of 'modern rationalism' to a high point in *Star Trek: The Next Generation*. We argue that the two later series, *DS9* and *Voyager* (and the film *First Contact*) make a decisive move away from modern rationalism, incorporating both religious belief and irrationality – even insanity – into their frame of reference. The parallel that is drawn in *First Contact* between Captain Picard and the deranged Captain Ahab in *Moby Dick* is the best place to start to consider the influence of this iconic sea-going novel on the world of *Star Trek*. *Moby Dick* may be one of those books that is much referred to, while not necessarily read – the digressions being longer than the story. The book reflects Melville's experience working on whaling ships in 1841–2 (he deserted one and left another as a mutineer, so this was clearly a formative experience). The narrator opens the book rather guardedly with 'Call me Ishmael': Ishmael turns out to be the only survivor of a voyage led by Captain Ahab. They set off on what is apparently a commercial whaling trip in the *Pequod*, but Ahab's obsession with a huge white sperm whale becomes, it is clear, the reason for the voyage. Ahab had lost a leg to this whale on an earlier voyage, to which his first reaction had been a delirious, raving craziness that caused his shipmates to tie him up in a strait-jacket for their mutual safety. Repressing his insane level of rage, he harboured his ambition for revenge under a more normal demeanour. Ahab determined to find *Moby Dick* again and kill him – at whatever cost. The cost – and for nothing – turned out to be not only his own life, but that of his crew and the destruction of the ship too.

Ahab has not only lost a leg to the whale; he has lost his reason: 'his torn body and gashed soul bled into one another; and so interfusing, made him mad'.[25] He moves into a register of psychic disaster, in which everything is subordinated to his ungovernable need for revenge. Blind and self-destructive revenge as the motivation for irrational action has also been written into *Star Trek*. Usually, there is little sympathy for the avenger, but in the case of *First Contact*, it is – more interestingly, perhaps – a trope that is written around the hero, Captain Picard. He, too, has a torn body and a gashed soul to deal with, from an earlier encounter with the Borg. Picard is taken over by the Borg as a spokesman for them – he is renamed 'Locutus of Borg' (*locutus* is the Latin for 'having spoken'). His assimilation involves bodily mutilation: 'I had their cybernetic devices implanted throughout my body', he later recalls. As Locutus, he had supplied the Borg with information from Starfleet that, we are subsequently told, directly resulted in the death of 11,000 of his own people, and the destruction of thirty-nine ships. Picard's body has been torn and his soul gashed; he plans to resign. In *First Contact* an explicit argument about *Moby Dick* dominates a key segment of the film. But Melville's book figures as an influence on the film in a much more general way. The Borg, like the whale, are presented as a force in nature, as supernatural, as something that only the captain really understands. Both captains abandon their real missions. For both, this decision is shown to be destructive; murderous rage ensues.

Like Ahab, Picard is at first seen as being particularly well placed for the task at hand. Riker tells him that 'your experience makes you the best man' [to fight the Borg]. Melville writes that on Nantucket, 'far from distrusting his fitness for another whaling voyage, on account of such dark symptoms, the calculating people of that prudent isle were inclined to harbor the conceit, that for those very reasons he was all the better qualified and set on edge, for a pursuit so full of rage and wildness as the bloody hunt of whales'.[26] The task for both is ostensibly reasonable, but in terms of its real psychic meaning it is insane. 'Now, in his heart, Ahab had some glimpse of this, namely: all my means are sane, my motive and my object mad.'[27]

Picard's explicit confrontation with the Ahab inside him is brought about by Lily Sloane. He has been acting against the wishes of his crew; in particular he has fallen out with the (normally battle-hungry) Klingon security chief Worf over his refusal to destroy the *Enterprise* and take the Borg down with it. He orders his men to 'stand their ground' in suicidal fashion, to 'fight hand to hand' against the over-powering technology of the enemy. The crew's position is clear: the only rational solution is to 'blow up the damn ship' and escape to a remote island, but Picard's rage stops him from seeing this. He simply cannot face affording the Borg this victory over his ship – 'we have made too many sacrifices already', he explains. But Lily, beamed aboard Picard's twenty-fourth-century *Enterprise* from the primitive times of twenty-first-century earth, functions as the voice of reason amid his chaotic emotion. Lily accuses him of wanting revenge, of enjoying killing the Borg. To his smug claim that 'in my century we don't succumb to revenge', she says 'Bullshit!'. Picard becomes so angry that he smashes the glass cases in the conference room where this stand-off is taking place. They contain models of spaceships and sailing ships. As they lie broken, the camera lingers on the smashed model of the *Enterprise D* – this is the one that has won our affection over the course of the *TNG* series, the one where children are on board. Picard has destroyed his own ideal. Lily laconically observes, 'You broke your little ships. See you around, Ahab.'

It is only when he destroys his own beautiful models that Picard sees where his madness is leading them all. In smashing the ships, he is symbolically destroying not only his own ship but the entire culture of rational exploration and enlightened governance that Starfleet stands for. It shows us how selfish he has become – to satisfy his own desire for revenge he is prepared to watch over the death of all his crew. He is willing to sacrifice them (even to assimilation by the Borg, which he regards as worse than death), in pursuit of his personal 'mad object'. For Picard, the vendetta is not purely personal, as it is for Ahab. The *Enterprise* represents humanity. Picard says: 'we have not lost the *Enterprise*; we are not going to lose the *Enterprise* . . . not to the Borg.' To lose the *Enterprise*, even if this meant saving the crew and destroying the Borg, would be giving in. It would be allowing the Borg to take from him his personal symbol of humanity.

The Borg are the antithesis of humanity, and represent a refutation of the ethical dimension of reason. Their subordination of every goal and value to finding the most 'efficient' means of doing something is a debased and mechanical variant of modern rationalism. Finding an efficient solution to a technical problem takes priority over ethical considerations.[28] Like Ahab again, their means are sane, however mad we may find their object. The Borg are described, when encountered by *Voyager*, as like a force in nature.[29] *Moby Dick* has much to say about the whale as symbolizing nature, and everything against which humanity struggles. But as nature is associated with the divine, Ahab's crusade (like that of the Ancient Mariner) is not only insane but courts the charge of blasphemy. At least, there is a misperception of the whale as the embodiment of all evil. It is this that, at a very dramatic point in the film, leads Picard to quote directly (as he thinks) from Melville: 'he piled upon the whale's white hump the sum of all the rage and hate felt by his whole race'.[30]

Verne and vengeance

Ahab's revenge is personal. Picard's claims to be on behalf of human-ity. A common resonance for the *Moby Dick* motif is the quest for vengeance for the death of others, typically a wife and children. The vengeful villain is often the man who claims our sympathy for the murder of his family. The enigmatic and threatening figure of Captain Nemo, inventor, owner and autocratic captain of the submarine *Nautilus* in Jules Verne's *Twenty Thousand Leagues Under the Sea* (orig-inally published in 1869), is an ideal type of this man. It is only towards the end of the book that we discover that he is driven by 'a monstrous or sublime hatred that time could not quench'.[31] As he prepares to sink a large two-decker warship, Nemo declares that he represents 'right and justice'. The ship must be destroyed, because 'It is through it that all that I loved, cherished and venerated – country, wife, children, father and mother – all perished!'[32] Nemo's motiva-tion is left somewhat oblique. Ostensibly, he is driven by patriotism. He visits the sacred burial ground of a ship – the 'glorious wreck' of the appropriately named *Vengeur*. We are told that this ship had sunk, to the cry of '*Vive La République!*', rather than surrender. Nemo, however, sinks the ship of an enemy (whose nationality is never specified) in a distinctly dishonourable way: by using the *Nautilus* as an underwater ram, he simply holes the ship below the water-line, where she is unprotected. This is not even a clean fight, still less glorious warfare: it is mass murder. The steel ram of the *Nautilus* went through the wooden ship 'like a needle through sailcloth'. The real emotional force of Nemo's driving passion for revenge is, we discover, familial. Described as 'that terrible avenger, a perfect archangel of hatred', Nemo turns back from the slaughter to his room, the narrator (Professor Aronnax) following: 'I saw the portrait of a woman still young, and two little children. Captain Nemo looked at them for a few moments, held out his arms to them, and, kneeling down, burst into sobs.'[33]

If Melville gives us the theme of personal vengeance, Jules Verne – sometimes known as 'the father of science fiction' – gives this the specific inflection of the grief-mad husband and father. In the increasingly 'intertextual' forms of *Star Trek* that are now being produced, we find ironic allusions to (and even jokes about) the legacy of these nineteenth-century classics of literature about the sea. Picard's quotation from *Moby Dick* in *First Contact* is deadly serious, as is the Melvillian treatment of revenge in the second *Star Trek* film, *The Wrath of Khan*. In some more recent episodes of *Voyager*, however, the literary trope of vengeance is mercilessly sent up. In 'Year of Hell', it turns out that all *Voyager*'s terrible troubles are being caused by a Krenim leader who has a time machine. Officially, he is entrusted with the task of the restoration of the Krenim empire, but in fact he has a more personal agenda. His wife and children have been killed and he is trying to restore a timeline in which the particular colony they had lived in ('Kiana Prime') would survive. To this end he is subjecting his crew to appalling sacrifices (they have been suspended in time for hundreds of years and by now their loved ones are dead), to the point where in the end a young man refuses to co-operate further with this monomaniac. Tom Paris and Chakotay have been taken prisoner and are on board the Krenim vessel. The leader, in a pun that glancingly takes in the geeks of cyber-culture as well as Professor Aronnax of the *Nautilus*, rejoices in the name of Anorax; Tom Paris – more accurately – simply refers to him as 'Captain Nemo out there'.

A later *Voyager* episode reprises this theme, in relation both to Melville and Verne. The main storyline concerns a huge organic being that represents itself as a wormhole through which the ship can get back to earth from the Delta Quadrant, where they are stuck. In fact, it thrives on a diet of spaceships (it eats anti-matter) and is luring them into its capacious stomach. Knocking around in its innards (like the Jonah much referred to in *Moby Dick*), *Voyager* makes an alliance with a ramshackle fellow called Katai who is in there seeking to avenge the meal this organism made of his wife and family. He has spent nearly forty years (thirty-nine years, two weeks and four days, he says) getting back into it and trying to destroy the thing from the inside. As *Voyager* heads off with relief, they fail to persuade him to let them help him. They leave him preparing for another bout of his pathologically repetitious behaviour. Katai is impressed with the doctor's range of skills and suggests that perhaps he might join him in this project. 'An Ishmael to your Ahab? No thank you,' is the reply he gets.

Much of what we examine here under the rubric of the 'nautical metaphor' concerns the great age of sailing. In particular, the fighting ships of the Napoleonic Wars are a point of constant resonance and reference. In a rather different way, there is an interesting parallel between the existential experience of space – the shock of reflection upon a world that we see from the outside – and the experience of the underwater medium that we find in the Jules Verne story. In *Twenty Thousand Leagues* there are passages far more striking than those addressing the themes of politics and vengeance: they concern the startling experience of existence in an impossible environment for human beings: water. Professor Aronnax is a scientist and when he is effectively kidnapped on board the *Nautilus* he finds much to wonder at in Nemo's collections of treasures from the oceans of the world. But the greatest sources of wonder are reserved for the moments of indescribable existential shock.

Verne invests with a great sense of drama their first sight of the submarine universe. In fact, the staging is not unlike the image with which we began – the sight of the earth from space. (Except, of course, that in this case it is drawn entirely from the imagination.) The impression is that of a mixture of astonishment and recognition. The moment when they first see where they are is very dramatic – panels in the wall of the saloon are slid back and panes of glass illuminated:

> The sea was distinctly visible for a mile round the *Nautilus*. What a spectacle! What pen could describe it? Who could paint the effect of the light through those transparent sheets of water, and the softness of its successive gradations from the lower to the upper beds of the ocean.
> ... Lost in wonder, we stood before these windows, and none of us had broken this silence of astonishment . . .[34]

Aronnax subsequently describes the submarine equivalent of man's first space walk. First we hear of the 'impervious dress' that is worn, the metal helmet for the head, the 'pumps and regulators' providing air to breathe. The physical protection required, and the need to provide oxygen, are of course shared by sea and space. Of the actual walk on the sea-bed he says that 'words are powerless to describe such marvels'. The marine environment is represented in a way that is to some extent analogous to space; 'The solar rays easily pierced this watery mass and dissipated its colour. . . . The water around me only appeared a sort of air, denser than the terrestrial atmosphere, but nearly as transparent.'[35] And, just as *Star Trek* posits the colonization of space, Captain Nemo dreams of a human population on the ocean floor: 'I could conceive the foundation of nautical towns, agglomerations of submarine houses, . . . independent cities!'[36]

'Mongrel' mariners

The vessel created by Verne forecasts an important – and extremely contentious – aspect of the fiction set in space. The crew of the *Nautilus* speak 'an incomprehensible language'; it is one that Captain Nemo has imposed upon them. Only towards the end does Aronnax discover – in a gruesome manner – that one of them is in fact, like him, a Frenchman. This poor sailor is the victim of a giant squid and in his dying call for help he reverts to the '*à moi*' (to me, to me) of his mother tongue. Aronnax reflects that the crew is a 'mysterious association, evidently composed of individuals of different nationalities'.[37] The *Nautilus* is not alone in this. As we shall see, the multiracial, multinational (we might now say 'multicultural') composition of the fictional crews of both sailing-ships and spaceships is the source of much highly politicized discussion. This was an important aspect of Melville's nautical imagination. The *Pequod* in *Moby Dick* has been described as 'inherently international' by one critic:[38] 'Melville wants the whole world in . . . a Gayhead Indian, a Negro, a Polynesian, a bunch of Parsees, as well as a Maltese, a Tahitian, an Icelander, a Chinaman, a Dane, and so on.' One of Melville's descriptions of the crew of *Moby Dick* provided C. L. R. James with a good book-title: 'mariners, renegades and castaways'.[39] Another gives an even clearer indication of the *Pequod's* complement; he says the crew is 'chiefly made up of mongrel renegades, and castaways, and cannibals'.[40]

Melville devotes an entire chapter of *Moby Dick* to a philosophical rumination around the question of 'the whiteness of the whale'. He is at pains to disentangle that which is appalling in the whale's whiteness from what 'we' – as it were – normally think of as the superior qualities of whiteness. In this context he says (of the colour white itself) that 'this pre-eminence in it applies to the human race itself, giving the white man ideal mastership over every dusky tribe'.[41] In a later chapter of this book we shall return to the semiotics of whiteness and colour in analysing race in *Star Trek*. At the moment we want to draw attention to the treatment of one particular character: Queequeg. In *Moby Dick* we are told he hails from 'Rokovoco' in the southern seas. In some limited respects, Queequeg is a model for Commander Chakotay in *Voyager*. Chakotay, presented in terms of his indigenous American heritage,[42] insists on his cultural integrity and refuses to adhere to the usual Starfleet belief system. He follows his 'animal guide', ritually incants 'far from the bones of my fathers', goes on spiritual quests and so on; Queequeg, too, resists the cultural practices of his ship. They also share the element of an impressive facial tattoo. An early source refers to him as a 'native American "Queequog" [*sic*] person whose people have renounced Earth and live as expatriates on another planet'.[43] Perhaps a more obvious reference to Queequeg, however, is found in Worf, in *The Next Generation*. As a human-reared Klingon he is often seen as an outsider, but, like Queequeg, he has some aspects of the 'gentle giant'. His unusual cultural beliefs often cause amusement to the crew but he is accepted as a worthy and loyal officer. While Queequeg hurls harpoons at oncoming whales, Worf is the master of his ship's photon torpedoes. When thought to be dying Queequeg is very upset at the prospect of a burial at sea. He is particularly appalled at the idea of being sewn up in his hammock – a nautical custom described in detail in *White-Jacket* (as in many other sea narratives). Surprisingly, Queequeg is offered the ship's carpenter to make him a wooden coffin. This undertaking goes so well that it is almost presented as a factor in his recovery. Eventually the redundant coffin is recycled as a ship's buoy – much to the annoyance of the carpenter, who has to remake and seal it.

The tale of Queequeg is told in an odd register – it is reasonably benign, but at pains to categorize him as both alien (or other) and somehow other-worldly. Ishmael is surprisingly tolerant of Queequeg's cultural practices, though he views them as slightly odd: 'I cherish the greatest respect towards everybody's religious organisations, never mind how comical.' For his new friend's sake he even accompanies him in idol-worshipping. This respectful attitude to other cultures is exactly the sort of behaviour a good Starfleet officer engages in. Queequeg is described, with irony, as a 'cannibal' and his manifestly gentle and friendly demeanour is made apparent. Ishmael is initially horrified to hear that he will be sharing a bed with someone 'engaged in such a cannibal business as selling the heads of dead idolaters', but this common myth of 'the other' is quickly exposed. The Nantucketers' view of Queequeg calls to mind the little boy who asks Worf in fascination, 'Is it true you can kill someone just by looking at them?'[44] Queequeg thus functions as both 'the other' within human society and also, at least to some, as an 'other-worldly' signifier pointing beyond that boundary.

Conrad's colonial horror

Conrad is the one figure who is regarded as the premier 'writer of the sea' and it is to his work that we now turn. What is the influence of this colossus of maritime literature on the nautical imagination that runs through the heart of *Star Trek*? The legacy is a difficult one because it is around Conrad's work that the most heated controversy about racism and literature in recent years has emerged. The reasons are not hard to spot. Let us look first at what is sometimes claimed as the greatest English sea novel: *The Nigger of the 'Narcissus'*. Yes, this really is a story about a black man and a ship called the *Narcissus*. The book was written and published in 1897; to some extent this contextualizes the language of the title (the first American edition was published under the title *The Children of the Sea*). The book describes a voyage from Bombay to London. The voyage itself is eventful, with an appalling storm that almost wrecks the ship. Narrative, however, is subordinated to a depiction of the enigmatic presence of the eponymous character James Wait. At embarkation he is greeted with more than hostile racism; he is perceived solely through a negative reading of his colour. His very appearance causes the ship's cook to say: 'I thought I had seen the devil.'[45] Wait is indeed enigmatic, principally in that he is ill but it is not clear how ill he is. Like Queequeg, there is an implication that he is able to control whether he will die (that he can choose to die) or not. In any case, he spends most of the voyage sequestered from the rest of the crew – for part of the time because he has defined himself as too ill to work, for the latter part of the voyage because the captain refuses to allow him to redefine himself as now well enough to work. In the event, James Wait dies just as the ship, which has been becalmed, picks up the wind that will enable it to complete its journey.

Interpretation of Conrad's 'position' is difficult. It may be overdue to remind ourselves again that these are novels we are discussing – and that novels are not political manifestos, nor even primarily organized along an axis of truth and error. Novels are works of the imagination; they are fictions. *The Nigger of the 'Narcissus'* is indeed the very novel for which Conrad wrote a celebrated preface in which he aligns fiction with 'temperament', rather than 'persuasion'. 'All art, therefore, appeals primarily to the senses, and the artistic aim when expressing itself in written words must also make its appeal through the senses, if its high desire is to reach the secret spring of responsive emotions.'[46] Conrad's own conclusion might lead us away from shock at some of the explicit racism uttered in the text, and towards a more complex analysis of what our *felt* response might be. In this book there is no narrator, nor protagonist, that can be simply identified with the author. There is no figure in this book that can be held to represent Conrad's own views. What we have is a balance of two tendencies in the text. The first is the articulation of a quite open and appallingly racist mode of perception. Wait is described as having 'a face pathetic and brutal: the tragic, the mysterious, the repulsive mask of a nigger's soul'.[47] His eyes are given to rolling widely and showing their whites. As he lies at the point of death, he is described through what we can easily recognize as very unsympathetic racial codes: 'Wait shook his head; rolled his eyes; he denied, cursed, threatened – and not a word had the strength to pass beyond the sorrowful pout of those black lips. It was incomprehensible and disturbing: a gibberish of emotions, a frantic dumb show of speech pleading for impossible things, promising a shadowy vengeance.'[48]

One tendency of this text is to fix James Wait in a vocabulary drawn directly from an extreme anti-black point of view. On the other hand, Conrad creates a situation in which the reader's sympathy is quite unequivocally on Wait's side, by casting him as the victim of a particularly offensive crime. In the last seconds of life, he is robbed by Donkin. To take a key from under the pillow of a man in the process of dying, raid his money box and return the key is a peculiarly unpleasant exploitation of the most vulnerable moment of a person's life. Jacques Berthoud comments that 'the viciousness of this deed has been felt by every reader'.[49] 'Felt' is precisely the right word: the novel makes us feel appalled on James Wait's behalf, notwithstanding the way he has been pejoratively racialized in the text. Berthoud suggests that in this regard Conrad is able to expose the cocktail of seamen's rights and xenophobia that Donkin represents as a precursor of fascist *ressentiment* rather than the solidarity of the oppressed – and he concludes that Conrad is more 'politically prescient' than is often thought.[50]

Perhaps most tangibly present in this novel is the representation of James Wait as alien. In an obvious sense, this is done directly through the issue of race: Wait is the racial 'other' against which the predominantly white crew (it includes a Russian Finn and two Norwegians) define themselves. More interestingly, perhaps, Wait is an object (literally) on to which others project superstition, the irrational, the *un*-natural. He therefore houses that which modern rationalism – science, technology, exploration – cannot accommodate. As we shall see, the cracks in the patina of rationalism explored in Conrad's fiction lead us from the apotheosis to the collapse of this model in the imaginative world of space fiction. Nowhere is the phenomenon of the supernatural more powerful than in the description of Wait's burial. Like Queequeg, James Wait has been appalled when brutally reminded by Donkin that his corpse will soon be tipped overboard. In the event, the occasion is tense and horrifying, as his body refuses to ship out. It is compulsory in British and American maritime fiction to have a description of burial at sea – as it was compulsory for the whole crew to attend them.

The idea of burial at sea has a considerable literary presence. Perhaps the most well known is Byron's romantic address to the ocean ('Roll on, thou deep and dark blue Ocean – roll!'), where he describes the phenomenon '. . . like a drop of rain / He sinks into thy depths with bubbling groan, / Without a grave, unknell'd, uncoffin'd and unknown'.[51] Funerals in space, are closely based on nautical precedent. Spock's funeral, for instance, in the second *Star Trek* film, gives us the perfect iconography of a naval burial transposed on to space. A black casket is ejected through a port into space, its departure prefaced by a ceremony in which the dead officer's colleagues stand in an honour guard to the accompaniment of bagpipes.

At sea, the sailmaker was summoned to sew up the dead sailor in his hammock; weights were put at his feet. In naval tradition these are cannonballs; in the merchant marine whatever hardware might be to hand. The body is put on a bier of two planks nailed together, with the feet positioned at a porthole. The captain reads the order of service for a burial at sea and when he gets to the words 'commend to the deep', the head end of the planks is lifted up and the body slides out ('splash!' as Donkin callously put it the day before), sinking immediately. In the case of James Wait there is a hitch – they heave the end of the plank as high as they can reach and the body simply will not move, defying gravity. It turns out later that the carpenter had left a nail sticking out of the wood and the boatswain had forgotten the usual trick of the trade – a dab of grease on the planks. 'The chap was nothing but trouble . . .' they say, 'from the moment he came aboard.'[52]

At the time of the burial the atmosphere is extremely tense. James Wait's only friend, Belfast, intervenes dramatically. His words are remarkable: 'Jimmy, be a man! . . . Go! . . . Go, Jimmy! – Jimmy, go! Go!' As he touches the corpse, it shoots off 'with the suddenness of a flash of lightning'. The predominant emotion is fear. Jimmy 'won't go' because of fear; the lifting party are stammering; the men are 'profoundly disturbed'; the reader of the prayers is 'perspiring abundantly'.[53] The exhortation to Jimmy to 'be a man' is double-edged; he must be a less cowardly man and face up to death, but he is also being addressed as if – now immortal – he were still alive. High tension and superstition both inform what happens next. The wind suddenly arrives, the sails fill, the ship rushes before a freshening gale. Superstition is rampant – it is Wait's departure that has made their progress possible. James Wait houses not only the alien, the 'other' of a racialized world, he embodies the irrational, the supernatural, that lurks at the borders of the orderly world of the ship.

At various points the question is raised as to what kind of man James Wait is. In Conrad there is a continuing exploration of the question of what constitutes humanity. Although, as we shall see, this takes offensive forms in regard to race, it is an important point of comparison with the questions central to *Star Trek*. The crucial point of difference can be simply identified: *Star Trek* uses alien species, non-humans (albeit organic, cybernetic or whatever) to ask questions about how humanity is to be defined. Conrad asks questions about the definition of humanity, but he does it by comparing humans of different races. He is enquiring whether 'savages' are to be thought of as human at all. Curiously to us now, this was done from the point of view of rejecting the hard and fast line between colonizers and the colonized 'savages'. So certainly one may say that Conrad was asking questions that problematized the imperialist and racist assumptions of his time. The history of western colonization is also a history of racialized discussion about what constituted humanity. Slavery is predicated upon an assumption that human rights are not universal; that some people are not 'human' in the full sense. *Star Trek* involves an elaborate discussion of these issues, mainly through the device of projecting human differences on to fictional species in space. There is much critical debate about whether or not this avoids the charge of racism. Nevertheless, the fact that there is such a preoccupation in *Star Trek* with questions of race and humanity is an important link to the literature of modern exploration on earth. Exploration, by sea or in space, provokes these questions.

The most discussed version of Conrad's treatment of these issues is the novella *Heart of Darkness*. This story dates from 1899 and draws heavily on Conrad's experiences working for a Belgian ivory trading company, in the Congo, in 1890. He did not spend long there, as he became ill and was invalided out. While in the Congo he made one significant journey up the Congo River to the settlement of Stanley Falls, by means of a tiny steamboat – the *Roi des Belges*. On the return journey one of the company's agents (Klein, the model for Kurtz) died of fever and they buried him. This experience was to be the basis of a most extraordinary piece of writing, in which unease, menace, corruption and sickness all loom very large. He claimed that it was 'experience pushed a little (and only very little) beyond the actual facts of the case'. His intention was as follows: 'That sombre theme had to be given a sinister resonance, a tonality of its own, a continued vibration that, I hoped, would hang in the air and dwell on the ear after the last note had been struck.'[54] This turns out to be a very modest account of its effect on the reader. One striking aspect of *Heart of Darkness* is how difficult it is to shake off the very unpleasant atmosphere and mood that it generates.

One wonders what Conrad would have made of the fact that there is now available a painstakingly assembled record of the empirical experience underlying this most atmospheric of texts. It is indeed strange – such is Conrad's fame – that people have gone and found the very old lady who remembered the day, seventy-eight years previously, that Klein was buried by the banks of the Congo River. There is even a photograph of the grave of Georges Klein, engraved headstone and all; Conrad's only comment in *Heart of Darkness* is: 'I am of course aware that next day the pilgrims buried something in a muddy hole.'[55] We have a photograph of the steamer captain who was murdered and whose place Conrad took, photographs of Stanley Falls at the time, contemporary records of negotiations about ivory, photographs of the individual agents described in the novella, even a photograph of the *Roi des Belges* itself.[56] Rightly or wrongly, the existence of this factual archive makes it more difficult to ignore Conrad's authorial presence in *Heart of Darkness*, whose voice is ostensibly that of the narrator Marlow.

Heart of Darkness is a troubling account of a period of shocking colonial exploitation. The reiterated and much-requoted phrase 'The horror! The horror!' carries a plurality of meanings. Certainly, it is important to stress the extent to which the book springs from Conrad's own horror at his experience, and his appalled account of the greed and brutality of the colonizers. He described what happened in the Congo as 'the vilest scramble for loot that ever disfigured the history of human conscience'.[57] It is also useful to point to the passage at the beginning, in which Marlow imagines the experience of a young Roman soldier during the invasion of Britain, appalled by the 'utter savagery' that had closed round him. There can be no doubt that much of Conrad's own motivation was the desire to evoke the complex horror of colonial predation in its worst form. On the other hand, the book articulates rather than criticizes a form of racism, as opposed to colonialization, in the ways in which the Africans in the book are dehumanized (as James Wait had been). The indigenous inhabitants of the Congo are presented to us quite simply as savages, who are likely to kill whites. Much is made of the threat of cannibalism. The question that Conrad asks is about the definition of human nature. A key passage in the novella is introduced by Marlow's description of a sighting of a settlement of what he calls 'prehistoric man': 'a whirl of black limbs, a mass of hands clapping, of feet stamping, of bodies swaying, of eyes rolling, under the droop of heavy and motionless foliage'. Marlow is both wise enough and manly enough to see that these savages are also human. Unlike his small-minded colleagues, he can accept the tiniest identification with them. The passage is significant enough to quote in full:

> It was unearthly, and the men were –. No, they were not inhuman. Well, you know, that was the worst of it – this suspicion of their not being inhuman. It would come slowly to one. They howled and leaped, and spun, and made horrid faces; but what thrilled you was just the thought of their humanity – like yours – the thought of your remote kinship with this wild and passionate uproar. Ugly. Yes, it was ugly enough; but if you were man enough you would admit to yourself that there was in you just the faintest trace of a response to the terrible frankness of the noise, a dim suspicion of there being a meaning in it which you – you so remote from the night of first ages – could comprehend. And why not? The mind of man is capable of anything – because everything is in it, all the past as well as all the future. What was there after all? Joy, fear, sorrow, devotion, valour, rage – who can tell? – but truth – truth stripped of its cloak of time. Let the fool gape and shudder – the man knows, and can look on without a wink.[58]

Conrad's *Heart of Darkness* has become a notorious war zone for the politics of textual reading. In 1975 the writer Chinua Achebe changed the ground rules of critical discussion of Conrad, arguing that he was a 'thoroughgoing racist'.[59] For our purposes here, the relevant core of Achebe's argument is contained in two points: that the reduction of Africa to a mere backdrop for the torment of one European mind is preposterous; and secondly, that the novel fosters and celebrates a 'dehumanization' of Africans. Achebe rightly refers to the 'agonies and atrocities' that have flowed from the kind of prejudices and insults paraded in the book. He regards it as an 'offensive and deplorable' book – 'a story in which the very humanity of black people is called into question'.[60] In this, Achebe is undoubtedly right – notwithstanding the efforts of many subsequent critics to emphasize instead the extent to which *Heart of Darkness* excoriates the white colonialists. To say that the text was critical in respect of imperialism – as indeed was the author – is not the central point. Nor, really, is the issue of how much Conrad himself is expressing his views through those of his narrator, Marlow. It might be worth noting, however, the comment of a reporter who met Conrad around 1907 and observed: 'He dislikes certain broad types of people virulently, and says so in a downright fashion. At such times he sloughs off his elaborately courteous demeanour he reveals himself as a man of devastating force of character. He grows fierce, passionate, violent . . . triumphant and obliterating and sweeping away his carefully calculated suavity of speech.'[61] As Chinua Achebe put it: 'Irrational love and irrational hate jostling together in the heart of that talented, tormented man'.[62]

Conrad is *the* maritime novelist, the 'writer of the sea' *par excellence*. It is no coincidence that these chronicles of ocean travel should have triggered such an explosive argument about racism, colonialism, and what we would now call 'cultural difference'. In Conrad's case, the issue is whether the 'nigger' of the Narcissus (to reverse the quotation marks) and the 'savages' of the Congo are part of humanity. In this, there is a reprise of the debates generated by earlier explorers as to whether the indigenous peoples 'discovered' should be regarded as human beings or not. *Heart of Darkness* is the inspiration for the Vietnam War film *Apocalypse Now*. The shared imagery used in the depiction of colonial violence, the expression of dehumanization, is striking. There is nothing in *Star Trek* in the register of either of these brutal and bleak stories. Colonial and patronizing tendencies it may have, but those who accuse it of racism might usefully look at this earlier literature to get a bearing on the scale of the crime.

The physicality of sea and space

Before leaving Conrad, there is one further point to consider, and it is precisely raised by the 'nautical' question. It concerns the role of the sea, and the question may also be asked of space: is it a player itself, or simply the backdrop? Conrad himself, as Jacques Berthoud explains, felt this distinction strongly. He preferred to write about sail rather than steam not because it was more romantic, but because his knowledge of how to relate to the action of the sea came from sailing, and thus he was able to make it more of a player in his fiction. He disliked the popular novels of Marryat, in which the sea was merely a background for the antics of midshipmen, preferring those of Fenimore Cooper, where the sea 'interpenetrates with life'.[63] Conrad, even more than Melville before him, brought to maritime fiction a detailed knowledge of the operation of the sea. Conrad joined the French Merchant Navy at the age of seventeen, and obtained his British Master's certificate twelve years later; he spent twenty years mainly at sea before retiring to become a writer. Novels set at sea vary in respect of whether they engage with the sea itself as a factor, or simply use it as a *mise-en-scène*. For example, a comparison between C. S. Forester's *Hornblower* tales, and the sequence of Patrick O'Brian novels about Aubrey and Maturin will reveal that every detail of naval activity is shared, but that the behaviour of the sea itself is only a significant element in *Hornblower*. To say that the sea is a player in the text is not to impute any motivation or agency to the sea, nor to endow it with supernatural qualities – although, of course, this has been done many times (perhaps the most famous example being Coleridge's 'Rime of the Ancient Mariner'). Rather, it is to see the water as something other than a blank and flat space: it is to pay attention to actual and predicted wind direction and force, currents, squalls and other such phenomena.

We can look at this question initially by considering a very frivolous example. It is a little-known fact that the idea of a 'wormhole' in space, one of the most striking of the phenomena of space and much used in fiction about space travel, was actually invented by none other than Herman Melville. *Moby Dick* gives a description of the earth's oceans in which the possibility of wormholes is made quite apparent. A wormhole is best explained to the reader uninitiated in astrophysics by comparing it to the secret passages on a Cluedo board linking the kitchen to the study and the conservatory to the lounge. Instead of using up several throws of the dice to plod from one end of the house to another, you can take a short cut (through another dimension *behind* the board) and get there in one move. A wormhole is a 'subspace' tunnel between two points in normal space; it allows an immense shortcut to a region that would otherwise take years to travel to.

Einstein's equation of the four-dimensional curvature of space/time in relation to matter and energy, elaborated in the general theory of relativity, is the basis for a more technical understanding of wormholes. Lawrence Krauss offers us some simple diagrams, showing how the bending of space/time offers the possibility of wormholes: 'If spacetime is curved, then perhaps there are different ways of connecting two points so that the distance between them is much shorter that that which would be measured by travelling in a "straight line" through curved space.' He also indicates that (as happens in *Star Trek*) they could facilitate travel through time as well as space.[64] The possibility of finding a wormhole leading back to the Alpha Quadrant (where earth is located) is psychologically important to the crew of *Voyager*. For the series *Deep Space Nine*, the politics and wars fought over the Bajoran wormhole, which has the status of a key port or ocean gateway (rather like the Bosphorous and Dardanelles) constitute the central dramatic pivot of the narrative.

Although Melville is not generally thought of as a science fiction author, it seems that *Moby Dick* preceded Einstein on this one. The problem he needed to solve was brought about by superstition and 'unearthly conceit' – people thought that Moby Dick was ubiquitous: 'that he had actually been encountered in opposite latitudes at one and the same instant of time'. Certainly, the ways of sperm whales in general remained 'unaccountable': 'especially concerning the mystic modes whereby, after sounding to a great depth, he transports himself with such swiftness to the most widely distant points'. Melville resolves the mode of transport of the whale as follows:

> Hence, by inference, it has been believed by some whalemen, that the Nor' West Passage, so long a problem to man, was never a problem to the whale. So that here, in the real living experience of living men, the prodigies related in old times of the inland Strello mountain in Portugal (near whose top there was said to be a lake in which the wrecks of ships floated up to the surface); and that still more wonderful story of the Arethusa fountain near Syracuse (whose waters were believed to have come from the Holy Land by an underground passage); these fabulous narrations are almost fully equalled by the realities of the whaleman.[65]

It is increasingly understood that space involves complex weather systems that affect us on earth – particularly now that so many of our communications systems rely on satellites in space. So 'the weather' in space affects our activities – solar flares can interfere with mobile phones, for instance. Knowledge of space plasma phenemona, chemical kinetics, and the very nautical-sounding question of the relationship of 'solar wind speed' to 'solar latitude', are all now available to the lay person.[66] (There is no need for 'fabulous narrations' here.) But is space simply a backdrop for the activities of starships, or is it 'interpenetrating with life'? Here, there is a difference of emphasis between the various series of *Star Trek*. The nautical metaphor applies much the most strongly to the imaginative world of *TNG* and *Voyager*. It is, perhaps, not surprising that the original series was not particularly attentive to the technical vagaries of space.

Kirk's apartment: spot the ships

As we know, the idea of a space setting was related to the prospects of getting a progressive, multicultural crew past the gatekeepers of what a popular audience would tolerate. So it is predictable that in *TOS* we would see the spaceship functioning more like a James Bond car than anything else.

In one of the films based on *TOS*, we find an explicitly nautical story. *The Wrath of Khan* is in many ways deliberately set as a sea-epic. Kirk's apartment has models of sailing ships among its clutter, for a nice historical touch. The final battle consists of cannon-like barrages as the two ships sail past each other through a nebula that impedes accurate sighting, rather like a storm of the naval tradition. This mode of attack is in particularly striking contrast to later *Star Trek*'s emphasis on aerial dog-fighting as the model for space combat. The music, too, brings out a decidedly maritime atmosphere. Before we have even met Khan himself, the camera zooms in meaningfully to focus on a copy of *Moby Dick* in his book pile. He paraphrases Captain Ahab in such a way as to transpose the quoted passage explicitly to the space environment, to explain his own passion to revenge himself on James Kirk: 'I'll chase him round the moons of Nibia and round the Antares maelstrom and round perdition's flames before I give him up.'[67] Khan's avenging mission is modelled explictly on the Melville theme that was to inspire so much later Star Trek. It also incorporates the Jules Verne/Captain Nemo twist, in that Kirk had been responsible for the appalling death of Khan's 'beloved wife', a particularly cruel death that had robbed her of her sanity first. Khan's own last words are another quotation from Moby Dick: 'from hell's heart I stab at thee; for hate's sake I spit my last breath at thee'.[68] He dies, and Kirk escapes, just as Ahab dies and Moby Dick escapes. The themes of The Wrath of Khan – which includes Spock's funeral – are both explicity and implicitly in line with the nautical metaphor.

Even so, there is not much in TOS to compare with the reality of the materiality of space that we find in TNG. This second series abounds with the spatial equivalents of currents and wind formations, including neutron stars, black holes, energy fields, sinkholes, temporal rifts, stellar winds, stellar clouds, nebulae, binary stars, wormholes, quasars, even tidal forces. Voyager is similar in this regard: the phenomena of real astrophysics – supernovae, Bok globules, filamentary dust lanes, dark matter, interstellar dust, spatial 'tornadoes'[69] – are real players in these stories.

Deep Space Nine is a series set on a space station rather than a ship, and for that reason, perhaps, is less attuned to space phenomena. This might sound paradoxical, given that the discovery of the Bajoran wormhole is what makes DS9 an important location. But it is worth stressing that the predominant force affecting the wormhole – a crucial portal between the Alpha and Gamma Quadrants – is not astronomical but religious. The wormhole is controlled by its resident 'prophets' rather than by processes which science can hope to analyse. In some ways, this is what is most significant about DS9 in relation to the underlying world-view that motivated Star Trek in the earlier period. DS9's exploration of religious faith – which we discuss in detail later in the book – is a massive change from the 'modern, rational' outlook in Star Trek until that time. It is noticeable that the second spatial phenomenon of any importance to DS9 is the region of space they – like children in a story with a crude moral at the end – call 'The Badlands', where electromagnetically active nebulae generate cosmic 'masers', and produce rogue plasma shock waves. Sensors will not work there, and navigation is difficult.[70]

There is, however, one very interesting episode of DS9 to look at in this context. In 'Explorers', Benjamin Sisko decides to build a tiny craft, powered only by 'solar sails' to test the theory that the ancient Bajorans could have reached Cardassia by this means of transport.

The historical model is Thor Heyerdahl's *Kon-Tiki* voyage, which showed that it was possible to sail from South America to Polynesia in a sail-powered raft. The scientific model is Tsander's theory that the sun's radiation pressure could be used to travel through space by exerting acceleration on lightweight sails.[71] Sisko and his son Jake do end up in Cardassia, but the voyage shows them to be hopeless sailors. Sisko senior talks confidently about spritsails and the like, and they both enthusiastically turn little handles on cog wheels to adjust the sails, but credibility is stretched. They lose various sails and spars, cannot get their communication or navigation systems to work, and have no idea at all of where they are. Sitting there waiting to be rescued, they suddenly find that they have arrived at their goal: hurled along by tachyon eddies their vessel has followed the path of its Bajoran forbears and arrived in Cardassian space. Although celebrations are in order for their triumphant proof of the prowess of the ancient Bajorans, the whole attempt is so much a victory for good luck that it reinforces their lack of any nautical skill.

Another sign that *DS9* has moved away somewhat from its nautical moorings is given in the episode 'The Reckoning', where Worf and Odo are arguing about which quarters to assign to various Federation dignitaries. Worf, a character carried over from *TNG*, is outraged at Odo's lack of respect for the minutiae of diplomatic regulations. 'It is naval tradition,' he emphatically protests at his colleague's lack of interest in the procedures. The shapeshifter's response is curt: 'So is keel-hauling, but right now we should focus on accommodation.' It seems the earlier romance of the age of sail has drifted away somewhat in the port environment of Deep Space Nine.

Star voyager

Voyager, on the contrary, is very much a sailor's ship. The concept underlying the *Voyager* series is epic. There are, indeed, parallels between the story of the starship *Voyager*, facing a journey of seventy years to get back to earth from the position in the Delta Quadrant to which she was catapulted at the opening of the series, and the story of Odysseus himself. (It is to be hoped that Janeway's eventual return to earth will not precipitate a slaughter along the same lines as the carnage that Odysseus found necessary in order to resume his rightful place.) *Voyager* has epic qualities in other ways too, most obviously shown in the dramatic two-parter 'Year of Hell'. Anorax's motives for giving them hell have already been mentioned (see pp. 22–23); let us now look at *Voyager*'s response. The depiction of a ship brought to the brink of destruction by war is comparatively rare in *Star Trek*. Much of the ship is damaged beyond repair and the maintenance of life becomes very difficult. The crew become progressively more dishevelled and filthy in this protracted battle: Janeway has been disfigured by burns, Tuvok has been blinded. In this episode we actually confront the unthinkable, and the command to 'abandon ship' is given to all but the senior officers (because 'asking you to stay would mean asking you to die'). It is, in fact, only thinkable in this story because the reality we are seeing is an 'alternate', or parallel, timeline to that of the eventual outcome. The plot is complex: Anorax (on a ship not unlike the description of the submarine *Nautilus*) is attempting to restore the Krenim empire by using a 'temporal weapon' to rejig history. When *Voyager* gets involved, they develop 'temporal shields' to protect themselves but then they, too, become players in a temporal battleground in which millions are being 'erased from history' in order to restore the Krenim 'Imperium'. Eventually, Captain Janeway, alone on *Voyager*, uses the ship as a kamikaze weapon and drives *Voyager* itself through the Krenim temporal warhead (like Captain Nemo, she is using it as a battering ram) – thus erasing the whole of this nightmarish timeline and restoring *Voyager* to the status quo ante.

The nautical atmosphere of 'Year of Hell' is striking. Through small details, an overall impression of a sailing-ship is built up. As well as the feeling conveyed, explicit allusions to the age of sail are manifold. The opening is set at the point when *Voyager* is celebrating the development of a new astrometrics facility, which uses Starfleet and Borg technology to map the stars ten times more accurately than their existing system – and allows them to shorten the journey home. Chakotay's introductory speech begins: 'Before there were maps and globes, let alone radar and subspace sensors, mariners navigated by the stars. We're returning to that tried and true method'. Later, Chakotay attempts a highly symbolic birthday gift – he has replicated the chronometer of a nineteenth-century British Navy captain, whose ship was thought lost in the South Pacific but eventually limped home with its crew intact. Janeway, however, tells him it must be recycled: so short of materials are they that it might save a life. Later still, after Chakotay has been taken captive by the Krenim commander, she finds it in his quarters (he has disobeyed her orders and kept it) – and at that point she decides to wear it.

The ship takes such a battering that a new protection system is developed: 'transverse bulkheads that set up emergency force-fields between all decks and every section in the event of a cataclysmic hull breach'. 'I was inspired by an ancient steamship,' says Tom Paris modestly, claiming to have made some improvements since the time of the *Titanic*. It is also Paris who reveals to Chakotay the desperate state of morale on the Krenim vessel by another nautical reference: 'Does the name Captain Bligh mean anything to you?'[72] In the second part of the story, things get even worse. As the pressure rises and the captain starts taking more and greater risks, the Doctor questions her ability to retain command (for health reasons), and moves formally to relieve her of duty, on pain of a court martial. Janeway's reply is defiant: 'Before I give up command, you're going to have to shoot me'; and she even threatens to shut down the Doctor's program if he continues to question her ability. As the protracted battles draw towards their conclusion she declares her right as captain to stay on board the crippled *Voyager*: 'The Captain goes down with the ship – right?' *Voyager* is much more than an inanimate object, she declares: 'right now it needs one of us'.

The reference in 'Year of Hell' to a possible court martial of the captain links this epic story to a common feature of maritime fiction. A captain who lost or surrendered his ship, for however good a reason, faced a Navy court which would either end his career in disgrace or acquit him honourably. This nautical convention is followed in the original series on several occasions. In *TNG*, one is convened after Picard's loss of the starship *Stargazer* – and we are later told how much he resents the zealous officer who conducted it.[73] The model of a naval captain's court martial is best drawn by C. S. Forester in the dramatic case of Hornblower.[74]

This court martial is dramatic because it concerns a situation where the stakes are particularly high. Hornblower, as captain of the *Sutherland*, has been ordered into a battle (this is in 1810 in the Mediterranean) in which he is hopelessly outnumbered. He disables four French ships but his own has been dismasted and is shipping water. More than half the crew have been killed or taken out of action. Eventually Hornblower 'strikes his colours' and surrenders to the French in preference to further carnage that could serve no strategic advantage.[75] He is taken prisoner and bound for Paris, to face exemplary execution. (This disgrace would entail a court martial whatever reverse of his fortunes might follow.) Hornblower escapes in transit to Paris, and hides throughout the winter in the safety of the house of a Bourbon sympathizer. Eventually he daringly recaptures a British ship in the harbour at Nantes and manages to rejoin the British fleet. By then, Hornblower is presumed a British martyr to the tyrant Napoleon. His return makes him a hero. So the martyr and hero – fast becoming a major celebrity – is also the man being court-martialled for surrender. Hornblower, like Picard, may be a man of action but he is immensely introspective and proud. He experiences the trial with real fear: he is so anxious that when he goes in for the verdict he can literally see nothing but the 'one little space' where the symbol of the decision is placed. His sword has the hilt towards him – he is acquitted.[76]

Star Trek's creator, Gene Roddenberry, once commented: 'Horatio Hornblower was a great hero of mine,';[77] but are *Star Trek* captains rightly described as 'Hornblowers in space'? There are several points at which we might want to draw a parallel between these two extended narratives of sea- and 'space-faring' life. The first concerns the context of exploration in a time and space where the ship is alone. We have already mentioned the emphasis in *Hornblower* on the absolute authority of the captain – how he has the power not only to marry and bury, but to condemn to death with no appeal. The captain's total command over the crew is complementary to his role as an autonomous, decision-making ambassador. Reviewing one decision, Hornblower notes that there was nothing a captain could not do 'in a ship detached far from superior authority'.[78] The *Hornblower* novels themselves contain a certain amount of discussion about historical changes in communications and transport, with some bearing on the compression of time and space. An interesting passage in an early novel gives a description of the 'miracle of modernity' that was brought about by the new canal system of the Industrial Revolution in Britain. Hornblower himself has a go at steering the canal boat as it races along at nine miles an hour (eight knots to him), pulled by cantering horses on the towpath. The Sapperton tunnel is the 'marvel of the age'. The fact that one can get to a market twenty miles away from home and back in a day-trip astonishes him. The canals, he notes, had 'changed the economic face of England'.[79] What is most interesting is that the *Hornblower* stories are set at the moment that this modern compression of time and space – through new transport and communications systems – is changing the assumptions of the old world. *Star Trek*, by using a setting in space, is going back to the pre-modern parameters of a looser, emptier, and – paradoxically – *slower* world. Escaping from rural France by river, trying to minimize contact and discovery, Forester tells us that 'on that big lonely river it was almost like travelling through an uninhabited country'.[80] Many of the routes of *Star Trek* are through uninhabited, even 'undiscovered' countries.[81]

Ocean-going sea voyages and space travel have in common a complete dependence on the ship. As is repeated in countless examples of both genres: if the ship goes, we die. The crew's fate and the fate of the vessel are completely entwined: survival beyond the bounds of the ship itself is unlikely. Certainly the 'man overboard' and the individual casualty from a spaceship cannot survive without something to help them continue to breathe. On a more prosaic level, but equally important, is the question of the maintenance of life on board. It is only on *Voyager* – whose situation is most like that of a real ship at sea – that we hear about the enormous significance of provisions. In *Star Trek* generally, there is an Olympian attitude to food, which is simply replicated to order. Every dish in the universe can be got, customized to your taste, from the equivalent of a foyer drinks machine; only eccentrics do any actual cooking. *Voyager*, however, is not in this happy position: we hear constantly about food rations, attempts at hydroponic cultivation on board, raids on passing planets for ingredients, experiments by the ship's cook Neelix, and Janeway's relentless personal quest for a good cup of coffee. The *Hornblower* books spell out these issues with the importance they deserve. At one point Hornblower, after seven months at sea, is able to replenish the stores on the ship: he requires an unimaginable consignment including 200 bullocks, 500 pigs, 40,000 citrus fruit (scurvy being a big worry), five tons of tobacco and so on. He is particularly pleased at being able to conjure up more supplies of the obligatory rum for the sailors.

Sea and space fiction share a realm of political debate around the issue of modern democracy. The indexical reference-point is the Napoleonic wars, in which France is represented as the tyrant and Britain and its allies as the standard-bearers of the rights of the freeborn. Nelson, whose victory and death at Trafalgar in 1805 turned the fortune of the war at sea, is the iconic figure, yet his emphatic support of the slave trade cannot be reconciled with the fight against tyranny. This wide-ranging debate encompasses, perhaps not surprisingly, many such contradictions – particularly apparent around the issue of slavery and individual rights. This question is a crucial one in the rhetoric of *Star Trek*. It is a contentious one in *Hornblower*, too, particularly as the abolitionist movement intersected with British/Amercian tensions. In Forester's stories, Hornblower is explicitly identified with Nelson. In the first place, he suffers from seasickness, as did Nelson; like him he is 'nervous', 'not strong'; as a young captain, Hornblower's first post is to supervise the naval funeral procession escorting Nelson's body up the River Thames to St Paul's. Forester is somewhat equivocal on the issue of slavery, painting Hornblower as requiring enormous tact in his dealings with the American authorities. In *Hornblower in the West Indies* there is a description of his mixed feelings at using sabotage to capture a slave ship: clearly not an honourable strategy for a sailor, but to set against this was the fact that over 300 slaves were freed by it.[82]

The Napoleonic Wars are also the central reference-point for the enormously popular series of books by the late Patrick O'Brian, featuring Captain Jack Aubrey and Dr Stephen Maturin. These novels (begun in 1970) are in many ways indebted to the legacy of *Hornblower*: certainly they draw on the same historical sources. On many issues, the O'Brian series is more outspoken than the Forester books. The treatment of sexual behaviour, for instance, is far more explicit. O'Brian also tells us that Nelson, and therefore his admirer Jack Aubrey, was in favour of slavery: 'he said that the country's shipping would be ruined if the trade were put down. Perhaps it comes more natural if you are black'.[83] Captain Aubrey is the sort of fellow who regards Tom Paine as having 'wild, regicide revolutionary ideas'. The character Stephen Maturin is a foil for Aubrey's rather simple 'king and country' mentality. For Maturin, the fight against Bonaparte is more genuinely part of a fight against tyranny wherever it may be found: 'I think I feel more strongly about slavery than anything else', he says.

Starfleet models itself on the conception of a global ('anti-Bonapartist') alliance. To round off this discussion of the nautical resonances in *Star Trek*, we will look briefly at an example from the quasi-official world of the *Star Trek* mass-market novel. These works are a publishing phenomenon in themselves. They are extraordinarily popular – every title since July 1986 has gone into the *New York Times* bestseller list; their worldwide sales top 30 million copies. Within the overall list, there are many sequenced titles associated with the four *Star Trek* series – six books on one theme, four on another and so on. They are published by Pocket Books, which is a division of Simon & Schuster; the books are copyrighted to Paramount, the owner of all *Star Trek* rights: all these players are in the huge Viacom conglomerate. The novels, however, are not generally written by the official *Star Trek* writers, and editorial control is certainly much looser – things happen in these novels that would not happen in the prime-time family show. The writing style tends towards the dramatic-formulaic. One particular writer – Diane Carey – has picked up on the nautical model of *Star Trek*. As we might expect from what we have said so far, the most convincing are those based on the characters of *TNG* and *Voyager*. Even James T. Kirk, however, is allowed a little reflection along nautical lines: 'he felt that esprit with sailors from centuries past, who understood what a ship really was, how a bolted pile of wood, metal, and motive power could somehow be alive and command devotion as if the heart of oak actually pumped blood'.[84]

The *Voyager* novel in the *Captain's Table* series has a field day with nautical metaphor. The plot is barely relevant to this argument. In short, Janeway escapes the destruction (as she thinks) of *Voyager*, signs up on the rather pathetic vessel that found her, eventually becomes captain of it, leads a bold and brave assault on an enemy, and meets up again with *Voyager*. The scene for Janeway's telling of her story is an English pub (in the Delta Quadrant), where captains hang out spinning their autobiographical sea yarns. The language of the great sailing ship is immediately heard – mauling gales, hoving to, spare spars, jury rudders and the like. Propping up the bar is a man that all we readers are to recognize from the description alone: he has pale hair, is thin, not tall, wears dark uniform with medals and ribbons, has a pinned-up sleeve – yes, it is Lord Nelson himself! Embarked on her story, Janeway describes how she had to dispose of the body of another captain – the tragedy being that neither of them had been able 'to go down with our ships'. Reminding him of the conventions of 'burial at sea', she ejected his body from the airlock of the escape pod (aka lifeboat) into space. The ship she ended up on, the *Zingara*, had a view screen with an open aspect that created the illusion of being in space with no structure to contain them: 'we might as well be on an open-decked vessel in the middle of an ocean' – it was as if you were underwater but could still breathe. A phenomenon called 'spaceborne quicksand' appeared, dragging them down. The *Zingara* was a 'warranter' – a private vessel authorized by the government to raid and salvage. Janeway pointed out that the warranters are 'privateers', often licensed by a 'letter of marque' to differentiate them from pirates (a terminology strongly associated with the Napoleonic wars). Up comes the identification with a ship: 'As seafarers and spacefarers had for thousands of years before the two of us, we both knew the ship we were on meant our very lives. If it died, we died.'

After she became deck boss, Janeway taught her men to get everything ship-shape: 'let's start by squaring away' she instructed ('squaring away' means to 'clear the deck'). Next she got them to follow the Navy convention of repeating orders, and even adding 'aye' – 'so I know you heard me clearly and understood'. ('Customary acknowledgement of an order' is the naval definition of the term 'Aye, aye, Sir'.[85]) She instituted new station bills and watch schedules, reflecting that in running a ship there were similarities in management that made sense – as shipfarers from long ago had discovered. Later, Janeway had recognized the similarity between the 'warranter' and 'the old-time pirate ships on earth': the captain is elected by the crew. The climax of the story involved an old naval manoeuvre: the use of a 'fire ship'. Janeway explains that the 'oceanfaring navies on my planet in the past' would pack a ship with combustibles, light it up and send it among enemy ships. This tactic she proposed for a battle in which they were going to be decisively outnumbered, musing that such odds should be taken on, as 'well, Nelson did it at Trafalgar'. Back in the pub at the end of her story, 'the man with one arm' is trying to learn from her experiences.[86]

The book *Fire Ship* is interesting in its sustained use of the nautical metaphor, which transposes the language and assumptions of a sailing-ship on to a spaceship. Another Diane Carey book, also with a sailing lexicon, raises more important issues of content; this is the portentously titled *Ancient Blood*, the first book in the *Day of Honour* series. This has an 'A' story about political intrigue and corruption on a world that is divided as to whether it wants to be part of the United Federation of Planets. The Klingon Starfleet officer Worf (an important character in two of the series) is the key player, and because he cannot tell a lie, a family friend gets brutally killed. The 'B' story, tightly interwoven, concerns Worf's twelve-year-old son Alexander, who needs to study for the Klingon 'Day of Honour' festival; since Worf himself is away he asks Picard to supervise the boy. Instead of choosing a Klingon ancestor, Alexander produces a holo-program from the archives of his human foster-grandparents, for him and Picard to run. It is a dramatization of the diaries of one of his distant (and human) ancestors. When they start the program, they are part of the crew of a British Navy frigate in action against the colonists in the American Revolutionary War: the year is 1777. One might think that this was an obvious reference-point for a historical incursion in *Star Trek*. However impeccably the nautical theme is developed in the book, we are not allowed to lose the point that the underlying emotional reference-point is not this war, but the Napoleonic Wars. Picard is trying to place things – 'He didn't even know which battle this was.' 'Not my best period,' he muttered. 'Couldn't you have had a Napoleonic relative?'

This book paints a dramatic picture of the physical realities of battle in such a ship. Alexander watches the tearing of flesh rather than an anodyne phaser wound, and sees men die in great pain. The technical side of managing the vessel is dealt with in great detail. When we first join the program, an officer charges past, barking out incomprehensible orders to do with heads'l sheets, braces, the weather side, shrouds and so on. Picard tries desperately to remember what he knows about sailing, as he is an officer in the program and has to give orders to others. Here, the author uses a device that also allows the technical vocabulary to be explained to the reader: Picard gets a midshipman (junior officer) to give Alexander (programmed in as a ship's boy) 'a quick lesson in the structure of this ship and its rigging'. Though horrified, 'Mr Nightingale' obligingly defines and explains the working of the sailing aspect of the ship with a technical vocabulary: stays, shrouds, deadeyes, lanyards, chainwales, fore mast, main mast, mizzen mast, lower and upper tops'ls, t'gallants, royals, fore-and-aft spanker, squares, yards, yardarms, brace lines, clews, bunts and sheets. Picard rightly mutters to Alexander that it sounds like a discussion in the engine room of the *Enterprise*. Nightingale's disquisition, in fact, covers only a small part of the technical vocabulary needed to understand these vessels – which is why many books on sea-power have glossaries included. For the modern reader of this fiction, some device has to be found to introduce the lexicon. Patrick O'Brian does it in the first novel of his series by getting another good-natured midshipman, Mr Mowett, to explain it all to a landlubber. He does it by taking Dr Maturin aloft, and giving him an aerial view, which – notwithstanding vertigo – facilitates a detailed lesson (eight pages of text) in 'sea terms'.[87]

Why does Janeway address Tom as 'Mr Paris'? Why is Kirk's helmsman called 'Mr Sulu'? (We even have 'Mr Savik', who is a woman.) The use of the title 'Mister Picard' is what alerts Picard, in the simulation, to the fact that he is likely to have been cast as an officer – a look at his clothes confirms this. It is a title that is used selectively. It functions to keep alive, in certain circumstances, the conventions of sailing – associated with rank and status rather more than polite manners. Such conventions are the tip of an iceberg of underlying attitudes. Picard's reflections on the parallels between the sailing vessels of Chesapeake Bay and his own starship bring this out. Whimsically, he regrets having tried to get 'the marlinspike seamanship course' dropped when he was at Starfleet Academy: he now finds a use for tying knots and repairing lines. More pertinently, he murmurs that the organization of HMS *Justina* is 'not so different from the way a starship is run'. Most significant of all, in this novel Picard is given the role of making a connection between the technological and the ideological: 'He knew how the Revolutionary War would come out, but he still shivered with excitement at seeing this. The brilliant technology of his own time was allowing him and Alexander to see the technologies upon which it was built. And even more, the attitudes that built it.'[88]

These attitudes are, in the novel, complex. Alexander's ancestor is a British officer who still believes in the Divine Right of Kings and the treasonous nature of the fight for independence; his cousin is now an American colonist. The issue of how to define 'honour' is ostensibly the main theme of the story, and brings out a curious similarity between the notions of honour among Klingons and the eighteenth-century British aristocracy. Perhaps more interesting is the way the issues of colonialism and independence are addressed, a theme to which we return later on. One might assume initially that an identification would be made between the underlying attitudes of Starfleet (proposed as a kind of progressive colonialism) and the Delaware colonists, but in fact the novel deals with the issue in a far more complex way. Picard and Alexander, because of their structural situation as members of the British Navy, as well as the boy's admiration for his dashing but blinkered ancestor, are put in the rather perverse position of having to see things from the British point of view. In this, the 'B' story connects eventually to the 'A' story: the planet wanting to secede from the protective mantle of the Federation is in danger of instability, weakness, hunger, invasion. Picard, however, has learnt a lesson that is quite threatening for his colleagues in the beloved Federation. He insists that the colony should be allowed its independence as of right: he refuses to put himself 'in the position of the British'.

These formulaic mass-market paperbacks wobble on the line of official *Star Trek* output. Many of them, however, offer the opportunity to explore more freely a connection that is quite significant in the more formal products – in this instance the association of *Star Trek* with the metaphor of sailing.

The nautical model

It is time now to round up the salient elements of the nautical theme in *Star Trek*. The literature in English on seafaring goes a long way back. As we have already explained, there is a difference between setting a human drama against a flat and passive backdrop of the sea (or land or space for that matter) and engaging actively with the changing force of the marine element. Jonathan Raban's collection on the sea[89] gives some interesting and amusing examples of writers in whose work the sea figures – but only to be studiously ignored. Hakluyt's account of colonial travels construes the sea simply as a road to a destination, with only limited glimpses of the water beneath. Celia Fiennes's journeys around England in the seventeenth century took her often to the sea but she neither saw it nor wrote about it. It was a blank – 'a vacancy on which she wasted no words'.[90]

Raban himself eschews what he calls 'nauticalia', whether technical, naval, travel or whatever, in favour of a focus on the sea in literature. He begins with the anonymous Anglo-Saxon poem 'The Sea-Farer', anthologized in the year 904. The poem has had many translations and many readings, and is naturally the subject of much scholarly dispute: does the evocation of a sense of hardship and exile in the poem displace that of the desire to travel? Raban looks at the construction of the sea in the eighteenth century in terms of the then (as now) fashionable theory of 'the sublime'. Joseph Addison in 1712 first identified the 'agreeable horrour' of a tempest at sea as constitutive of the sublime: a 'troubled ocean' offering one of 'the highest kinds of pleasure'. Edmund Burke, elaborating the role of terror as the ruling principle of the sublime, cites perception of the ocean as a type case.

In English literature the sea assumes another set of meanings as romanticism takes hold. Samuel Taylor Coleridge's poem 'The Rime of the Ancient Mariner' (1797) is a legendary text; to the catalogue of its many cultural influences we could add its resonances in the recent anti-rational and 'post-modern' forms of *Star Trek*. Byron's nautical interests have already been mentioned. Shelley's fatal passion for the sea and sailing is well documented. Marine discourse is entertainingly mocked in Jane Austen's description of a man who, in talking of the sea and sea-shore, 'ran with energy through all the usual phrases employed in praise of their sublimity, and descriptive of the *undescribable* emotions they excite in the mind of sensibility'; 'rather commonplace perhaps' is the narrator's comment.[91]

No such cynicism is apparent in the world of *Star Trek*, where the sea of space takes on a beauty and wonder of its own. The lavish nebulae and other astronomical phenomena encountered are treated with much reverence. The mere sight of the Bajoran wormhole opening to admit a ship is often depicted as a moment of spiritual revelation and Starfleet crews regularly take detours to witness some dramatic stellar phenomenon at first hand. In one episode of *Voyager*, the crew is sent into deep depression by a vast expanse of starless space.[92] Janeway suffers a crisis of command, retreating to her quarters like Ahab in recluse; the crew begin fighting with each other over petty issues and Neelix suffers an acute psychosis, brought on by a 'fear of nothingness'. Empty – one might say inactive – space is clearly no good for anyone. Ezri Dax in *Deep Space Nine* has a literally queasy relationship with the universe; she can barely set foot on a shuttle without suffering severe 'spacesickness'.

It is, however, with the writing of Melville – and the later writers whose work we have discussed – that fiction about the sea becomes immediately relevant to the imaginative world of *Star Trek*. British maritime supremacy, in all its aspects of colonialism, commerce and naval victory, had been (Padfield argued) crucial for the development of an open-minded modern, western, democratic political culture. It is this 'modern' culture, built on the co-operation required by trade and on a secular rejection of religion and tradition in favour of science and exploration, that *Star Trek* classically represents. The Napoleonic period is iconic for *Star Trek*, albeit only sentimentally, because this was the period when British supremacy was decisively challenged in the early nineteenth century by the invention of the American clipper. As Jaques Berthoud points out, memories of Britain's glorious naval victories over Napoleon tend to obscure the fact that British shipping was then becoming obsolete in the face of the very fast clipper design. By the mid-century, the entire trading superiority of the Atlantic and Pacific passed from Britain to America; by the time of *Moby Dick* (1851) American fiction had 'transformed the imaginative representation of the sea in western literature'.[93]

Of course, this is not without its ironies. The Baltimore clipper was, as Paul Gilroy notes, 'the fastest ship in the world' – the only ship fast enough to outrun the British blockade of the slave traffic.[94] *Hornblower in the West Indies* provides the example of the British Navy crew reduced to covertly attaching a 'drogue' to the rudder of a slaver, and thereby bringing it to a halt, as they could not keep up with it in open water. In *Star Trek III: The Search for Spock*, Scotty pulls off a similar manoeuvre and succesfully grounds the USS *Excelsior*, whose mission is to relieve Kirk of the *Enterprise*. Subsequently, however, British and American fortunes were again reversed; by 1900 British steamships had reconstructed a commercial superiority in world maritime trade routes. As Berthoud points out, the British Merchant Marine may have controlled 50 per cent of total world mercantile tonnage by the turn of the century – but it could certainly not supply the manpower for them.[95] Hence the case of Conrad, a Polish recruit to the British Merchant Navy; hence the multinational, multicultural crews of such ships throughout the nineteenth century; and hence, perhaps, a model for the explicitly multinational (and later multi-species) crews we find in the ships of Starfleet.

The nautical metaphor in *Star Trek* operates at lexical, imaginative, historical and interpretative levels. The modern world evoked in

Twenty-fourth-century sailors

the classic conception of *Star Trek* is one where the relationship of time and space is changing. The place of 'man', of the human being, within that changing world is constantly challenged in *Star Trek*. There is an unprecedented interest in, even an obsession with, human identity. What does it mean to be human? This is the question around which much of *Star Trek* revolves. Part II of the book investigates this insatiable interest in *Star Trek* in the issues of human identity, the nature and rights of individuals, the definition of sentience and consciousness. These questions are common to all the different series of *Star Trek*. In the third part of the book we look at what is different about the forms of *Star Trek* that we might want to describe as critical of the 'modern', rational, western world – they are, literally, 'post-modern' in their strategies of presenting issues. They may be post-modern but they are not 'post-nautical'. Janeway and the *Voyager* series represents a high point of nautical referencing. Perhaps the most 'post-modern' of nautical references comes in the film *Star Trek: Generations*. The crew of the *Enterprise* is on the holodeck, entertaining themselves by playing at being the crew of what looks suspiciously like a frigate of the Napoleonic period. Riker has acquired a good grip on sailing terminology, referring to studdingsails quite naturally by the colloquial 'stuns'ls'. An emergency super-venes, and they are recalled from their holodeck to the bridge of the starship. The image of the *Enterprise* staff on their bridge, dressed in the impracticable ceremonial uniform of early nineteenth-century naval officers, shows the nautical metaphor going strong in a new and stylistically 'post-modern' context.

Part II

Humanity on Trial

Europe's early modern maritime explorers soon became the colonizers of a New World. When Christopher Columbus sailed across the Atlantic in 1492, he reached an island in what is now the Bahamas; from the ship he could see – and noted in his log – that it was inhabited. Nevertheless, at first light the landing party stepped ashore and immediately unfurled the flag of the Spanish crown. Columbus declared that he was taking possession of the island for the King and Queen, that it was a part of Spain and its inhabitants were Spanish subjects. As well as Spanish it was to be Christian. So next he put up a cross and named the island San Salvador (Holy Saviour).[1] We might think that this was a form of arrogance that history has caused us to regret. Far from it. As you gaze up at the moon one night, you may recall that the Stars and Stripes is proudly flying up there. The moon is even graced by a plaque signed by Richard Nixon.

The mission of *Star Trek* – to explore 'strange new worlds' – has painted a picture of nautical exploration on the wider canvas of space. Is this, by definition, a colonialist project? Is it possible to be an explorer without also being a conqueror? This anxiety is fully recognized within the *Star Trek* narrative, for example in the fact that Starfleet's most fundamental principle, the 'Prime Directive', is the requirement not to interfere in any way with other cultures. Much of the discussion about the 'politics' of *Star Trek* is a discussion of the issue of colonialism. The issues of race and racism, and of wars fought over territorial expansion, recur again and again. An interesting episode of *TNG*, entitled 'First Contact', depicts a culture where, although the technology for space travel has been developed, the suspicion of the motives of the *Enterprise* in coming to greet the emergent space-faring society is considerable. A dispute breaks out between those welcoming the new era of space travel, and those bitterly unwilling to go down this route for fear of colonization. In the end, the chancellor decides to halt the space programme (allowing the scientist who had developed warp drive to choose exile from home and to join the *Enterprise* in space travel) and divert the resources to 'education', in the hope of breaking down public resistance in the longer run.

The most recent indictment of colonialism in the *Star Trek* universe is in the 1998 film *Insurrection*. Featuring the cast of *The Next Generation*, it is in many senses an embodiment of the 'modernist' ambition and high moral preoccupation of that series. The story is a shocking one to the long-term follower of *Star Trek*: an official edict from the Federation Council has ordered the forced relocation of a group of settlers. This is in order to extract their planet's unique

Stars and Stripes

rejuvenating properties, a process that will render the planet itself uninhabitable. Captain Picard is characteristically principled about the matter: 'We are participating in a violation of everything the Federation stands for,' he tells the admiral in command; 'It's an attack on its very soul.' The Federation is quite clearly betraying its own Prime Directive (a doctrine of non-interference) for nothing other than personal benefit. Picard leads the 'Insurrection' against his own Federation's authority and protects the inhabitants of the planet himself, explaining that he is happy to face a court martial where the truth will have to be heard.

Despite the auspicious prospects of this self-evidently righteous theme, the film floundered with low ratings and critical indifference, a failure made particularly striking when compared with the success of the previous cinema offering, *First Contact*. It seems that many reviewers, and – by extension – audiences, remained unconvinced by the captain's position. If moving 600 people against their will would grant you everlasting youth, would it not be insane to refuse? The high-minded utopian humanism of the 1980s had failed to find support in the selfish and cynical late nineties. More recent *Star Trek* episodes have presented moral ambiguity and downright immoral behaviour by leading characters. The high-minded modernist assumptions of *The Next Generation* have begun to be eroded, in line with shifting opinion among *Star Trek*'s audience.

Underlying the recurring discussion of colonialism and race is a more general debate about humanity. As is often observed, *Star Trek* traditionally offers a peculiarly optimistic view of the world; without going so far as to say that it views human nature as essentially good, we certainly could say that it seeks to defend humanity against the charge that it is evil. Whereas most science fiction comes into the category of dystopia, *Star Trek* deals with the same issues with optimism and humour. The comedy aspect of *Star Trek* is an important element of its outlook. The *Alien* films, and *Blade Runner*, come to mind immediately as far more gloomy treatments of some comparable material.

The underlying issue around which *Star Trek*, in all its manifestations, revolves is that of the qualities and morality of humanity – an issue that is dramatized for us in its starkest form in the opening and closing of the series *The Next Generation*. As we shall see, it is often in *TNG* that the values of *Star Trek* in general are most crisply articulated. In this instance, there is a particular framing of the series in which the basic question is posed: can humanity be defended when charged with its manifest crimes? The character of Q appears at the beginning of the first episode of *TNG*, 'Encounter at Farpoint'; it is not without interest that on this occasion he has chosen to take the form of an Elizabethan sea captain such as Sir Walter Raleigh. Q then convenes a court scene, reminiscent of a surreal Spanish Inquisition, in which the characters in the dock are the captain and crew of the *Enterprise*. 'Before this gracious court now appear these humans to answer for the multiple and grievous savageries of their species.' Seven years later, as the final episode ('All Good Things . . .') concludes, Captain Picard finds himself back in the same courtroom, he hopes for the last time, he says. Q's reply sums up the series, and the whole of *Star Trek*'s interrogation of human morality: 'You just don't get it, do you, Jean-Luc? The trial never ends.'

Picard defends humanity

Star Trek is itself this trial. In the main, what we get is the defence: humanity's attempts to put wrongs right, to improve society and prevent war. According to *Star Trek*, the world of the twenty-fourth century has eliminated poverty, famine, social class and money. These are all seen as primitive problems that have been solved by an enlightened galactic democracy. The story is told from the viewpoint that the human race is more than morally credible; its crimes are all in the distant past. In *The Original Series* this utopianism was in the context of the troubling Cold War situation, but later series have maintained the same values, even if their relationship to the present has changed. A good example to look at here is the *Voyager* episode 'In the Flesh', which, though made thirty-odd years later, reads a lot like an episode of *TOS*.

The story involves *Voyager* in what is essentially Cold War espionage, when they discover a secret base containing a perfect replica of Starfleet Headquarters on Earth, complete with a seemingly human population. It turns out that Species 8472 are training to infiltrate Starfleet – it is they who are running this operation, their genetic make-up disguised by surgery. The *Voyager* crew is fearful of the threat they pose – as Tuvok points out, 'they did threaten to purge our galaxy of all life'. Meanwhile Captain Janeway, though ordering a massive weapons production effort, begins to worry about her responsibility as a diplomat. 'Directive zero one zero,' she muses: 'Before engaging alien species in battle any and all attempts to make first contact and achieve non-military resolution must be made.' Most of Voyager's crew see 8472 as nothing more than 'the enemy', however. Seven of Nine's attitude is typical: 'This species intends to purge our galaxy of all life; it's time you resisted your Starfleet philosophy . . . [they do] not deserve our compassion.' While Janeway and crew are pondering the situation on ship, Chakotay has been infiltrating the mock-up of Starfleet Command, involving himself with an 8472 who has taken the form of a young woman officer. It soon becomes clear that there is a fundamental misunderstanding between the two sides: 'They'll attack any species that's not part of their Federation,' she informs Chakotay. Yet just as Janeway is having doubts on board Voyager so too is she on the starbase: 'At first glance they're so primitive – genetic impurities, no telepathy, violent – and yet they've invented so many beautiful ways to communicate their ideas: literature, art, music.'

The Cold War analogy is very clearly registered: both sides have devastating weapons – on Voyager they even discuss the concept of deterrent weaponry. The 8472 leader acts like a typically eccentric foreign commander, pouring drinks while he interrogates Chakotay. Of Seven of Nine he remarks, 'once a Borg, always a Borg'. Tom Paris, ever the voice of history, even brings the parallels right to the fore in explaining the purpose of the installation: 'Back in the twentieth century the Soviets used to build American towns to train their agents to infiltrate the United States.' In the stand-off that ensues it is up to Janeway to show her enlightened Starfleet (human) ideology and do her best to prevent an armed conflict. 'As long as we keep spying on each other, making assumptions,' she explains, 'we probably will go to war.' In an act of sensational diplomacy that her predecessor Kirk would be proud of she takes a staggering risk in order to secure their co-operation – she orders the disarming of Voyager's weapons: 'One of us has to take our finger off the trigger – it might as well be me. . . . Our defences are down. What will you do now? Blow Voyager to high heavens? Or do we keep talking?'

In the dramatic scene that follows Janeway successfully negotiates peace between the two forces and they agree to exchange with each other the technological secrets of their weapons. This vindication of Starfleet philosophy is a refreshing reminder of the values that have sustained Star Trek's stories for over thirty years. Ever sceptical, Seven of Nine is surprised at the resolution: 'I believed they would take advantage of your human weakness.' In solving the problem so successfully Janeway secures her place in the annals of enlightened leadership that the program has always stood for.

While most of *Star Trek* is wholeheartedly behind this defence of human morality, it is a large part of *Deep Space Nine*'s agenda to show us the case the prosecution continues to make. *DS9* is notable for this descent from the rather sqeaky-clean morality of the other three series. In *DS9* we see people, even the captain, doing what is necessary to get what they need or want. In one story his teenage son realizes his own capacity for 'cowardly' behaviour: that 'the line between courage and cowardice is a lot thinner than most people believe'. In this, as frequently in *DS9*, there is an evident cynical tone to the proceedings. The characters are far more flawed, more realistic, more 'human' than the heroic paragons that run the other three series. The departure of *DS9* from many of the core values of *Star Trek* will be examined in some detail in Part III of this book. Meanwhile, it is important to stress that what all the series share is the trial itself – a preoccupation with what constitutes humanity, and what the moral status of the human individual is. In this focus, at times bordering on an obsession, on the question of 'human nature', *Star Trek* is decidedly unfashionable in terms of contemporary social and cultural theory. Here the prevailing winds blow in the direction of seeing the entire debate as couched within an irredeemably 'essentialist' set of assumptions.[2] While this is not the place to expand upon these theoretical arguments at length, it will be useful to make some introductory points about the definition of the 'human' and how this might affect the way we interpret *Star Trek*'s treatment of the issue.

To look at the question of humans in space we propose to start by looking up two terms in the dictionary: 'human' and 'universe'. The first is particularly complex – so much so that we might see how thirty years of *Star Trek* has not cracked it. The term 'human' derives from the Latin word *humanus*, for a human being. This draws on the Latin word *homo* (plural *homines*) which means the generic man as opposed to other animals. The Latin for man (*vir*) as opposed to woman (*femina*) are words still much used in modern English when speaking of virility and femininity. The old Latin word *homo* is the source of several confusions. It connotes in one sense the 'better qualities' of man; in another, man's propensity to error. The use of 'my man' to refer to a servant is also there in the Latin. This is the *homo* of *Homo Sapiens* (the human characterized by wisdom, prudence, sensual and metaphorical 'taste'), but not the 'homo' of homosexual, which comes from the Greek word '*homo*', meaning 'the same'. Greek runs a distinction between the male ανδρος ('*andros*'), and the female γυνη ('*guneh*') from which we might deduce that Data is indeed an android (made in the appearance of a male human) whereas his daughter might more accurately have been described as a 'gynoid'. The Greek equivalent of *humanus* is the generic ανθρωπος ('*anthropos*'), also the word used to signify mankind, humanity.

These terms are the background to the variety of complex uses of the word 'human' in English. Thus, if we consult a modern dictionary, we will find the following broad uses of the term (not always compatible) identified:

1 the quality or condition of being human; characteristic attributes of humans;
2 the secular, as opposed to the divine;
3 from 'humane': kindness, softening, 'civilizing';
4 the 'humanities'; the language and literatures of humanity (as opposed to theology);
5 manhood – conflating the generic human with the specifically masculine.

One of the difficulties in following an argument about what is meant by the term 'human' is the directly conflicting connotations that the term has historically had in different contexts. To be human is both to be noble and to be capable of error. In a notorious political scandal of the 1990s, the wife of a disgraced politician described him as 'more human than most'. A 'man' can be both a representative of human dignity and freedom, or a personal servant. A 'man' can be both a representative of the generically human, or specifically a male. In this regard, the term 'human' has as perverse a history as the idea of a 'person'; the word that we now think of as a reference to individuality and sovereign self-identity derives from the word for an actor's mask (a residue of which is found in the vocabulary of *dramatis personae* in the theatre).

Of particular interest is the issue of the secular – of the human as opposed to the divine. *Star Trek*, in its most 'modern' rational incarnation in *The Next Generation*, is militantly secular. 'Horrifying', shuddered Picard, at the prospect of being taken for a god by the inhabitants of a pre-space culture.[3] The implication of 'humanism' is the displacement of God and the elevation of humanity to the top of the moral tree. This move has a distinguished philosophical history. In some way the ethos of *Star Trek* is comparable to the beliefs of Ludwig Feuerbach, who argued that humans should take their place at the moral centre, rather than projecting all that was good on to an outside being (that is, God) and internalizing all that was bad as 'sin'.[4] It is no coincidence that Feuerbach was an important influence on the early thinking of Karl Marx, whose theory of 'alienation' is a theory that man has an essential 'species being' – construed by Marx as optimistically as it is in *Star Trek* – which exploitation in wage labour was eroding and 'alienating'.[5] It is surprising that from the USA in the 1960s there should have emerged a utopian world of the twenty-third century, where food is replicated on command and money does not exist, that resembles the ideal of Marx's communism – 'from each according to his ability, to each according to his needs'.[6]

In *Star Trek*, we see a great deal of 'humanization', which raises the question of how benign it is. Captain Kirk famously used the expression 'everybody's human', by which he really meant that everybody he liked was human. The issue of 'humanization' is quite a lively one in contemporary thinking about our nearest relatives. Should the higher primates have 'rights' equivalent to human rights, now that it has been shown that they have some near-human capacities and sensibilities? The campaign against the solitary confinement of great apes is a case in point. At stake here is the boundary between the human animal and other animals, a boundary that the ecological movement is currently having some success in showing to be quite arbitrary. In *Star Trek*, there is a comparable process of redefining beings as human as a means of interrogating what the definition of humanity really is. Is a robot human? Is a Borg drone human? Is a hologram human? Obviously not – but in many ways, *Star Trek* is able to 'make it so'. What is interesting is that *Star Trek* offers the reverse of the usual process of exclusion. In the colonial history of earth the trend is towards a restriction of who is deemed to be human; in *Star Trek* the issue is to 'humanize' as many people as possible. Kirk's insistence at the funeral of his half-Vulcan friend Spock that 'of all the souls I have encountered in my travels, his was the most human' is merely the first of a long line of invitations to alien species to define themselves within the human family. Whether this is the result of an inability to tolerate difference or simple native human chauvinism, rather than a more innocent pluralist agenda, is not entirely clear.

If we then turn to the second term triggered by the idea of space travel, let us consider what we understand by the 'universe'. At first blush this is a matter of grand cosmology. John Barrow's *Theories of Everything: the quest for ultimate explanation* is wittily headed by a remark from a sketch by the comedian Peter Cook: 'I am interested in the Universe – I am specialising in the Universe and all that surrounds it.'[7] Our project here is merely to look at what the word 'universe' generates in an English dictionary. Two points emerge. The word is made up from the Latin *unus* (one) and *versus* (past participle of *vertere*: to turn); the word itself involves the activity of 'turning' things into one. The basis of the universe is not – to put it simply – that it *is* one thing, but that we *turn* things into one by perceiving them as a unified system. Hence the definition 'all created things *viewed as* constituting one system or whole' (our emphasis).[8] Modern dictionaries tend to delete the idea of creation, and substitute the existence of matter, arriving at a formulation such as this: 'In modern astronomy, the totality of all that is in the cosmos and that can affect us by means of physical forces'.[9] This more neutral definition is, of course, more scientifically satisfactory. It is perhaps worth remembering, however, that the very concept of a *universe*, as opposed to the 'multiverse' we encounter via quantum physics, is part of a creationist tradition in thinking about the cosmos.

Secondly, it is worth drawing attention to another aspect of what has been implied by the term 'the universe'. We find a slippage between what humans have conceived of as a unified system – indeed, have *turned into* a unified system – and humanity itself. The whole of creation slides silently into the operation of human beings. The *OED*, for instance, defines the universe in the following elements: (1) 'The whole of created or existing things regarded collectively; all things (including the earth, the heavens, and all the phenomena of space) considered as constituting a systematic whole'; (2) 'the world or earth, esp. as the abode of mankind or as the scene of human activities'. (This leads to 'mankind in general'.) Lest it be thought that these archaic meanings do not apply to the vocabulary of today, let us consult the Millennium Edition of the Collins Dictionary for a bang up-to-date definition of the universe. The first two senses given are: (1) *Astronomy*, the aggregate of all existing matter, energy, and space; (2) human beings collectively.

Thus, on the one hand, we find a lexical tradition of conflating the whole of the cosmos with the biological species *homo sapiens*. On the other, it can be argued that the vocabulary of 'the human' is itself linked directly to the earth in the most literal fashion. Tony Davies explains that the root of the Latin *humanus* is *humus*, the earth. This is the humus still to be found in garden compost and the exhumation of bodies. The derivation of *humanus* is one that stresses the earth in the literal sense of the soil, and a being that exists at ground level: 'The root-word is, quite literally, humble (*humilis*), from the Latin *humus*, earth or ground; hence *homo*, earth-being, and *humanus*, earthy, human. The contrast, from the outset, is with other earth-creatures (animals, plants), and with another order of beings, the sky-dwellers or gods (*deus/divus, divinus*).'[10] Of course, the whole point of space travel is to become a 'sky-dweller' – the human aping the divine, perhaps? To summarize: when we look at the complex histories of the use of the words 'human' and 'universe' we can find not only the proposition that the human is specifically earth-derived, but also the contradictory notion that the entire universe is the site of human action. It is, perhaps, not surprising that *Star Trek*, in its unrelenting focus on the question of human identity beyond the context of the earth, has found a rich vein to mine.

To badly go . . .

Star Trek presents a range of concerns with human nature, including human existence and knowledge, but it is centrally focused on the issue of human morality. It began in the 1960s, and is indebted to the political culture of the Civil Rights movement in the United States. It is not surprising, then, that we find issues of race, slavery and discrimination recurring again and again in the history of the show. Particularly significant wars in recent American history also feature prominently, including the war in Vietnam as well as the struggle against fascism in the Second World War. The two most appalling moral crimes against humanity in *Star Trek*'s world are both connected with ethnic and racial power and its abuse: slavery and the Holocaust. In the majority of cases, the moral 'crimes' are presented as committed by others: Starfleet officers are the ones who encounter and respond to them, rather than initiate them. In this regard, as in many others, the third *Star Trek* series, *Deep Space Nine*, differs from the other three in the quartet, as it is willing to question the strength of *Star Trek*'s own moral foundation. Doctor Bashir very clearly lays down the anxieties that underlie this philosophical dilemma: 'If push came to shove, if something disastrous happened to the Federation, and we got frightened enough, or desperate enough, how would we react? Would we stay true to our ideals, or would we end up . . . right back where we started?'[11]

DS9 is less of an optimistic myth than the other series, and no doubt for this reason it is rather less 'popular'. The young children's audience in particular appears to have moved from *The Next Generation* to *Voyager* and has tended to leave the somewhat less safe *DS9* to a young adult audience. In terms of the 'trial' of humanity that is staged throughout *Star Trek*, there is plenty of evidence piling up on the *DS9* space station.

Benjamin Sisko, the first black figurehead of a *Star Trek* series, is not an *Enterprise* captain, but the commander of a complicated

Kirk in the dock

border outpost which is very far (and not only in light years) from the headquarters of Starfleet. Both Captains Kirk and Picard got themselves court-martialled by Starfleet, and on various occasions made it clear that their own moral values were superior to those of their superiors. In 'The Drumhead', for instance, Picard succeeds in proving that the Starfleet admiral investigating a presumed sabotage on the *Enterprise* has turned it into a witch-hunt, which he gets stopped. Similarly Captain Kirk is most unhappy when 'kicked upstairs' as an admiral and most in his element when ignoring his orders and doing what he knows to be right (not unlike the Nelson who put a telescope to his blind eye and audaciously declared that he 'had not seen' the signal to withdraw at the battle of Copenhagen in 1801). There is no sense, however, in which the command structure at Starfleet is seen to be generally unworthy of respect in either *The Original Series* or in *The Next Generation*. Moral questions in *DS9* are significantly greyer. Since the whole of the *Voyager* series is conducted with virtually no contact between the ship and the San Francisco HQ, there is limited opportunity to put Janeway's loyalty to the test.

As far as *Deep Space Nine* is concerned, the benign management by Starfleet seen in the previous series has been eroded. Starfleet has not quite become the evil Galactic Empire of Terry Nation's *Blake's*

7, but it has certainly lost some of its moral credibility. This development is also made clear in the 1998 *Star Trek* film *Insurrection*, which positions the Starfleet authorities in a very dubious light. On Deep Space Nine, the mysterious 'Section 31' gained much attention. Its members are citizens of the United Federation of Planets and should therefore be policed by Starfleet, but it is presented as a special security operation that is not constrained by the normal ethical protocols. The implication, that some members of Starfleet are covertly involved in its work, is troubling. The goals of Section 31, as well as its illegitimate methods of brainwashing and torture, are deeply questionable. By the end of the series, Section 31 has been shown to be responsible for the crime that *Star Trek* most opposes – genocide. It transpires that a disease, which has been killing the species known as 'the founders', has actually been introduced by Section 31 with the deliberate aim of killing them all and thus destroying the power of their 'Dominion'. Sisko and the Deep Space Nine officers are aware of this, as they infiltrate Section 31 themselves to find a cure to use on the one founder on the station, Odo. But they collude with Section 31, and Starfleet, in not blowing the whistle on this murder of a people – effectively, they keep quiet about an appalling crime.

It is not simply other people who are committing moral crimes. The responsibility is frequently that of the characters we know and love. One episode, 'Rocks and Shoals', imaginatively reworks the iconography of the trenches of the Western Front in the First World War. This time it is Sisko and his staff who are put in the position of simply mowing down a detachment of infantry walking towards them. They are Jem'Hadar, subordinates whose superior has betrayed them into the ambush; their sense of duty and honour requires them to walk to what they know to be certain death. Sisko, though he tries to avoid this conclusion, has to take responsibility for the massacre. In another episode with strong Great War overtones, a young soldier (Nog) has lost his leg in conducting reconnaissance. His new prosthetic leg is supposed to be painless, but in a reworking of shell-shock Nog has a lot of 'hysterical' pain that he cannot control. His extreme youth at the time of the injury leads to comment (from his uncle, who is also in the field) on the appropriateness of sending him on the mission in the first place – a question paralleled by the much-discussed cruelty and lack of honour in the Dominion's hidden mines, which evoke current campaigns against the use of land mines. The episode 'The Siege of AR-558' shows clearly that these deadly hidden mines make the crew of DS9 aware of the horror of war. However, as soon as they get hold of the technology, Sisko and 'our' side in the war start using these mines, too – raising serious questions among the senior staff, some of whom oppose the captain's decision.

Generally speaking, the morally dubious actions of Starfleet officers are called for by some overriding principle (in the above cases the simple condition of being at war). Unlike the mad villains of previous series, the people responsible for these decisions are very clear about what they are doing and the moral implications of their actions. 'In the Pale Moonlight'[12] takes the form of Sisko's personal log, as he recounts the story of how he manipulated the Romulan government into joining the Federation's side in the war. ('I have to justify what's happened, what I've done,' he explains.) The captain has some serious questions to ask about his own behaviour: 'I lied; I cheated; I bribed men to cover the crimes of other men; I am an accessory to murder.' He had enlisted Garak, a former spy, to convince the Romulans that the Dominion were planning to attack them and, on his advice, arranged the forgery of a holographic clip to that effect. (As the Cardassian explains, 'You came to me . . . because you knew I could do those things you weren't capable of doing.') Ultimately, the forgery is uncovered and Garak kills the two men who know about it, making the 'accidental' death of the Romulan look like an act of Dominion sabotage. Sisko is furious, but Garak convinces him that this behaviour was worth the price since the Romulans do indeed sign up for the war effort: 'all it cost was the life of one Romulan senator, one criminal and the self-respect of one Starfleet officer . . . I'd call that a bargain'. The captain's log shows him trying to identify the moment at which his behaviour crossed the line into the immoral – when 'I had stepped through a door and locked it behind me'. His motives were always good, and he finds himself frustrated by the difficulty of his position: 'People are dying out there, every day. People are struggling for their freedom. And here I am worrying about the finer points of morality.' Sisko ultimately decides that his behaviour was immoral but necessary – 'the road to hell is paved with good intentions . . . I'd go to any length because my cause was just, my intentions were good'. 'The most damning thing of all,' he concludes, is that 'I think I can live with it'.

The shift represented by *DS9* is towards seeing the moral ambiguity of war through the eyes of those we as viewers have identified with, rather than as the 'fault' of outsiders of various kinds. The character of Kira Nerys is a good example here. Portrayed as having been a passionate fighter in the long years of the Bajoran resistance to the occupation by Cardassia, she is a character whose religious faith, national identity and sense of self are all completely bound up in a loathing of the evil Cardassians. Yet she at some point has to recognize that her mother's relationship with the Cardassian leader Dukat was more a voluntary affair rather than the sexual violence she had always assumed it to be ('Wrongs Darker than Death or Night'). And as the war that dominates the last two seasons of *DS9* becomes an ever more shifting sand of alliances, Kira is herself forced to work with Cardassians against a common enemy – and of necessity to query some of her most dearly held beliefs. The question of loyalty is crucial to *Deep Space Nine*.

However, it does not necessarily take war for characters to re-evaluate their convictions, and see the justice in what they once thought was immoral. When Odo's Bajoran 'father' (the scientist who discovered him) visits the station in 'The Begotten', the 'changeling' finally realizes that the methods by which he was taught to shapeshift were more necessary, and less cruel, than he had always assumed. In this episode Odo is looking after a baby changeling that had turned up on the station. His interactions with it are extremely affectionate and he explains his bitterness at the methods of his own upbringing: 'I spent months in the lab being prodded and poked by a scientist who didn't realize I was a life form. . . . He never talked to me. . . . I was lost, alone. But it's not going to be that way with you. . . . I promise I'll never treat you the way I was treated.'

When Doctor Mora (the Bajoran scientist) arrives on the station, Odo is resentful of his presence and the two revert to arguments about the past. 'You enjoyed watching me suffer,' Odo says to his 'father', listing the cruel experiments that were conducted on him: the 'vacuum chamber', 'protein decompiler' and 'cytoplasmic separator'. He suggests that Mora had no respect for him as an individual: 'you could sell tickets on the promenade – Doctor Mora's Chamber of Horrors!' Mora is contemptuous of Odo's gentle methods – 'without discomfort . . . it'll just lie there . . . never living up to its potential'. He sums up his own philosophy as 'spare the rod, spoil the child'. At first Odo ignores him, but when Starfleet starts demanding results and he has nothing to show for all his work, he reluctantly begins using the 'contraptions' that Mora has brought along. 'Now you understand the kind of pressure I was going through,' explains the scientist to Odo. With a combination of the two approaches to child-rearing Odo manages to teach the child effectively, while remaining on good terms with it, something that impresses Mora greatly. Odo comes to realize that the scientist's actions were not without compassion and that his 'father' clearly cared a lot for him: 'I think I finally understand how much I meant to you and what you must have gone through when I left.' Despite this conclusion, however, the episode's message is clear: Odo's compassionate (Starfleet) methods were not working. It seems that force is required to get things moving.

Earlier versions of *Star Trek* have certainly engaged with the perception of moral ambiguity, but it has rarely been entirely attributable to a member of the crew. Instead it would tend to be revealed by an 'alien' of some kind, to whom we are intended to feel superior. The moral 'dilemmas' of *The Next Generation* were generally debated without the constraints of personal interest.

'The Begotten' shows a character who changes his own beliefs to reflect what is perhaps a less ideal world than he had previously believed in. As with Sisko in 'In the Pale Moonlight', Odo is well aware of the decisions he is taking and their implications towards his conception of self. In *Voyager* we are shown what Janeway's crew could have become if they had abandoned their own principles in their desire to get home. In the episode 'Equinox' *Voyager* encounters another Federation starship, the *Equinox*, which – like them – has been stranded in the Delta Quadrant, under the leadership of a distinguished Starfleet diplomat. This ship, however, has lost touch with its Starfleet principles: the crew are on informal first-name terms, have no interest in Starfleet Protocols and their attitudes are somewhat coarse in comparison to those on *Voyager*. 'Once we get back to earth there'll be plenty of women,' the captain comments to one officer. It soon transpires that the crew of the *Equinox* is conducting unscrupulous (and fatal) experiments on an innocent alien race, coverting them into fuel to speed up their journey home. (We are told that killing a further sixty-three aliens will get them safely back to earth.) This behaviour goes against everything that the Federation stands for. Captain Ransome is fully aware of his own position, as he tries to explain to Janeway when his actions are uncovered: 'We started to forget that we were explorers – and there were times that we even forgot that we were human beings.' She is appalled by the actions of the *Equinox* crew and has them arrested immediately, reminding the captain that his mission is 'to *seek out* life – not destroy it'. 'It's never easy,' she explains, 'but if we turn our backs on our principles we cease to be human.' The title of the episode suggests that Janeway represents daylight while Ransome is the embodiment of night; in terms of morality they are clearly polar opposites. The episode contains an interesting exchange between Seven of Nine and a member of the *Equinox* crew, who comments: 'You said you wanted to learn about humanity – I guess we're not prize examples.' Seven's response is coldly factual: 'On the contrary, you've taught me a great deal.' The *Equinox* doctor (another copy of the program on *Voyager*) behaves without the normal Hippocratic constraints – as he explains to his counterpart: 'They deleted my ethical subroutines.' What *Voyager* shows us, however, is that it is not only holograms whose ethics can be rewritten, but respected Starfleet officers.

A similar trend in the evolution of *Star Trek* concerns the question of class, a social phenomenon that has become increasingly visible in *Deep Space Nine*. *The Original Series* and *TNG* presented us with a supposedly classless utopian society, and when the former did deal with the issue it was in alien surroundings. 'The Cloud Minders' (*TOS*) deals with a 'totally intellectual society' of art and music that is only supportable by the efforts of a sub-race of 'Troglytes' [Troglodytes] working in the underground mines. As Spock comments: 'Those who receive the rewards are totally separated from those who shoulder the burdens.' The description of these Troglytes as physically 'inferior' calls to mind the opposing classes of H. G. Wells's *The Time Machine*, in which the human race has diverged into two species – one that only works, the other that only plays. Those of the 'intellectual' race in 'The Cloud Minders' pride themselves on their 'complete separation of toil and leisure'. Unsurprisingly, their social system is in for something of an upheaval as the Troglytes reject their inferior existence and call for greater equality.

On Deep Space Nine, however, the question of social class is much closer to home – it is a part of the great melting pot that the station represents. The Cardassian Garak is of a notably high-ranking family, while Doctor Bashir's father is depicted as a downmarket Londoner. Sisko's father owns a Creole restaurant; Ezri's mother owns an interstellar mining operation; Major Kira's Bajoran caste system dictates she should be an artist, despite her evident lack of ability. While one could perhaps *read* some class into the previous series (Spock and Picard are palpably posh), these differences were never up for discussion. In *DS9*, however, the question of class is raised quite explicitly. The episode 'Past Tense' takes us back to the earth of *Star Trek*'s past (our future) in which 'social problems . . . seem too enormous to deal with' and the poor and unemployed are simply ghettoized to keep them out of the way. One crewmember finds herself living in the high society of this period in an 'ultra-modern' suite with a 'million-dollar view of the bay'; others endure appalling housing, food and medical shortages in the ironically named 'sanctuary' for the socially excluded.

The juxtaposition of these two extremes serves to highlight the dangers of our own society – in *DS9* it is *our* earth, not some alien world, that has descended into a class-based repression. Back on the station we find the Klingon General Martok, whose career was sabotaged by simple class prejudice. The council member who rejected his application to the military was 'of the blood – born to rule. . . . He couldn't bear the thought of someone like me joining the elite officer ranks.' When this same council member finds himself in trouble he is rapidly rescued by his friends in high places. 'That's the difference between his name and mine,' comments Martok; 'his opens doors, mine closes them.' It is interesting, given the volume of literature on gender and race in *Star Trek*, that an analysis of the class and status systems in play has not yet come to our shelves. The treatment of this issue is consistently a critical one: class divides stand very much in the way of the idealized utopian vision.

Star Trek's list of the moral crimes of humanity is headed by slavery. Personal freedom is its most valued objective. It must be said that on occasion this can sound a little like the Cold War injunction to 'Live Free or Die!' still emblazoned on car number plates in the fervent state of New Hampshire.[13] Giving it the benefit of the doubt, it is worth pointing out that the issue of slavery is the focus of the very first *Star Trek* ever, Gene Roddenberry's rejected pilot, in which Jeffrey Hunter played the short-lived Captain Pike. In the story, Pike is captured by a race who have selected him to breed with their one human female; it turns out that they are a brainy super-race and need humans to service their needs. Pike is given a fantasy existence of exactly what he most desires, and the Talosians cannot understand it when he objects both to his own imprisonment like an animal (the episode is called 'The Cage'), and the idea of breeding 'a whole race of humans to act as slaves'. In some astonishment, they let him go, realizing that his species has 'a unique hatred of captivity' such that they 'prefer death'.

An opposition to slavery is a key element of the *Star Trek* world – it underlies the emphasis on the rights of all 'sentient' life forms that is enshrined in Starfleet practice. The *TNG* episode 'The Measure of a Man' uses the analogy with slavery to make a case against the use of 'disposable people'. The issue of racism in more recent American history is dealt with extensively in the later as well as the earlier series. An example might be an episode in the original series 'Let that be Your Last Battlefield', which is patently about 'race'. It concerns two groups, both with bi-coloured black and white faces, locked in an unending conflict. They are divided according to whether it is the left or the right side of their face that is black or white: to the viewer they are like identical twins. Kirk fails to bang their heads together and we leave them, apparently to pursue this utterly pointless conflict for eternity. The *Star Trek* characters are completely puzzled by this; Chekov comments: 'there *was* persecution on earth once – I remember reading about it in my history class'. Although the episode

could be said to have its heart in the right place, in drawing attention to the arbitrary nature of the markers of racial difference, it is
none the less also rather smug in the attitude of superiority from
which the situation is presented.

Slavery and racism are issues on which *Star Trek* has systematically delivered a critical account. This is perhaps not surprising, given
their centrality to the troubled political consciences of the liberal
strand in American thought and culture that was, and remains, the
impetus behind *Star Trek*. The *DS9* episode 'Far beyond the Stars' is
a particularly powerful indictment of racism, set in the 1950s and
featuring Sisko as a writer of science fiction whose stories about a
black spaceship captain are censored and the magazine that dared to
print them pulped. There are those who believe that *Star Trek* itself
reproduces the evils it claims to criticize: we are aware of these arguments, but leave them to one side for the moment. Our point here is
simply to look at the extent to which *Star Trek* revolves as a drama
around making a 'case' against humanity – and a defence. Disturbing conflicts in American history can be expected to figure. An
episode of *The Original Series* – 'A Private Little War' – was made
about the war in Vietnam. More provocatively, the episode 'Nemesis'
of the more reflective *Voyager* series raises further historical doubt
on the subject. Chakotay finds himself in a jungle guerrilla war in
which the other side are apparently desecrating the corpses of their
enemies; the morality of the situation seems quite clear to him and
he joins in as a participant. It is only in the denouement that he discovers he has been fighting on what he must conclude was morally
the 'wrong' side.

Vietnam and the Second World War are the two wars of the twentieth century that have the most powerful hold on the imagination of
the makers of *Star Trek*. From a European point of view, it is easy
to see the cultural influence of other wars. We have dealt at some
length with the 'nautical metaphor' in *Star Trek*, and could argue that
the history of the Napoleonic Wars has a strong legacy in the series.
Similarly, there are a number of ways in which the tropes of the Great
War are reworked in *Star Trek*, particularly in the bleak and costly
alliances and endless casualty sheets that characterize the protracted
'Dominion War' in *DS9*. Nevertheless, these are influences of historical feeling and resonances of the imagination that refer principally
to how conflicts are represented. The substantive conflict to recur in
much of *Star Trek* is the Second World War, on which (unlike the
Great War of 1914–18, the Vietnam War or the Cold War) the verdict
of historical hindsight is very clear. This was not a war in which self-
interest predominated; it was a 'holy war', a politically just war

against the immoral force of fascism. The extent to which the definition of the Second World War as, retrospectively, the fight against fascism is justified is a larger question. (The worst crimes of the Nazis were only appreciated as the war ended.)

There are direct references to the Second World War in several of the series, explicitly so in *The Original Series* and *Voyager*. In *TOS*, 'Patterns of Force' is the first episode to show the horrors of Nazism, depicting a society in which a certain group is being exterminated. The celebrated episode 'City on the Edge of Forever', featuring a romance between Captain Kirk and a youthful Joan Collins, also revolves around the theme of the Second World War. Kirk's gorgeous girl has to die, since in this 1930s moment – rather improbably – her survival was linked to a timeline in which Hitler went on to win the war. The most extended explicit discussion of the Second World War occurs in *Voyager*. The fiftieth anniversary, in 1995, of the dropping of the atomic bomb on Hiroshima was the occasion for *Voyager*'s allegorical treatment of its consequences. The invention of a 'Metreon Cascade' super-weapon ended a war by destroying an entire inhabited moon, and this wiped out Neelix's entire family. The scientist who invented the weapon, fifteen years later and towards the end of his life, is trying to make some reparations. Neelix, forced to come to terms with his own failings of the time (he had left the moon himself and been branded a deserter) is eventually able to articulate a note of forgiveness.

It is not without interest that it should be the Allies who can – by extension – be forgiven. The Nazis are themselves more difficult to 'forgive'. There is, however, an innovative spin put on their crimes in the double episode 'The Killing Game', in which the *Voyager* crew act out the French resistance as well as American liberators in the Second World War. As Joe Menosky explained, his co-writer Brannon Braga thought it would be 'cool' to put the alien species currently harassing *Voyager* into Nazi outfits, and the eventual ending – in which the hostile Hirogen follow one dissident and turn towards merely 'virtual' holographic hunting of their prey – is a 'kind of *Star Trek* message where this guy becomes a good guy, and Janeway ends up working together with him'. Rather engagingly, Menosky concludes: 'So what started out as "Let's watch some shit blow up and see World War II material", and had an action-oriented or more visual inception, turned into a story with a thematic *Star Trek* basis.'[14]

No such spin, whether the optimistic *Star Trek* 'message' or postmodernly coded 'cool', is appropriate for raising the issue of the Holocaust – which 1990s *Star Trek* repeatedly does. In *Deep Space Nine* there are a number of episodes in which a clear parallel is drawn between the brutal occupation of Bajor by the Cardassians and the concentration camps of Nazi Germany.

The occupation of Bajor (a precursor to the events of the series itself) is represented very much in terms of the Nazi model. The Cardassians have stolen from Bajor, raped and murdered in labour camps, used Bajorans as lab rats for their experiments, had them work as personal slaves and mistresses, and tried to suppress their traditional religion. *Deep Space Nine* begins with a very fragile Bajoran government (the first for over half a century) and all the diplomatic problems one might expect from this situation. The Bajorans are, without exception, vehemently opposed to all things Cardassian, and to any opportunity for co-operation. Major Kira sums up much of her people's feelings in one episode ('The Darkness and the Light'):

> None of you belonged on Bajor; it wasn't your world. For fifty years you raped our planet and you killed our people. You lived on our land and you took the food out of our mouths. And I don't care whether you held a phaser in you hand or you ironed shirts for a living – you were all guilty.

'Duet' deals with the aftermath of one of the Cardassians' worst atrocities – the events of the Gallitep labour camp in which countless Bajorans were worked into their graves. When an unknown Cardassian arrives on the station he is identified as having been posted at this camp and is held by the Bajorans to be a war criminal, simply by virtue of having been there. Major Kira, particularly, is in favour of trying him in court: 'If you had been there twelve years ago when we liberated the camp. . . . If you had seen the things I saw. . . . All those Bajoran bodies. . . . Starved, brutalized . . . the rape of mothers in front of their children. . . . Husbands beaten till their wives couldn't recognise them. . . . Old people buried alive because they couldn't work anymore.'

As the episode unravels, much confusion abounds about the identity of this Cardassian. Initially claiming to be a filing clerk, he is later revealed as 'The Butcher of Gallitep' himself, the detested Gul Darhe'el. As Darhe'el, the Cardassian freely regales Major Kira with the attitudes behind the occupation: 'What you call genocide, I called a day's work,' he boasts. When Kira digs deeper into the past, however, she finds evidence of cosmetic alterations performed on this Cardassian, coupled with (reliable) reports that Darhe'el himself is dead and buried. When she confronts him with this information, the prisoner becomes hysterical; he tries to ignore her and calls for security to rescue him from Kira's questioning. It turns out that this man is the filing clerk Marritza after all and to Kira's assertion that Gul Darhe'el is dead, he becomes increasingly agitated, and eventually begins to break down:

> That's not true! I'm alive! I'll always be alive! It's Marritza who's dead! Marritza; who was only good for cowering under his bunk and weeping like a woman.... Every night, covering his ears so he wouldn't have to hear the Bajorans screaming for mercy while we killed them.... Covering my ears.... So I wouldn't have to hear those terrible screams! You don't know what it's like to be a coward. To stand by and let such horrors take place, and do nothing.

Kira is shaken by this story, and cannot understand Marritza's motivation in the deception. She even begins to forgive him as a member of the Cardassian occupying forces: 'You were only one man,' she tells him. Marritza pleads with her to maintain the charade: 'I have to be punished. We all have to be punished.... Cardassia will never survive unless it stands in front of Bajor and admits the truth. My trial will force Cardassia to acknowledge its guilt. And we are all guilty.'

Deep Space Nine shows us the overpowering guilt of a man who was by all accounts completely powerless to prevent that for which he blames himself. Major Kira's acceptance that Marritza is not a 'bad' person is highlighted by the events which follow his interrogation and the public revelation of his true identity: on his way to a transport which will take him from DS9, he is killed by a Bajoran civilian. 'He's Cardassian. That's reason enough,' is the man's explanation.

Perhaps the most eloquent of all these reflections on the Holocaust is the elaborated analogy drawn in the *Voyager* episode 'Remember'. Here, B'Elanna Torres, the half-Klingon/half-human hybrid who is the ship's chief engineer, has the strange experience of re-enacting the memories of a dying woman who has managed to transfer them into her mind – so that some historical record would remain and the crimes could be investigated. In her own life the woman, daughter of a society leader, had fallen in love with a young man from a group defined as 'regressives' and treated as pariahs. He, with his family and friends, had been transported to a 'resettlement' labour area, but the whole population had in fact been exterminated. So extensive was the cover-up, that within this woman's own lifetime, she had become the only one who could remember what had actually happened.

The theme spelt out in this (for once) very plain episode title – 'Remember' – points towards the increasing interest in *Star Trek* in the manipulation of the historical record: an issue itself stemming from the dangerous rise of 'revisionist' or 'denial' scholarship about the Holocaust. The notion of 'remembering' the dead with poppies and so on is heavily ingrained in our society – as long as we *remember* we can avoid the mistakes of the past. The issue of revised and doctrine-driven histories is dealt with on several occasions in *Voyager*. One episode concerns a society that simply cannot face the truth of its own evolution. The model for the treatment of scientists with unpleasant truths to tell is the punishment meted out to those such as Galileo, whose astronomical conclusions contradicted the religious belief of their time. The furore caused in the nineteenth century by Darwin's theory of evolution is paralleled in the people of this culture, who simply cannot accept that they are originally descended from earth.

Human morality is bound up with the truth of the historical record: the rewriting of history is one of the crimes that humans are prone to commit. (*Voyager*'s Doctor commented: 'Revisionist history! It's such a comfort.') *Star Trek* has approached this complex question from several points of view. Worf has the unique distinction of playing a major role in two of the series. He is a Klingon who has become a Starfleet officer, and the resulting clashes between the requirements of his captain and his commitment to a Klingon definition of 'honour' provide the basis of much conflict and negotiation. Klingon honour is modelled on a family-based concept of honour: a disgrace to one is a disgrace to all. In Worf's case his own life is overshadowed by questions about his father, Mogh – was he a Klingon hero or a traitor? At various points his father is convicted of treason, for which Worf is publicly ostracized and formally 'discommended'; Mogh is later thought to have suffered the shame of having been taken prisoner; subsequently he is rehabilitated and so on.[15] In all this, Worf's actions are an attempt at allowing what he knows to be true to stand – but not if the truth would cause more damage. He accepts the appalling ceremonial 'discommendation' as a coward, for instance, in order to prevent the war that revealing the truth would have provoked. So even in a character for whom 'honour' is a mantra (his relentless rehearsing of 'honour' is parodied by Ezri Dax on *DS9*), the question of what stands as the historical record is a complex one.

One episode of *Voyager* deals explicitly with the question of how history sees the guilt (or otherwise) of human action. In 'Living Witness' the ship's holographic Doctor finds himself reactivated in a museum 700 years in the future. The crew of *Voyager* are here recorded as sadistic warriors whose desperation to get home led them to make a deal involving the use of a genocidal biochemical weapon. An audio-visual simulation depicts what to us is a very 'alternative' Captain Janeway. Drawling such lines as '... violence – it's the Starfleet way ...', she is staged as an object of hate for the visitors to the museum. Janeway's hair is cropped, Chakotay's elegant forehead tattoo has spread all over his face, the entire officer complement wears black leather gloves. The hailing message is: 'This is Captain Janeway of the Warship *Voyager*.' It is claimed by future historians that *Voyager* has 'assimilated' other species and pressed them into its crew. This self-reflexive moment is rendered safe, as the Doctor – a 'living witness to history' – manages to convince the historian/curator that the latter's version of history is wrong. Nevertheless, the gesture of rehearsing an unfavourable historical verdict on *Voyager* is an index of a preoccupation with the record of human guilt.

'Living Witness' is an example of the *Voyager* crew's being presented to us as evil: in this respect it is analogous to the episodes of *The Original Series* and *Deep Space Nine* that are set in a 'mirror universe' in which they exist largely as morally alien versions of themselves. In the case of *Voyager*, the crew do appear in other contexts, particularly in other time frames (for example, in 'Future's End'), but their moral integrity is rarely questioned. The prosecution against human morality is far more likely to come from *Voyager*, and it is often influenced by what we might call a post-Holocaust moral sensibility. The biological experimentation associated with the Nazi camps and the work of Josef Mengele seems to haunt them. In 'Nothing Human', B'Elanna Torres is dying of an illness for which there is a cure, but she flatly refuses it on the grounds that it was developed in the camps on Bajor during the Cardassian occupation and she will not be contaminated by it. In the episode 'Scientific Method', Janeway is enraged that an alien species have infiltrated the ship and are conducting covert but lethal 'medical' experiments on the crew. In the showdown she accuses them of 'exploiting another species for your own benefit' and declares that 'my people decided long ago that that was unacceptable, even in the name of scientific progress'. The vocabulary is of 'mutilations', 'deformities', 'fatalities'. To shake them off, Janeway flies through a binary star, with an estimated one-in-twenty chance of success; death is preferable to becoming a 'lab rat'.

Each series of *Star Trek* explicates the crimes by humans against humans in a different way. It is perhaps not surprising, for instance, that the first series (1966–9) does not offer much of a critique of environmental crime. The issue was not sufficiently high up the political agenda. The later series, however, raise the problem in their own distinctive ways. High-minded and rational, *The Next Generation* crew discovers (in 'Force of Nature') that warp travel is destroying the universe they love to explore. The result is a Federation Council Directive instituting a speed limit of warp 5, except in extreme emergencies. *Deep Space Nine* persistently presents us with a world made infertile by the occupying Cardassians and the problems this causes for future generations. In *Voyager* some dramatic encounters are staged on what is obviously regarded as an important issue. Tom Paris is demoted and punished when he disobeys orders and tries, against the Prime Directive, to save a society from environmental destruction ('Thirty Days'); while in an episode somewhat indebted to *The X Files* ('Juggernaught'), *Voyager* encounters a weird monster created from the ingestion of toxic waste. The Me'lon are a race of beings known to us only for their unprincipled dumping of such waste.

The point, however, is that although the series may choose different issues, and treat them differently, they all share the common theme of an orientation towards questioning human morality. Q's indictment, citing 'the multiple and grievous savageries of your species', is the charge *Star Trek* seeks both to illustrate and defend themselves against. Underlying this elaborate discussion of human morality is the more difficult issue of human nature. It is 'difficult' for a number of reasons, yet it is the question that *Star Trek* poses most consistently. In this respect, *Star Trek* is running against the tide of opinion in social theory, which has for many years been dominated by an implacable opposition to 'humanism'.[16] The universe in *Star Trek*, on the other hand, is viewed from a profoundly 'humanist' position. *Star Trek* is more in tune with the history of western humanist thought than it is with the anti-humanist position of its critics.

The racial/spatial problem

One theme is explored in all the series of *Star Trek* – and in the films and all the peripheral materials. Uniting them all is the desire to answer one basic question: what constitutes humanity? How can we define the human? The whole idea of going into space is designed to enable us to focus back on ourselves – perhaps understand ourselves better. Locating the *Star Trek* enterprise as part of a long tradition of the imaginative writing of modern human exploration (as we have already done) is a help here. In 'Living Witness', 700 years later, the

Doctor says indignantly: '*Voyager* wasn't a warship – we were *explorers*.' Such exploring moves, in earth's history, have in the past precipitated very fraught debates about the definition of the human. There were debates, for instance, about whether various indigenous peoples were even to be regarded as 'human' by the western colonizing cultures. (As we saw in Part I, the charge that Achebe laid against Conrad was precisely that his writing had 'dehumanized' Africans.) It is perhaps not surprising that a less malign version of the question follows from the exploration of space. In this section of the book, we look at the various devices that are used to put this issue of the definition of humanity under the spotlight, throughout the four major series, with a surprising coherence and constancy. In Part III of the book, we shall be looking – by contrast – at what the two later series do very differently from the earlier ones. For now, however, let us address what all these versions of *Star Trek* have in common – the interrogation of human nature.

There are two main groups of devices that *Star Trek* has elaborated to pose the question of what human nature 'really is'. They consist, first, of anomalous situations brought about by various aspects of space physics; and second, the markers of conflict or difference that are assigned to various 'species', 'races' and so on. We shall first examine the way in which 'race' – a highly contentious topic – is addressed. *Star Trek* dealt with the question of race, from the outset, through the national and ethnic composition of the crew. Like the multicultural crews of the merchant marine in the days of Conrad, the crew of the first *Enterprise* was multi-ethnic: it included Sulu (Pacific Asian), Uhura (African American) and – just as significantly at the height of the Cold War – Chekov (Russian). Having said that, the flirtation with 'difference' in the person of the half-Vulcan Mr Spock, was scarcely – by more recent *Star Trek* standards anyway – adventurous. Mr Spock's only visible difference from his white male colleagues is the top of his ears, which are a bit pointed. 'Difference' is found in this original set-up – but mainly in relation to the weird and wonderful aliens they meet in space, rather than within the crew. Captain Kirk was even shown to express explicitly anti-Klingon views, a prejudice justified within the narrative by the fact that his son David had been killed by Klingons. Later series have found it possible to integrate more and more 'different'-looking species into the insider crews.

It would be surprising if a popular television entertainment – explicitly set in the future to enable it to be more liberal in its treatment of race issues – did not encode elements of the racist perceptions we all inevitably bring to bear on our worlds. Every watcher of

Star Trek could no doubt identify examples where the wrong note has been struck. The portrayal of the black Ligonians in 'Code of Honour' stands out as particularly 'unfortunate' at the beginning of the first series of *The Next Generation*. In general, the issue is whether *Star Trek* has been able to raise questions about race without employing the kind of stereotypes it might hope to avoid. Complex and contested definitions of 'ethnicity', 'race', and 'species' are all in play here. In order to address this, it is necessary to give a brief run-down on how *Star Trek* presents what we might call 'racial differ-ence' – visible (bodily) markers of difference. It is particularly important to do this, as *Star Trek* has over the years quite flatly refused the categorization that any sociologist of the United States might consider appropriate. Klingons or Vulcans are played by both white and black actors: their identities as Klingon or Vulcan are vouchsafed in insignificant 'phenotypical' markers such as the ears or facial ridges, as well as by 'ethnic' characteristics that are quite patently cultural (concepts of reason, or honour, for instance). These differences have generated a lot of debate, particularly among the fans of *Star Trek*, about whether they can be linked to characteris-tics of existing groups on earth. Were the Klingons meant to be the Soviet Russians? Are the Cardassians modelled on the Nazis? These sorts of questions – not usually bearing much fruit – echo around the fan communities.[17]

Initially, it might help to classify the various visibly 'marked' groups in *Star Trek* in such a way as to highlight their function within the narrative as a device for defining humanity. Before describing them, one point has to be made about the significance of the word 'humanoid'. It may readily be observed that *Star Trek*'s universe is populated by many species or 'races' who look very similar to – but not the same as – human beings. Within the narrative, *Star Trek* even-tually offered an explanation for what had started off as a personal preference by creator Gene Roddenberry (no funny-looking aliens on the show, please) but was becoming a point of debate. In the episode 'The Chase' in *TNG*, it is shown, through the co-operative effort of humans, Klingons, Romulans and Cardassians to solve a four-billion-year-old genetic puzzle, that the DNA for many humanoid races arose from one originating species of ancient 'progenitors'. Whether or not one is convinced, this is 'the line' explaining why there should be so many 'humanoid' species with such a close similarity to humans.

Let us look firstly at an important category through which a great deal of conflict and power, rather than mere 'difference', is carried. This is the group of most frequently featured <u>organic humanoid species</u>. *Humans* (they are invariably privileged so we might as well put them first) are emotional, conflicted, disorganized, but they have a rational scientific side and high moral principles as well as a romantic sense of idealism; they will 'die trying' to live up to what they believe in. *Klingons* were for many years the representative of anger ('wrath') and the chief opponent of the Federation; latterly they have been brought into an uneasy alliance and the trait by which they are most frequently represented is traditional, family-based 'honour'. The *Romulans* are rivals to the Federation, defending their proud empire beyond the neutral zone; they are at the same time cast as something like humans in disposition, though perhaps more closely resembling their genetic cousins the Vulcans. The Romulans are a very serious bunch and liable to cause much trouble behind one's back – they are the mysterious 'Men in Black' of the Alpha Quadrant. One of Starfleet's most consistent enemies in recent times are undoubtedly the *Cardassians*, characterized by deviousness in the context of an apparently strong social order. Their judicial system is purely for show; the secret intelligence 'Obsidian Order' is really in charge. They are perhaps best known for their ruthless occupation of Bajor, but in a twist of dramatic irony they come to mirror their victims at the hands of the 'Dominion'.

Klingons, Romulans and Cardassians traditionally carried the most sustained conflict with the values of humanity encoded in Starfleet. As the magazine *Star Trek Monthly* candidly tells us, 'There's a distinct technique for coming up with a villainous alien race for *Star Trek*. What you do is emphasize a Human trait or quirk at the expense of all the others, blow it up out of all proportion and keep playing off it.'[18] *Vulcans* are depicted as majestic, ambassadorial and above conflict, valuing logic over instinct and passion. They are perhaps the nearest in *Star Trek* to Hamlet's evocation of 'a man': noble in reason, infinite in faculty.[19] The group of four 'humanoid' species who discover their ancient common ancestry are the more mortal – perhaps one might say more *human* – Klingons, Romulans, Cardassians and humans.

There are several other organic humanoid species in *Star Trek*, some with a significant role in the developing narrative. *Deep Space Nine* was constructed around the *Bajorans*, a people characterized by their elaborate religious faith and calm dignity as well as their bold resistance in the face of oppression. Temperamentally the opposite are the *Ferengi*, first introduced as unpleasantly acquisitive, but later shown as having a braver and more generous disposition. The war with the 'Dominion' brought in other species, such as the *Breen* – whose presentation of self owed something to Darth Vader of *Star Wars*. The situation of *Voyager* has facilitated a new use of alien organic species. As *Voyager* is progressing through the Delta Quadrant, we are passing through the space of particular species in residence. Rather like Odysseus on his winding voyage, we tarry awhile with each group and then move on. Hence particular species, with identifiable characteristics, play an important role for a few episodes, giving way to a new 'story arc' as we move out of their range. The warlike and feuding *Kazon* are superseded by the sick and unprincipled *Vidiians*, then by the master hunters the *Hirogen*, and so on.

   Star Trek history contains a very long list of organic humanoid species encountered in space. They may be given specific personalities or characteristics, but these do not form part of a continuing story. The *Star Trek Encyclopaedia* lists scores of such species, from the Axamarians and Aldeans to the Zaldans and Zibalians.[20] In most of these cases a species is identified, but not given particularly significant attributes from which to reference aspects of human nature. Sometimes quite important characters are given a species identification that is specific to them but does not 'carry' any real difference or conflict. An example of this might be Neelix on *Voyager*. Neelix is a *Talaxian*, and he has a very unusual hairstyle and a freckly facial décor. There is no sense, however, in which his personality is the product of what we might call his 'species-being' as a Talaxian; in fact, he is a recognizably 'human' type of the most obvious kind. So, confusingly, *Star Trek* is working with two different categories of organic humanoid aliens: those who 'carry' the burden of meaning of significant difference (such as a wrathful Klingon), that will probably lead to conflict, and those who, like Neelix, simply register 'difference' in their bodies and appearance. In this, a strategy disrupting the expectation that ethnic difference is connected to visible appearances of 'race', *Star Trek* is treading a path that provokes a liberal response.

   A second category marks a significant break with the limitations of the human (as seen in *Star Trek* anyway). There is quite a range of characters who are <u>superhuman</u> in the precise sense that they have abilities and capacities which humans – as far as we know at present – do not. At the strong end of this continuum, they are beings who can assume an organic, flesh-and-blood form, but exist also as forms of energy (or possibly spirit). To take the weakest form of the phenomenon, let us look at characters who have 'empathic' perception. It is quite routinely a feature of *TNG* that some people, or peoples, are innately 'empaths'. The most well-known case is Deanna Troi, the psychological counsellor of the *Enterprise*, who is half-human and half-*Betazoid*. Since the Betazoids are a race of telepaths, she has some empathic (though not truly telepathic) ability: she can sense conflict, fear, and so on, and is able to converse in her head with telepaths if she chooses. The entire frame of reference of Captain Picard's leadership is rational and scientific, yet such is the certainty about Troi's empathic means of communication, that Picard will take decisions on the basis of what she has told him she has 'sensed'– he simply accepts that she has access to information that he does not. (There is some debate, in 'The Drumhead' as to whether it is ethical to 'use' empaths to determine innocence or guilt in a criminal context, however.) The category of 'an empath' is what we might call an 'essentialist' one, and in *Star Trek* it is construed as an attribute of particular species or 'race' (these categories are pretty much interchangeable in this world).

The character of Kes in *Voyager* is an *Ocampa*. By the time she left the ship (hoofed out to make way for the character of 'Seven') she had been developed as a being of *super*-natural (superhuman) capacity. Her parting from *Voyager*, in an episode appropriately entitled 'The Gift' involves her blowing the ship 10,000 light years on its way, thus knocking ten years off their projected journey time to get home. The audience has been prepared for this startling feat by the gradual development of Kes's supernatural powers. When Tuvok teaches her to meditate, to control her emerging psychokinetic abilities, they find that she can intervene with matter at the subatomic level. Kes is an operator in the world of quantum physics and in the end *Voyager* is just too limited an environment for her – her very presence poses a threat to the cohesion of the ship. Another character with superhuman abilities is Guinan, also trusted by Picard to the extent of his taking major decisions on the basis of her unprovable insights. He literally stakes his judgement on faith that she is right when he takes the awesome responsibility of sending the *Enterprise*, which Guinan knows is in the wrong timeline, to its destruction ('Yesterday's Enterprise'). Guinan is not immortal or omniscient, but she has been around for several hundred years and has seen places (such as 'The Nexus' in the film *Star Trek: Generations*) that humans do not readily have access to.

The being who *is* immortal and omniscient in *Star Trek* is, of course, Q. The name may have various sources; an obvious one is 'question' or 'query'. Another possibility is the gadget expert in James Bond films. It has one relevant history in Christian theology, where the so-called 'synoptic problem' of the authorship of the gospels is held by some to involve a 'hypothetical entity' responsible for the creation of parts of these texts not otherwise explicable. 'To postulate Q is to postulate the unevidenced and the unique.' Q is here a sort of residual category, invoked when need arose and now, it seems, the subject of much controversy.[21] The function of Q in *Star Trek* is also a topic upon which much speculation can be aired. As a god figure, he has the merit of being funny (the divine comedic effect) and the arrival of a female captain has added a sexual dimension to his repertoire.

The last of the supernatural characters that we want to identify (there are many more throughout the history of *Star Trek*) are the important category of 'shapeshifters'). These have appeared in earlier series but come into a major role in the religious ethos that informs *Deep Space Nine* (discussed in Part III). For the moment, we can identify them as 'the founders' (god-like beings who can assume any form they choose and revert to a merged experience with each other when they 'link'. The founders have an elaborate staffing support system; they can use the clonable 'Vorta' as subaltern officers disposing of the energies of the 'Jem'Hadar', a strata of slaves whose devotion is related to a chemical drug addiction (to 'ketracel white') that has been programmed into their DNA. Many of the superhuman entities in *DS9* have a religious dimension, most notably the 'prophets' of Bajoran religion. Odo, the security officer on the station, is refreshingly secular in his attitudes most of the time, despite being viewed as a god by the Vorta and Jem'Hadar. He has broken with the founders, but retains his ability to 'shapeshift'. The function of all these superhuman figures in *Star Trek* is to draw attention to the frail limitations of humanity, but also to show humanity in a good light.

The third group it is useful to identify are the hybrids. Although one might think that the post-modern climate underlying the values of *DS9* and *Voyager* would be particularly friendly towards hybrids, they have in fact been a feature of *Star Trek* from the beginning. Mr Spock is the first hybrid. He is, however, a relatively modest one, in the sense that Vulcans are cast as a 'top of the range' human species and the proposed organic differences between humans and Vulcans (such as the green blood and mating cycle of the latter) are a little unconvincing. Deanna Troi might be an example of a being who is technically a hybrid but with minor consequences – to all intents and purposes she is really a human with a sixth, empathic, sense (and an embarrassing mother). The two human/Klingon hybrids, Worf's son Alexander in *DS9* and B'Elanna Torres on *Voyager*, are treated somewhat differently. Alexander is conflicted in terms of his two cultural heritages: his dilemmas are strictly about beliefs and lifestyle. Torres, as we elaborate later on, is presented as a more biological hybrid: a being made up of two different DNA packages.

In addition to these rather lightly treated hybrids, *Star Trek* has created two types of hybrid that are a more significant challenge to assumptions about human nature: cyborgs and symbionts. These both feature in discussions later on in the book. For the moment, we need to draw attention to the cyborg entities created by the assimilation of humans into the Borg collective. Although there are several lesser examples, the two main characters to be developed in this context are Picard and Seven of Nine. Picard, kidnapped and turned into 'Locutus of Borg'[22] is not really a cyborg in any permanent form – though he has been physically mutilated Picard is able subsequently to restore himself to complete humanity, in a bodily sense anyway. Those who view a hip replacement as a form of limited cyborgia might be interested to note that the captain was already running with an artificial heart. The physical effects of Picard's assimilation, however, are largely temporary. Seven of Nine is a more interesting case, in that she had been so small at her assimilation as a child, that she had been fully psychologically acculturated as a Borg; furthermore (and unlike Picard), her Borg 'implants' have given her some lasting superhuman powers. Rather like Data in *TNG*, who at various points saves the *Enterprise* because of his immunity to some factor noxious to human physiology, Seven has capacities which enable her to play the same role on *Voyager*. In particular, we are told that her sight is superhuman – her prosthetic eye can 'see' anomalies in space/time, and aliens invisible to humans. As we shall see, the narrative of *Voyager* is directed towards the 'rehumanization' of Seven. She may be a hybrid, but the emphasis is increasingly on using her Borg capabilities in the service of quite specifically human values.

The 'symbiont' characters in *Deep Space Nine* are by far the most radical departure from the *conceptual* norm of 'the human' that we find in *Star Trek* – which is not to say that they actually look much different. The symbiosis involves the 'host' – a humanoid species called the *Trill*, who are distinguished from humans merely by a flourish of decorative skin freckling, and the 'symbiont', which is an unappealing slug the size of a mid-term foetus, which has to be surgically implanted in the host's abdomen. The point is that the symbiont has a life of centuries, the host is humanly mortal, and so the host Trill at any one time can be carrying the memories of the symbiont and its previous hosts. Thus the symbiont Dax has had two hosts (Jadzia and Ezri) whom the audience has seen a lot of, as well as one (Curzon) who is much spoken of as a friend of Sisko's, and several others to whom our access is via the memories of the present host. The gender neutrality of the symbiont, and the fact that the host can

Locutus of Borg

be male or female, gives rise to an unexpectedly bisexual subjectivity in the 'joined' host – a significant point to which we will return. In general, we can see that the symbiont/host duality is another strategy used by *Star Trek* to raise the question of whether human identity is unchanging or not – how far do we recognize the 'essential' Dax in the current behaviour of Jadzia or Ezri? Sisko's nickname for both attractive young women is 'old man', because to him they *are* his mentor and friend Curzon. Biological symbiosis is a strong variant of the theme of hybridity. In *Star Trek* it is used as a device to raise questions about the stability of identity and about sexual subjectivity and desire.

In considering the markers of difference and conflict in *Star Trek* – of which 'race' is one, but by no means the only one – a certain small category is worth indicating. The genetically engineered individual has featured only occasionally, but it is heavily weighted when it does. Khan, whom we have encountered earlier as the nemesis chasing Captain Kirk, is as dangerous as he is because he was a genetically engineered super-human with mental and physical resources that outclassed ordinary mortals. The Federation responded by banning the employment of any genetically modified person. As happened in the case of Julian Bashir, banning a practice drives it underground. Bashir (the doctor on Deep Space Nine) has an extraordinarily high order of reasoning, perfect hand-eye co-ordination, the ability to compartmentalize his own brain, and mathematical computational abilities that are far above the plausible. These abilities make him rather 'inhuman'. It transpires that as a boy his parents had been so disappointed by his weak progress at school that they had arranged for him to be genetically resequenced, with dramatic results. When all this emerges, his father is sentenced to prison but Julian is not struck off. He is somewhat relieved not to have to disguise his abilities, and more able to grieve the boyhood self that was taken from him.

Finally, we turn to the complex category of beings who are mechanical, rather than organic. The characters are used in a sustained commentary on the nature of the human. No doubt the best known is Data in *TNG*. Data is an android (a robot made in the form of a man) but he aspires to be human. He acquires the ability to experience emotion; he begins to dream and develop an unconscious; he plays the violin, learns to dance and he is an excellent painter. Under a ship-wide situation where inhibitions were lifted, Data had sex with a woman who propositioned him (Tasha Yar in 'The Naked Now'). The point about Data is that although he is strictly speaking an 'automaton', he is presented as embodying many aspects of the human (altruism, friendship, loyalty, responsibility, and so on). Data even has a family, although somewhat formulaic: scientist father, evil twin brother and sadly short-lived daughter. The episode about the tribunal that is convened to determine Data's status and rights is significantly entitled 'The Measure of a Man'.[23] Data is ruled to be a machine rather than a man, but he is given the quasi-human 'rights' that are extended to all sentient beings in Starfleet.

Other mechanical entities make an appearance in *Star Trek*. A scientist managed to create some little 'exocomp' robots that were deemed to be more than mere machines, scuppering her plans for using them as menial servants. The most important development, however, is the extension of the hologram and the challenge that is posed as to how such a being differs from a 'solid' human. In *The Next Generation* a holographic version of Professor Moriarty in a Sherlock Holmes simulation breaks out; he is subsequently enraged when Picard leaves him shut up for four years. The Doctor in *Voyager* (the EMH or emergency medical hologram) is on a trajectory of 'humanization' that parallels that of Data before him. He has been learning to sing opera, experimenting with a holographic wife and children, finding ways to exist in new locations, and so on. In a further twist in *DS9*, the holographic character Vic Fontaine is not only being used to blur the boundaries between a holosuite and life outside; in a 'mirror universe', he has been sighted as human: when shot he is all too literally flesh and blood. It is implied that his identity is not limited to his holographic physical state, any more than human identity, in *Star Trek*, is not reducible to its embodiment.

These are several different forms in which individuals are presented to mark difference both within the category of human beings, and beyond it. The function of organic non-human beings, and of mechanical entities, is to spotlight the question of how humanity is to be defined. The construction of difference by 'race' is certainly one element of this. But 'race' is confused, whether intentionally or not, in *Star Trek*; it is constantly replayed and its meanings re-negotiated. *Star Trek* is not afraid to confront the question of race, and we want to look at two examples where it offers a typically *Star Trek* 'philosophy'. The film *Star Trek VI: The Undiscovered Country* elaborates Kirk's anti-Klingon prejudice. When asked to escort the Klingon chancellor to a peace conference, Kirk pleads his loathing of them as a reason to get out of it. He fails, but his prejudice extends to his crew and when the Klingons come on board for a tense dinner the crew are rude to them. It transpires, after the assassination of the chancellor (of which Kirk is accused), that a conspiracy between Klingon and Federation anti-peace activists is responsible. The key point, however, is that the problem has to be solved by Spock, who works it all out while Kirk is languishing in a prison cell. Kirk's bigoted attitude – his racial prejudice – has made him unable to see what is going on. He has been unable to do his job properly. So while Kirk's racism is quite openly expressed, the resolution of the story makes it clear that it is only when free of such prejudice that he can retrieve his agency. Furthermore, in this instance it seems clear that the Klingons' conflict with Kirk is more plausibly read in terms of the Cold War than in relation to 'race'. The film was released in 1991 and featured the economic collapse (and hence forced peace) of the 1960s *Star Trek* enemy, the Klingons.

In the second example, from the episode 'Living Witness' in *Voyager*, we have an interchange that is very familiar. During a discussion of their own historical record, a Kyrian has called for the Doctor's execution as a war criminal against her people. The rather naïve liberal historian says, 'Please, this isn't about *race*,' while the angry Kyrian woman replies, 'It's *always* about race,' – and in one sense she is obviously right. However, the typically *Star Trek* resolution shows us some very different lines in the museum of the further future: we have become a united people and seen the damage that our racist antipathy to each other caused. No doubt some will see this is as a denial of racism. On the other hand, it is more plausible to put the *Star Trek* philosophy into the same category as one would moves towards 'truth and reconciliation' in contemporary political conflicts. The problem and history is stated, but a peaceful outcome is willed.

Star Trek is not afraid of engaging issues of race directly; *Deep Space Nine* in particular has made moves towards addressing this issue face-on, rather than in any more allegorical context. Captain Sisko is presented quite clearly in terms of his African heritage: he keeps traditional ornaments and wears neo-African clothing outside office hours. He occasionally comments on the imbalances of the past; in 'Badda-Bing Badda-Bang', he refuses to visit Vic Fontaine's holographic sixties casino. When pressed for further explanation he tells us: 'In nineteen sixty-two, the Civil Rights movement was still in its infancy. It wasn't an easy time for our people and I don't want to pretend that it was. . . . We can't ignore the truth about the past.' This reappraisal of the traditional utopian vision (and historical myopia) is not limited to *DS9*, however. In terms of the *Star Trek* representation of race, typically engaging divisions between different species, a recent *Voyager* episode has attempted to redress what might be seen as an imbalance in the past, and one traditionally tied in with a colonial racist agenda. As with most television, *Star Trek* usually presents us with 'good' aliens who look more or less human and 'bad' aliens who look increasingly ugly and disorienting. (The disease-ridden Vidiians are a good example here.) 'Nemesis', however, shows the danger of such generalizations – as we have already mentioned, this features Chakotay becoming embroiled in a Vietnam-style war. The people with whom he is fighting are phenotypically human in appearance, the enemy resemble nothing so much as the 'Predator' of eighties cinema.[24] The substantial shock-value of the episode rests in the conclusive realization that it is the human-like characters who have been perpetrating the moral crimes in this war and the ugly monster characters who are in the right. Despite knowing this to be true, Chakotay cannot shake the feelings he has formed around these people and he cannot look at them with anything but disgust. As viewers, the episode forces us to question our preconceptions.

The question of race in *Star Trek* should be seen as one of several strategies used to try and identify the parameters of human nature. Certainly *Star Trek* is *human-centric*, even if it has tried to give due respect to other species (perhaps more successfully in the later series than in the first two). But to conflate *Star Trek*'s undoubted prefer-ence for human beings over non-humans with racism is wrong. It is not at all clear that aliens are 'used' as metaphors for non-white peoples, and to suggest this might be thought in itself to reflect the very dehumanization of non-whites that is at issue. Some of *Star Trek*'s critics in this matter are very hard to please, perhaps the most extreme being Daniel Bernardi. Having spent a great deal of time claiming that *Star Trek* privileges the 'white', he then complains that the 'ancient progenitor' (an obvious god-substitute) of the galaxy is depicted as 'brown'. Instead of being pleased that this figure has been carefully presented as not white, has clearly been cast and made-up to look vaguely human but with no racial, species or colour charac-teristics, Bernardi then chooses to complain that *Star Trek* presents white humans as having 'evolved' from the non-white.[25] In the tri-bunal about Data's rights, which is about the rights of a machine (however engaging and human-centred), Bernardi first declares that Data is an 'allegory' of racism and then objects to people being 'racist' towards him. These arguments are, frankly, illogical. Another example of the problem is given by Jon Wagner and Jan Lundeen in their more reflective analysis of this question. They describe the fol-lowing situation: it is discovered that the destruction of Worf's entire family honour was brought about by another family; according to Klingon custom Worf has the right to take a life of a young repre-sentative; Worf is handed a knife and the boy set in front of him. The choice is either to kill the boy and act out a (racist) stereotype of innate Klingon aggression, or not kill him and demonstrate that Worf has sold out his Klingon heritage and been duped into absorbing Starfleet values. As Wagner and Lundeen point out, *Star Trek* 'can't win: if Worf drops the knife, the plot validates assimilation; if he uses it, the story racially essentialises Worf. Either way, *Trek* is racist.'[26]

Underlying these disputes is a thoroughgoing refusal to credit the fact that people are actually interested in how to think about 'human nature'. The category is itself so contaminated in cultural theory that it cannot be deployed: where it apparently is being highlighted in popular culture, it must be a 'displacement' of something else. So even though *Star Trek* does offer quite an elaborated discussion of the boundary between the human and the machine, Bernardi chooses to see the Data tribunal not as about what it says it is, but as *really* or 'allegorically' about race. Constance Penley makes a comparable move when she claims that in films such as *Terminator*, the (for her) central question of sexual difference, understood psychoanalytically, is 'displaced' on to the question of human/other difference.[27] The problem is that the theoretical anti-humanism underscoring these critical positions is simply not shared by either the makers or the audiences of *Star Trek*: they are fascinated by human nature and they incline towards 'humanist' values. To say this is not to deny the importance of race and gender; it is to suggest that these differences, in this context, are *sometimes* made to stand in for debate about humans in relation to the non-human. The relationship of humanity to other organic species and their rights is an important question, as is the interface between the human-organic and the mechanical-virtual. These questions are not resolved by being displaced on to issues of race, or gender.

If the representation of race is not best conflated with what we are calling a 'human-centric' universe, neither is it necessarily helpful to conflate it with the question of colour. What does it mean to say that the *Star Trek* project is 'white' in terms of its values, or to describe the *Enterprise* as a 'white' starship?[28] In recent years there has been an increasing recognition of the need for 'whiteness' to be understood, a move made in parallel with the recognition that the ethnicity (cuisine, clothes, and so on) of a dominant group is just as 'ethnic' as the ethnicity of minority groups. Richard Dyer's book on the representation of 'whiteness' in visual imagery gives an indication of the complex nature of these processes. In particular, although much of *White* is about the semiotic management of white 'unremarkability', of whiteness as a norm from which people of colour are marked off, the final chapter of the book has a very different inflection – death. The association of whiteness is not simply with death, but with aspects of death that are particularly fearful, horrible or bleak. Dyer here stresses a cultural connection between whiteness and the dead.[29]

The cultural history of 'white' is complex; it by no means functions in a unitary way as a colour of privilege. Cross-culturally, the associations of whiteness vary considerably. Within the western tradition of literature in English, whiteness does not function in any simple, benign way. A scene in Dickens's *Great Expectations*, for example, shows us Miss Havisham dressed in and surrounded by the unrelentingly white accoutrements of her aborted wedding many years before. Wedding white has moved seamlessly and eerily into the yellowy-white of decay.[30] Moby Dick, the 'white whale' who is the object of Captain Ahab's suicidal loathing, figures at many points in *Star Trek*. One of the most fascinating chapters in the novel is entitled 'On the Whiteness of the Whale', and it was this whiteness that appalled Ahab. He hated polar bears, too, whose 'smooth, flaky whiteness makes them the transcendent horrors that they are'. Next we have the 'white, silent stillness of death' in the white shark; Melville also speculates on the greyness or whiteness of the fearsome albatross in Coleridge's 'Rime of the Ancient Mariner'. Simply to cite references to 'nameless terror', 'strangely hideous', 'marble pallor', 'phantoms', 'spectralness', 'that hideous whiteness' – the white that 'stabs us from behind with the thought of annihilation' – does little justice to Melville's extraordinary indictment of the appallingness of whiteness. In *Star Trek* itself, the personification of evil – the Borg Queen – is startlingly white among her dark drones; 'white' is also the name of the noxious drug on which the Jem'Hadar depend.

Racial prejudice may indeed be expressed, whether deliberately or unconsciously, through the colour connotations of the English language: referring to the 'darker', often 'blacker', side of something, for instance, to indicate moral condemnation. The colour symbolism of language therefore has a layer of meaning that refers to 'race'. The problem, however, is that one cannot associate all colour symbolism with the question of race. The example of Melville's extreme and violent antipathy to the colour white is a pertinent case in point. Yet further complicating the situation with regard to *Star Trek* is the fact that there is an aspect of the politics of black and white that is less about colour than about lightness and darkness. Obviously the vocabulary of day and night, light and dark, has a racist inflection – in fact, Conrad's description of the terror induced in his febrile Europeans by the appearance of black Africans works precisely in this register. It must be said, however, that the entire history of the meanings of lightness and darkness cannot usefully be reduced to, or displaced on to, the issue of race. Taking the example of Conrad (discussed in Part I), we can note that even in the deeply anti-African lexis of *Heart of Darkness* there are contradictions. Cedric Watts has pointed out some of them: 'heart of darkness' might refer not only to the interior of Africa, or even to London, but to the 'dark' (as in mysterious, sinister, evil) heart of Kurtz; 'light' is associated with 'civilization' but also with the destructiveness of fire; whiteness is associated with hypocrisy ('whited sepulchre'), ivory, bones, death'; Kurtz's career may parallel that of Lucifer, whose name means 'light-bringer', evoking the conflation of light with knowledge.[31]

An episode of *Deep Space Nine*, appropriately titled 'The Darkness and the Light', demonstrates many of these issues. It concerns the heavily pregnant Major Kira, whose wartime comrades are now being assassinated by a Cardassian who was disfigured in an attack by their resistance cell. The obsessional Cardassian is preoccupied with the polarization of darkness and light. Kira, as a 'creature born in darkness' (the adversity of her planet's occupation) is 'blinded by the light' which seeks her repentance. She is described as dreaming 'dark dreams' – clearly for him she is the one who is evil. He explains that 'the light reveals the truth . . . no regret . . . no compassion'. Light is associated with both morality and honesty. Light, according to this Cardassian, is the tool of civilized man; Kira, as a person of darkness, is referred to only as 'the creature'. Yet the Cardassian himself frequently retreats into the darkness, and when he does so he reverts to muttering; it is only in the light that he is capable of conversation and interaction with the world. Kira's (surrogate) baby brings up yet more dramatic options – it is an 'innocent' and can thus be 'raised in the light'. The Cardassian plans to use a laser – a tool of light – to remove the baby forcibly from her womb. The question of innocence lies behind the obsessions of both characters. Kira views her associates as innocent freedom fighters ('you were all legitimate targets', she tells the Cardassian). He sees himself as an innocent bystander in a war that was not of his making ('I wasn't even in the military,' he says). Finally, the light is to be the site of Kira's death – the lightness of bones is brought into play. Fortunately Kira is able to outsmart the Cardassian, tricking him into a moment of compassion before shooting him in the chest. As the episode closes she explains: 'Sometimes innocence is just an excuse for the guilty.' From her perspective all Cardassians are guilty of the occupation of her world. Her conclusion that 'light only shines in the darkness' encapsulates the gritty feeling of *DS9* as a whole. Her captor's great mistake was to try to 'separate the darkness and the light' – the two are inextricably bound together in human morality.

One of the associative meanings of whiteness is lightness. Clearly lightness and darkness are crucially important to a narrative that is set in space, where light is at a premium. In *Star Trek* there are frequent appearances by phenomena that are represented as a dramatic form of light, and often they have superhuman powers. Light can be defined rather quaintly as 'that form of radiant energy which excites the sensation of vision', or more modernly in terms of the 'visible portion of the electromagnetic spectrum', or more quantumly as 'particles whose behaviour is governed by wave principles'.[32] Light is a category around which both energy and luminescence hover. There are many ways to define light and it is far beyond our scope here to look at the semantic history of these terms. It is, however, clear that the polarity between lightness and darkness, and its significance in human thought and culture, goes far beyond recent classifications involving the unsatisfactory terms 'white', 'black', 'brown', 'coloured', and so forth. Bernardi objected to the use of 'white light' in *Star Trek* but a moment's thought surely raises the question of what alternatives there are. There is no such thing as 'black light' which presumably would be more acceptable; white light is simply the amalgamation of all visible radiation; visible light *is* white.

Foucault has pointed back to the Stoic philosophers as one classical discussion of the darkness–light opposition: along with the water–fire polarity, darkness and light constitute one of the basic binaries of human existence. In his early essay on 'dream, imagination and existence', Foucault unpicks the phenomenology of dreaming: his analysis is an explication of the more abstract meanings, developed over time, of lightness and darkness. Light, in this analysis, is cast as 'the utter brightness of intuition', 'the lightning flash of inner vision', and contrasted with the limitations of sensory and discursive mediations. Foucault's essay on dreaming and the imagination is oddly resonant of the language of space: he talks in terms of 'cosmogony', 'the whole universe', and so on. The *epic* form of expression is characterized by 'departures, voyages and circumnavigations' – 'that Odyssey of existence'. The 'mesh of exile' and 'the stubborn return' of which he writes capture, uncannily, the texture of *Voyager*. In the lyrical mode, by contrast, existence plays itself out statically in the 'alternation of light and darkness'; in the tragic form of expression the truth 'hardly needs time and space'. Light and dark, in this essay, are explicitly linked to time and space. 'The future lies in the spatially distant', he says. Foucault's treatment of the dream, in this essay, is not only oddly – if conveniently for our purposes – aligned with the lexis of space, it is 'humanist' in a way that is surprising when contrasted with the relentless anti-humanism that characterized most of his work (until, significantly, the last years of his life). This younger and more phenomenological Foucault speaks unblushingly of 'the deepest human meanings', 'the freedom of man in its most original form', and 'the whole Odyssey of human freedom'.[33]

Foucault's essay provides us with one interesting treatment of the polarity between lightness and darkness, in the existential context of time and space. We have introduced it simply to register the many ways in which a discussion of lightness, whiteness, and so on, cannot usefully be restricted to the contemporary politics of race and racism. This is not to say that these issues about race are not important in making sense of *Star Trek*, for quite clearly they are. There is certainly a 'human-centred' agenda in *Star Trek*, but this is neither itself a form of racism, nor is it necessarily mapped on to a racist 'white' logic. *Star Trek* stages many 'racial' issues: that it does not always get it right is clear. On the other hand, as the Klingon dilemma showed us, the alternative is simply to avoid issues that are being negotiated in our lives. Violence that comes legitimated by cultural values is a fairly universal problem.

The racial question in *Star Trek* is part of the woof and warp of the text, rather than one issue about colour. It is there in the impulse towards exploration, itself a feature of modern culture. It is there in the importance of colonialism everywhere one turns in *Star Trek*. The 'Prime Directive' is well intentioned but necessarily much honoured in the breach. It is there in the setting of freedom as *Star Trek*'s main goal, and in its hostility to any form of slavery. It is there in the 'multi-cultural' crews of starships and space stations, playing out current debates about the limitations of this philosophy and strategy. It is there in *Star Trek*'s implacable opposition to the exploitation of one species by another. The issue of race and racism is there in the way *Star Trek* is haunted by the experience of black slavery in America, and by the Holocaust and its legacy. The *inhuman, dehumanizing* aspect of these two major historical assaults on our 'human rights' underlies the incessant questioning of the crimes of humanity in *Star Trek*, as well as its unambiguously 'humanist' values.

Space: the human frontier

The markers of conflict or difference that are assigned to various 'species' and 'races' are part of the way *Star Trek* examines what human nature 'really is'. Let us turn our attention now to another

way in which comparable questions are raised. Here we have situations – in which the issue of human identity becomes crucial – that
come about through technically described *spatial* events that could
not convincingly be relocated on earth. These situations rely on some
of the more popularized propositions of quantum and temporal
mechanics – as we shall try to explain. Here we are thinking both of
the predictable issue of time travel (predicated on the curvature of
space); also of the equally 'science fiction' idea of 'parallel' universes
or a 'multiverse' concept of space/time (the sum total of all 'alternate quantum universes'). We find in *Star Trek* an enormous number
of situations where anomalies exist, either in space / time itself, or in
the technology used to operate in space. This is the spatial equivalent of the maritime literature in which the physical characteristics of
the seas – currents, winds, whirlpools, and so on – are themselves
players in the action. In *Star Trek*, various forms of spatial and temporal mechanical anomalies are regularly used as devices to foreground the issue of how the 'human' is to be defined. In this sense,
'space' in *Star Trek* is not simply a convenient backdrop for the activities of explorers: it is part of the story.

Some of the implications of unpredictable spatial phenomena are
explored more mundanely in a device specific to the fictional world
of *Star Trek*: this is the celebrated 'transporter' system. As human
bodies are demolecularized and reassembled at the flick of a button
– a development that is unimaginable in terms of present knowledge
– it is easy to see that it would be tempting indeed to play with the
possible consequences of this technology's going adrift. Transporter
technology in present research has just about reached the capacity
to beam a photon (a speck of light) from one side of a desktop to
another. In the 1960s, it was invented for *Star Trek* as an economy
measure. This was a low-budget show that could not afford to film
endless sequences (involving models, lighting, sound, and so on) of
the starship or landing craft docking and leaving again. So they hit
upon the idea of the 'transporter', which would simply shift the personnel from the ship to wherever the landing party was going. The
transporter system is described in great detail in the 'technical
manual' of the *TNG* series. It involves scanners to determine a suit-
able arrival site; molecular imaging to derive a pattern that can be
converted into a subatomic matter stream; a buffer in which the
pattern is held and shifts between ship and site compensated for; and
transmission of the matter stream within an 'annular confinement
beam' to the site.[34] This is all most implausible, as Lawrence Krauss
has pointed out in some detail.[35] Most of the people in *Star Trek*
subject themselves with equanimity to a process which, as well as

being most unlikely to work, would also be very unpleasant. The nervy and neurotic character Lieutenant Barclay sensibly exhibits the equivalent of plane phobia and flunks the transporter. Perhaps he is right to do so, as transporter accidents are, in fact, alarmingly common in *Star Trek*.

Spatial identity problems

That transporter accidents are usually used to make a point can be seen immediately by looking at the early example of the malfunctioning transporter in the episode 'The Enemy Within', from the original series. A dog is being put on board. One might expect a dicky transporter either to lose the dog completely, or to produce part of a dog, or perhaps a blob of doggy DNA elements. One would not however, expect it to produce two dogs that are differentiated by moral rather than molecular qualities. In this fanciful plot, two dogs arrive – one viciously aggressive and the other a friendly ship's pet. An ensuing attempt to re-transport them together does reunite them into one dog – which unfortunately dies of shock. Meanwhile, Captain Kirk has arrived by the same transporter: there are now two physically identical Kirks roaming the ship, one good and one bad. The evil Kirk is crudely represented: his eyes glint and flash, his movements are jerky and exude guilt. He tries to rape a young woman. As captain, he callously gives the order to abandon the members of his crew who are freezing to death down on the planet below. The evil captain is certainly an 'imposter'; but the other Kirk is paralysed by his own niceness. He cannot act, he cannot decide what to do. Mr Spock has to remind him what he should be doing – and actually questions his ability to command the ship.

This rather silly story has (appropriately) two 'morals' at the end. The first is about the power of thought and the ability of reason to transcend moral weakness. The evil Kirk appears to be fading out and the good one enjoins him to 'think, and overcome what is happening to you'. This is the philosophy of Mr Spock, who has trained up his powers of logic inherited on his Vulcan side and played down his legacy of human emotion. He says to Dr McCoy: 'I have a human half, you see, as well as an alien half, submerged, constantly at war with each other. Personal experience, Doctor. I survive it because my intelligence wins out over both, makes them live together.' The second conclusion is less overtly rationalist. Dr McCoy says to Kirk: 'We all have a darker side; we need it; its half of who we are; it's not really ugly, it's human.' A binary complementarity of good and evil is asserted. Kirk is shocked to realize that 'I can't survive without him . . . a thoughtless, brutal animal, and yet it's me' – 'I've seen a part of myself no man should ever see.' The episode ends with a strong and dramatic closure. As soon as the weak-but-good Kirk accepts that the evil Kirk is also part of himself, his powers of agency return immediately. He bundles his malevolent other half into the transporter. When Captain Kirk re-emerges he is existentially whole, a charismatic figure lit up with confidence and leadership. He tells the crew to 'forget about' the bad guy, who is now 'back where he belongs'.

This conception of human nature is a little basic – we all have good and bad within us. In our second transporter accident, the device allows us to see something rather more complex. In this one, taken from *TNG*, the accident reveals not simply what is held to be essential or intrinsic to our individual natures; it encompasses what our circumstances might do to change our natures. The episode 'Second Chances' reviews an incident in the history of William Riker. When previously serving on the USS *Potemkin*, Riker had a narrow escape from a planet called Nervala IV, whose unusually unstable atmosphere offers only a small window for transporter use every eight years. Riker is now the first officer of the *Enterprise*, it is eight years later and they are back at Nervala IV. A shocking discovery is made: a freak transporter accident on the earlier beam-out created two William Rikers. While the Riker we know has been pursuing his career in Starfleet, the other one has been surviving alone on Nervala IV for eight long years.

So now we have Commander Will Riker and Lieutenant Will Riker, a challenge for Jonathan Frakes, who has to act both halves of the double character. Fortunately for the viewer, their uniforms are different colours, but they are otherwise identical in appearance. The passing of time has changed the two William Rikers in different ways, however, and particularly in terms of the relationship between Riker and Deanna Troi, the ship's counsellor on the *Enterprise*. Riker and Troi had been lovers at the time of the transport off Nervala IV eight years ago. Commander Riker decided to prioritize his career, and his relationship with Troi evolved into a friendship. Lieutenant Riker is still in love with her, having spent his lonely years yearning for her. When he emerges, Deanna has to decide whether to get involved with him again. She does, but finally concludes that this Riker will do the same as the other one, and so decides to protect herself from being hurt again by rejecting him.

What is most interesting is the difference that the eight years of contrasting life experiences have made between these two men. Lieutenant Riker is embittered; Commander Riker obviously feels unsettled and threatened by this disaffected *doppelgänger* and is reduced to pulling rank on him. Their unsurprising difficulties in getting on with each other give rise to an entertaining exchange between two of the non-human crew members. Data puts the problem down to the fact that, above all, 'humans value their uniqueness'; Worf thinks that what is uncomfortable for both the Rikers is that they are seeing 'something you do not like in yourself'.

Both Data and Worf turn out to be right. Lieutenant Riker, accepting a posting to another ship, decides to invoke their middle name and go under the name of Thomas Riker. Throughout the episode it is made clear that his experiences have made him critical of Starfleet – he is intangibly undisciplined compared with Commander Riker and it is this that Worf has registered. This theme is picked up later in *Star Trek*, when Tom Riker turns up on the *Deep Space Nine* station as a guerrilla fighter. He has joined the *Maquis*, and is attempting to steal the station's ship and fight with them against the Cardassians. Commander Riker's alter ego is both identifiable as him, and yet very different from him; the inference is that such divergences are the result of their different experiences, rather than reflecting intrinsic or essential differences.

'Second Chances' offers not so much a good and a bad Riker, as a contrast between one who is 'disciplined' and one who is not. The implication, that the Riker who remains on the *Enterprise* is 'better' than the one who eventually leaves Starfleet, is countered by the emphasis given to the different experiences that have led to these outcomes. In this sense, the transporter accident 'shows' us something more complicated than the fact that human individuals have good and bad aspects to them. The third series of *Star Trek*, DS9, is set on a space station where people routinely arrive by shuttle rather than by transporter. Transporters here have been used to kill people and to switch between universes, but they rarely bring about any staggering insights into the human condition. So we need to make a jump to the fourth series, *Voyager,* for the next transporter accident. In 'Tuvix' we have a story that is ostensibly at least as silly as the transporter on the original series that produced a nice and a nasty dog. Two people, Tuvok (ship's tactical officer, Vulcan) and Neelix (ship's cook and morale officer, Talaxian) go into the transporter separately but emerge as one character. The post-modern category of 'hybrid identity' is acted out here in a very literal fashion. Tuvix is a disconcerting entity, having some qualities (physical appearance, mannerisms, mental and emotional disposition) of each of these utterly different types. The story concerns this new being, who clearly has a separate identity from his two 'parents' (for want of a better word). What are the rights and status of this individual? The dilemma is acute, since if Tuvok and Neelix are to be brought back to life, this new character would have to die. Tuvix argues bitterly against the reversion – claiming that he has as much right to exist as they do. Clearly, it is a very difficult decision, and in the end Captain Janeway decides to separate these 'twins' that are joined in one body. The Doctor invokes his professional creed, and refuses to undertake the operation. Janeway therefore takes the controls, as well as the total responsibility, for the death of this new life.

The notion of hybridity as a key to identity has been present in *Star Trek* from the beginning, in the form of the Vulcan/human hybrid Mr Spock. It is developed in more depth in the later series, as we shall see later. For the moment, let us consider another episode from *Voyager*, in which a rather different 'device' is used to make an analogous point to the moral of 'The Enemy Within'. In 'Faces' this is explored through the character of B'Elanna Torres, *Voyager*'s chief engineer. Torres is also a hybrid, with a Klingon mother and a human father. Much of her part on *Voyager* revolves around the question of whether she can learn to control her violent Klingon inheritance. She left Starfleet Academy because of her frustration with its rules and discipline, a frustration made worse by the pressures of a complicated relationship with her absent Starfleet father. She is always getting into trouble for acting too aggressively (an interesting trait for a woman character). The plot of 'Faces' is set as *Voyager* is travelling through a region of space in the Delta Quadrant inhabited by the Vidiians, a people subject to a dreadful plague ('the phage'). Other episodes concern their unprincipled habit of 'harvesting' body parts from hapless visitors to keep the disease at bay among their own people. In this case, they have decided that Klingon physiology, being so strong, might enable them to infect a Klingon, who would survive, and deliver an antidote. The nearest to a Klingon they can find is B'Elanna Torres; she is duly kidnapped, after which the Vidiians split off her human DNA and proceed with their experiment on the resulting Klingon.

As in the two Kirks, and the two Rikers, B'Elanna becomes two independent beings – the Klingon and the human version. The Klingon B'Elanna is extremely brave and aggressive, but acts without thinking – she will die fighting to get away. The human B'Elanna is presented as weak, emotional, frightened. 'When they extracted my Klingon DNA they turned me into some kind of coward,' she says. Eventually, they co-operate, with the Klingon offering weapons cover while the human fixes the Vidiian computer to allow them to be beamed out by *Voyager*. The message is exactly the same as in 'The

Enemy Within'. 'So, you need me,' says the Klingon B'Elanna; 'I'm incomplete. . . . It doesn't feel like me,' says the human B'Elanna. The resolution is that the two are transported back together, the Klingon woman dying of her injuries. But the human B'Elanna is not viable without the Klingon DNA and the Doctor restores the hybrid – rather ghoulishly, from the corpse. 'So, she's saving my life again,' says the human B'Elanna. Her conclusion is: 'I guess I'll just have to accept the fact that I'll spend the rest of my life fighting with her.'

B'Elanna's experience here is odd, because ostensibly it is about her hybrid identity as half-human and half-Klingon. Yet the parallel between this episode, and the one where Kirk has to accept that his violent self is a part of his whole identity, is quite clear. The B'Elanna episode shows us a metaphor for thinking about human identity – that our selves are mixtures of the differing and often conflicting qualities that go to make up a (human) whole. This is *Star Trek*'s main concern. It is clear, however, that there has been some movement between the original conception of *Star Trek*, where human nature was prioritized above that of other species – the series developed on the hoof in this matter – and partly also because of the unexpectedly huge popularity of the character Spock. When they began, they were not sure that the public would accept the half-Vulcan alien. The outcry when he was killed off, and the fact that he had become the most instantly recognizable figure on *Star Trek*, meant that he had to be taken more seriously. Similarly, the android Data, in *Star Trek: The Next Generation,* has proved to be much more popular than many of the human characters. As we shall see, later versions of *Star Trek* have taken this on board and developed alien species that have their own integrity and respect – they are no longer simply foils for the reflection of human superiority.

Transporter accidents have been used as a device to split people into multiple personalities exhibiting specific traits; *Star Trek* has developed other devices to do this, too. This process is important in *Star Trek*, because it helps us to understand that human identity is a complex balance of what is endowed, or 'essential', what is chosen, and what results from chance. In one very well-known and much-discussed episode in *TNG*, a different device is used to create two Captain Picards – and to make him choose which one he prefers to be. 'Tapestry' is one of the most memorable and popular episodes in *Star Trek*, and it reads rather like *A Christmas Carol*. Picard has been mortally wounded and is in sick bay where Dr Beverley Crusher is trying to revive him. The problem, we are told, is with his artificial heart. He is dying now because, as a very young man, he got into a fight, was stabbed through the heart, and had a replacement put in. At the point of his death now, he is visited by a character who recurs at intervals in *Star Trek* – the omnipotent, omniscient joker named Q – who gives Picard the chance to re-run his life as a young man, avoiding the fight in order to avoid this senseless early death. Picard elects to do this. He dissuades his friend Corey from starting the fight, but loses his friendship; Corey says, 'I don't know who you are any more.' In every way Picard acts more timidly, more sensibly, than he did in his first life. We are shown what happens to this cautious version of Picard, when Q returns him to the *Enterprise*. Picard is now a humble astrophysics technician on the ship, a mere lieutenant ('Junior Grade') where we all expect him to be the captain. He asks Riker and Troi whether he could ever be promoted and they look embarrassed at the idea of this reliable no-hoper aspiring to a command post. 'If you want to get ahead, you have to take chances,' Riker tells him as he and Troi are bleeped away to a senior staff meeting on the bridge.

Picard eventually pleads with Q to undo this new life as 'a dreary man in a tedious job'. The new Picard is 'bereft of passion and imagination'; he is simply 'not who I am'. Picard insists that 'I would rather die as the man I was, than live the life I just saw'. Far from correcting the mistakes of his youth, Q's exercise has taught Picard that these mistakes form part of a preferable life. There were 'loose threads' in his earlier life, he says, 'untidy parts of me that I would like to remove' – but 'when I pulled on one of those threads it unravelled the tapestry of my life'. Popular narrative being what it is, Picard is not actually required to pay the price for his choice: he is revived and is grateful to Q for showing him that the foolhardy and fearless youth is a part of the senior officer he has become. Like Captain Kirk in 'The Enemy Within', having some aggression is a necessary part of being a good captain. Unlike the Kirk story, however, the recognition of this in 'Tapestry' is not a synchronic truth. As in the story of the two Rikers in 'Second Chances', the passing of time is necessary to bring out the consequences of an experience, and the importance of choice. Who you are now, in *Star Trek*, is a delicate balance of who you essentially are (that's just 'not who I am' says Picard) and the person that your choices and circumstances have made you into. In this, there is an awareness that many possible identities exist for any individual – a point with complex implications.

Duplicate identities

The notion of many possible trajectories has become quite popular. The film *Sliding Doors* is based on the notion that a woman's life could go one of two very different ways (depending on the exact moment that she got home one day). Alex Garland uses such concepts extensively in *The Beach*. At one point the protagonist explains to a girl he wishes were available: 'If you accept that the universe is infinite . . . there's an infinite amount of chances for something to happen, then eventually it will happen – no matter how small the likelihood.' They go on to discuss the various worlds floating around in the cosmos – 'in these planets everything that can happen will happen' – and he tells her stories about her 'parallel' counterparts. Finally he reveals the less metaphysical reason for his counterfactual fixation: 'I leant over and kissed Françoise. She pulled away, or laughed, or shook her head, or closed her eyes and kissed me back. Étienne woke, clasping his mouth in disbelief. Étienne slept. I slept while Françoise kissed Étienne. Light years above our bin-liner beds and the steady rush of the surf, all these things happened.'

The Beach as a whole is not so much a discussion of possible individual trajectories, as a meditation on how groups of people can go down one path or another together – the reality on the beach, as well as the protagonist's own identity, is quite alien to him in reflection and retrospect. Underlying this line of speculation is the notion aired authoritatively by Data in the episode 'Parallels', that in quantum reality everything that could happen does happen somewhere. 'For any event there is an infinite number of possible outcomes and our choices determine which outcomes will follow. But there is a theory in quantum physics that all possibilities that can happen, do happen – in alternate quantum realities.' The notion that the universe is full of slightly different versions of ourselves has proved irresistible to *Star Trek*. It must be said that the quantum physics allegedly facilitating this exploration is a little sketchy in Data's account. One problem is, as Roger Penrose has put it, that classical physics has given us a macro-model while quantum physics gives us a micro-model – but it seems likely that a physics that would bridge the two and explain something like human consciousness is still 'missing'.[36] Danah Zohar has embarked on an interesting attempt to show how quantum theory might be a good way of conceptualizing the self. Using the recognition that quantum phenomena can take the form of waves and/or particles, she suggests that consciousness could be thought of in a way that breaks down the rigid duality between mind and body. The quantum realm, she suggests, is one in which – like human life – existence and relationship are inextricable. Zohar claims that her argument is 'much more' than a metaphor – we leave that to those with competence in quantum physics to assess.[37] As a metaphor, it certainly is a suggestive one for thinking about the parallel trajectories we find in *Star Trek*.

The idea of 'alternate' trajectories can be seen in a very elementary way in the case of Molly O'Brien's dramatic experience. On a family outing Molly (aged eight) falls through a 'temporal gateway' and is lost 300 years in the past. In terms of time as she experiences it there, she is not rescued for ten years, during which period she has to learn to survive in the wild ('Time's Orphan'). When her parents Miles and Keiko finally get her back, she is not the child they knew. She has been disculturated to a shocking degree; in fact, she acts out the behaviour of a 'feral child' entirely raised outside human company. The introduction of the feral child into the *Star Trek* story has a particular significance. Social scientists have seen such children, from 'Victor' in the 1790s to 'Genie' in the 1970s, as a crucial key to understanding human nature, and have studied them with an intensity that some find troubling in that it treated already deprived and disturbed children as 'lab rats'.[38] The so-called 'nature or nurture' debate about how we should best understand human identity, is here reprised in *Star Trek*. The following season of *DS9* returned to this issue, with a story about one of the hundred 'changeling' infants who were dispatched alone into space to fare for themselves ('Chimera').

The notion of an 'alternate' reality for an individual is most strongly evoked if we consider the implications when a 'copy' or 'duplicate' (such as Tom Riker, whom we have already mentioned) is exposed to different circumstances. In the later series of *Star Trek*, duplication is looked at in quite a challenging way – and with a definite conclusion drawn in favour of the 'original' rather than the copy. As we saw in 'Tuvix', the originals were considered to have a better claim to life than the hybrid duplicate – a decision that Janeway took partly in response to an appeal from the partner of one of the two men who had failed to reappear. Both *DS9* and *Voyager* have run dramatic and emotive stories on this question, involving the crew itself rather than projecting the dilemma on to something outside. In *DS9*, the episode 'Children of Time' constructs a scenario in which the station's ship, the *Defiant*, encounters a planet populated by their own descendants. Apparently a 'temporal anomaly' had landed them on the planet two centuries previously and they had settled there – thus we have little children running around who are the direct great-grandchildren of the present visitors. Captain Sisko has to make an appalling decision: do they relive the accident, thus bereaving their own loved ones or do they escape from the anomaly, hence exterminating all their own descendants in this timeline? Interestingly, the *Star Trek* philosophy overrides Sisko's decision – he opts for saving the planet, but an unpredicted factor (Odo) gets them home instead (thus wiping out their descendants).

This episode of *DS9* is viewed largely, though not exclusively, from the perspective of 'our' crew. Very different is the extraordinary *Voyager* episode in which an existentially comparable situation is shown from the point of view of the 'duplicate' crew. 'Course: Oblivion' is the chillingly accurate title. The background is that some time earlier *Voyager* had visited a 'demon class' planet on which the away-team had effectively been cloned, with the copies only able to survive on this planet. Rather than leave them alone, the entire crew had volunteered for cloning and left an alternative but complete cast of characters when they left. Apparently, this duplicated crew had discovered a technique to allow them to function off the planet, and had eventually set off for 'home' in the wake of the real *Voyager*. 'Course: Oblivion' depicts them as the technique is failing – their bodies are starting to degrade and in the end they decide (but too late, it transpires) to return to the demon planet and abandon the attempt to reach earth. The episode is interesting for two reasons. The characters are completely in line with the originals – indeed, it is some time before they become aware that they are not the original crew. Even once this realization is made, Janeway says things like 'Duplicate or not, I'm still the same person,', and 'Our ship may be deteriorating but our humanity is intact,' while Chakotay is urging her to go back: 'Home isn't earth.' Paris insists that 'none of us are real' and that he's 'not sure why we're still taking orders from you'. Tuvok, when the truth is first identified about their plight, says of the duplicate crew: 'I've often wondered what happened to them. Are they flourishing? Do they continue to evolve?'

Tuvok's Vulcan nobility of spirit, in extending the hand of friendship to the clones (not realizing, of course, that he is one of them), is out of tune with the harsher fate that awaits them. Not only are the duplicate crew destroyed, but history is revised to exclude them. Janeway sets up a signal beacon, into which is downloaded the ship's database and all their personal logs: 'In the event we don't survive, there should be some record of our accomplishments.' But in fact, the beacon misfires and demolecularizes: 'all our history, gone', says Harry Kim, one of the last to die. The official record consists of the 'real' Janeway noting an anonymous casualty in the real *Voyager*'s log: ship destroyed, cause unknown, no survivors. It is rather extraordinary in showing us both the plight of a crew with whom we must identify, and what seems to be the *Star Trek* view that originals are privileged over copies. (In this context it might be worth noting that when Vic Fontaine has the temerity to appear not as a hologram, as he is on Deep Space Nine, but – in the 'parallel' station – as an embodied human, he is shot dead within seconds.)

The arguments for favouring the original over the clone are twofold: in the first place there is simply the favouring of 'originary identity'. Preference on this might have an age dimension, as in general cloning seems to be less feared by younger people. Proving, however, Zohar's point that existence and relationships cannot be disentangled, the arguments against the duplicates are strongest with regard to relationships. Tom Paris says to Harry Kim that if they did get back to earth they would come along after the 'real' *Voyager* crew had already been welcomed home by their loved ones. Their families will see them 'for exactly what you are – an imposter' he explains brutally. The issue of relationships is not only central for duplicates, it is a feature of long voyage narratives. In *Voyager*, Janeway's partner Mark has waited faithfully for her for years, and then given up and got himself another girl; next we hear (though from the lying 'pitcher plant' alien in 'Bliss') that he has disengaged himself again. The story of the return of Odysseus features the anxiety about waiting and the original partner – his arrival coincides with the moment after twenty years that Penelope has decided to accept one of the suitors and remarry. The idea of using an alternative trajectory to explore a different relationship had been used in two very popular episodes of *TNG*. In 'Parallels', Worf is transported to an alternate universe in which he is married to Deanna Troi and they have two children – an experience that causes him to regard her very differently when he gets back to the 'real' *Enterprise*. In the closing episode of *TNG* ('All Good Things . . .'), we are shown the future selves of Picard and Beverley Crusher, having been married and now amicably divorced.

The strongest version of this doubling and duplicating comes in the attempt to depict a systematically 'parallel' universe over a period of time. The notion of a parallel or 'mirror' universe is also held to rest on Data's little nugget from quantum mechanics (everything that can happen does happen). In this context, we cannot really speak of one universe – it would be more accurate to speak of a multiverse. It is quite striking that the staging of a temporally continuous parallel universe has given *Star Trek* the opportunity to put human morality rather than human existence under the spotlight. It is morality that features in what is, largely, a binary reversal of what we know of our characters. The 'good' Starfleet people have a mirror or evil variant, and the whole metaphor of the human moral condition is shifted into another existence. This universe, the most elaborated quantum alternative, shows what is essentially the evil side of the coin; it is peopled by the characters we already know, but in a largely malevolent guise:

as one says, 'the players are the same but everyone seems to be playing different parts'. This all starts with an episode from the original series ('Mirror, Mirror'), and reaches its most elaborate rendering in the sequence of episodes in *Deep Space Nine* entitled 'Crossover', 'Through the Looking Glass', 'Shattered Mirror', 'Resurrection' and 'The Emperor's New Cloak'.

In 'Mirror, Mirror' yet another transporter accident results in Kirk, Scotty, McCoy and Uhura materializing in an 'alternate' universe. The ship they find themselves on is owned by the Galactic Empire, a malevolent version of the United Federation of Planets. Everyone they come across seems to be an evil version of a familiar character – as Kirk comments: '. . . not our universe, not our ship, but something – parallel. . . . Everything is duplicated . . . almost.' Meanwhile the 'Imperial' *Enterprise* crew-members have materialized on the Federation *Enterprise*, where Spock quickly notices their odd behaviour and imprisons them. In order to return to his own universe, Captain Kirk is forced to seek help from the mirror version of Spock and he eventually persuades this Spock to embrace the Federation's ideals. The irony here is that the 'human' values of peace, compassion, kindness are here associated with the one non-human character present. With Spock's help, Kirk is able to return home and the duplicate landing party is also returned to its evil empire.

It is some 70-odd years, in the chronology of Starfleet, before the staff of Deep Space Nine encounter this other universe again. During that time, some complex political machinations have altered the foundations and balance of power there, and for humans it is a decidedly less desirable place. The return to the 'mirror universe' (in the episode 'Crossover') comes about as a result of yet another accident, this time the faulty collapse of a 'warp bubble'. Major Kira Nerys and Dr Julian Bashir are returning to the station when their runabout is transported to the mirror universe. Here the station is not called Deep Space Nine, but is known by its original Cardassian name, 'Terok Nor'. It is run by a Klingon–Cardassian alliance, and administered by the alternate Kira for the Bajorans. This Kira, in a similar role to the one she has on *DS9*, is here called the 'Intendant'.[39]

Kira, as the 'Intendant', explains how the current situation came about:

Almost half a century ago a Terran starship captain named James Kirk accidentally exchanged places with his counterpart from your side, due to a transporter accident. The Terrans were barbarians then, but their empire was strong. While your Kirk was on this side he met a Vulcan named Spock and somehow had a profound influence on him. After-

wards, Spock rose to commander-in chief of the empire by preaching
reforms, disarmament, peace. It was quite a remarkable turnabout for
his people. Unfortunately for them, when Spock had completed all his
reforms his empire was no longer in a position to defend itself against
us – the alliance, the historic coming together of the Klingons and the
Cardassians.

The Intendant is a sadistic perverted megalomaniac. For all Spock's
pacifist teachings this universe has returned to the state it was in
before. Indeed, perhaps this is what defines it – with the twist that
now it is humans who are the oppressed victims of a cruel empire.

The episodes in the *DS9* story-arc about the 'mirror universe' are
intended to show us how people can behave immorally in their
doubled form. Captain Sisko in the 'mirror' is having a distinctly
louche affair with this highly sexualised version of Kira, whereas on
'our' station sexual relationships are all about love and commitment.
(Mind you, as soon as he crosses the threshold, 'our' captain easily
takes over his counterpart's affair with Dax, even though in his universe the two are just old friends.) Yet while most characters display
a 'darker' mirror image, some are not so very different from how they
are on Deep Space Nine – Miles O'Brien, for instance, is portrayed
as basically still a good guy in difficult circumstances. Indeed, the
odious Ferengi Brunt is considerably nicer in his alternate 'mirror'
incarnation. That relationships are crucial can be seen from the
painful way in which Sisko's wife is brought back from the dead. Jennifer Sisko had been killed, in a typical *Star Trek* touch, in the devastating attack that resulted from Picard's period as a Borg – thus
giving the commander of the new series every reason to hate the hero
of *The Next Generation*. In a complex story Jennifer is brought back
– but in this reality their marriage is over and she is very hostile to
Benjamin. Their son, however, is completely seduced by this approxi-
mation of his dead mother. The story constantly questions the stability or otherwise of human identity. Is this tough, career-minded
scientist the same person as Jake Sisko's sainted mother? It seems not,
until her better side emerges towards the end. In the episode 'Resurrection', Kira's saintly lover on *DS9*, a religious leader named Bareil,
is brought back as an evil version of himself – he has even come to
steal a sacramental orb. The presentation of Bareil here, as was the
case with Jennifer Sisko, is not done through the mechanism of a
binary reversal: he decides not to go through with his crime. The
move is clearly redemptive; contact with the benign Starfleet universe
is able to turn round these versions who initially reflect the worst
side of the characters. It is with little surprise that in the final

mirror episode we see a mercenary Ezri Dax learning the value of compassion.

Humanization

We have suggested that one of *Star Trek*'s most central concerns is the question of how to define humanity. This is a double-edged project: on the one hand it is staged through the use of *non*-human species who are designed to function as a foil against which human qualities become more apparent. On the other hand, these non-human species themselves end up being progressively 'humanized'. (It is really only on DS9 that we see non-human species being left alone to get on with their lives as if they were different, yet perfectly plausible.) The tradition of what we might call a form of human expansionism – within *Star Trek*'s own value system – tends to take it for granted that it is better to be human. One strategy is for the alien beings to become progressively humanized – they are introduced as 'the other' and become steadily incorporated within a human value system. This can be seen, first, in the long-term transformation of Mr Spock. He began by valuing only his Vulcan heritage, where intelligence and logic prevail. In the film *Star Trek IV: The Voyage Home*, we find at the beginning that he is puzzled when asked in a computer test: 'How do you feel?'; his (human) mother has to explain to him that this is a relevant question to put to a being who is half-human. At the end of the film, he has learnt to deal in the currency of feeling. When asked by his father whether he has a message for his mother, he says: 'Yes, tell her I feel fine.'

This 'humanization' of Spock is one of the strategies whereby the alien, the other, the different, is incorporated into the world of human values. By the sixth film (*Star Trek VI: The Undiscovered Country*), Spock is saying such things as: 'Logic is the beginning of wisdom, not the end.' They are even able to joke about it: Kirk is pondering the traits of humanity; Spock points out: 'Captain, we both know I'm not human,'; Kirk replies, 'Spock, you want to know something, everybody's human,'; to which Spock responds, 'I find that remark . . . insulting.' By 'human' Captain Kirk does not, of course, mean that everyone is from the planet known as Earth – or that everybody is of the species *Homo Sapiens*. Kirk uses the word 'human' in relation to an evaluative concept of humanity, the essential qualities of compassion, respect, imagination and inquisitiveness found in many of the species in *Star Trek*. Spock finds the association of these traits with human beings to be human-centric arrogance, and objects to such sloppy use of language. Kirk is also underlining an abiding tendency of *Star Trek*, and much other science fiction: the alien beings, malevolent machines, insane creatures, and so on, are all there simply to represent aspects of humanity. In *The Original Series* the Klingons were thought to be Soviet Russians, and more recently the Cardassians have been seen as Nazis; but in any case their function is to highlight different categories of *human beings*. As Neil Mackinnon has commented: 'The aliens we encounter in *Star Trek* demonstrate that, in the writer's imagination, a Universe can accommodate all manner of "humanity". . . .'

By far the most dramatic example of humanization in the continuing world of *Star Trek* is the case of Seven of Nine in *Voyager*. Seven is a Borg 'drone' who ends up on *Voyager* as a result of a temporary alliance between Starfleet and their most hated enemy, the Borg. This alliance in itself is startling. The previously invincible Borg are being destroyed by a new enemy, 'Species 8472', who are using highly sophisticated biological weapons. Meanwhile, as *Voyager* has to get through Borg space in order to get back home, Captain Janeway believes that by making a 'pact with the devil' – offering technological help in defeating Species 8472 – they can negotiate for safe passage through Borg space. This Faustian pact nearly breaks up the *Voyager* crew, as Janeway's second-in-command, Chakotay, is strongly opposed to it, believing that the Borg are incapable of honouring any agreement.

The pact between *Voyager* and the Borg reaches a crisis when the Borg insist that, in order to work together on the new weapon, the two Starfleet officers involved must be hooked up to the Borg collective consciousness, so that their thoughts can be shared among all the Borg. 'Transceivers' are forcibly implanted in the necks of Janeway and Tuvok with the intention of letting them all think together. The Borg consider traditional 'linguistic communication' (talking) to be a primitive and 'inefficient' form of data transfer. Their hallmark is that they do not coexist with other species: they 'assimilate' them, adding the new knowledge to their existing 'perfection'. 'Your culture will adapt to service ours' is one of their mantras. But the transceivers are one step too far for Janeway and she suggests instead that the Borg nominate one representative to liaise with them.

In a rare display of co-operation (the trait Chakotay felt they would be incapable of showing) the Borg agree, and one drone is clanked free of its connections and steps forward. As she steps towards Janeway, this representative's first words are: 'I speak for the Borg.' The singular pronoun is a shock – the Borg have previously always referred to themselves as 'we', since they have a collective consciousness. This drone turns out to be called 'Seven of Nine' ('Tertiary adjunct of unimatrix zero-one'). Her attitude towards humanity is scathing: 'You are individuals, you are small, you think in small terms.' She much prefers the Borg mentality, where efficiency rules over ethics or compassion, where all minds think together rather than in a clash of differing opinions. As she says to Chakotay at a later stage in the episode: 'Every decision is debated; every action questioned . . . every individual entitled to his own small opinion . . . you lack harmony, cohesion, greatness . . . it will be your undoing.'

What follows is the most dramatic contest yet in *Star Trek* over its most central concern: the value of individuality. The Borg have been set up in a particular way, not just in *Voyager* but in several episodes of the earlier *TNG* series as well as in the film *First Contact*. Of all Starfleet's enemies, they are the most deadly, because they reject human individuality: they stand opposed to everything that Starfleet values, and they are relentless in their drive to 'assimilate' (and hence destroy) humanity. Janeway's decision to try to work with them is astonishing in the world of *Star Trek*. In the event, Janeway and Chakotay manage to outwit the Borg. To do this they have to disconnect Seven of Nine permanently from the Borg network, and she has to learn to live without the support system she has known most of her life. Like many of the Borg we have encountered before, Seven was once human. The next several episodes tell the tale of her struggle between the security and superiority of the Borg's collective consciousness, and the frail fledgling individuality of her human birthright.

In the first episode of this season, the word 'human' is used four times in the space of a minute. When she first appears, Seven of Nine is a repellent Borg – she has black implants and prostheses on her face and body, she has no hair, her skin is blotchy and horrible. Yet hardly having worked with her at all, Janeway says to her, 'You're human aren't you? . . . What was your name?' This is typical of *Star Trek*; an earlier episode of *The Next Generation* ('I, Borg') revolves around a temporarily detached Borg who is seen as an individual through the process of naming him. As 'Third of Five' (Borg designations reflect their membership of work groups), he was an expendable drone, but after Geordi names him 'Hugh' the other members of the crew begin to see him as more of a person, as he becomes curious about identity and individuality. Seven of Nine, however, has few memories of life prior to her assimilation – which happened to her when she was only a child. Her entire adult life has been with the Borg and she does not recognize herself as Annika Hanson (her human name). Seven denies her human identity, stating: 'This body was assimilated 18 years ago – it ceased to be human at that time', and when Janeway asks her her name she warns the captain not to engage in further 'irrelevant discourse'. Seven of Nine is very critical of humans, whom she regards as 'erratic, conflicted, disorganized'. The challenge to Starfleet is both to prove her wrong – to show that humans can work together in teams – and to prove that the advantages of individuality outweigh the lack of security and community.

As part of her efforts to re-educate Seven into the human way of life and to convince her that life without the Borg is possible, and indeed preferable, Janeway presents the drone with the information they are able to retrieve regarding her childhood. The process is not unlike forcibly 'curing' someone's drug addiction, or 'reprogramming' a member of a religious cult. Seven strongly opposes all efforts to humanize her; Janeway, however, perseveres, convinced that she has a moral responsibility to integrate this Borg into her crew and show her the benefits of humanity. As the captain says, 'Underneath all that technology she is a human being, whether she's ready to accept that or not. And until she is ready, someone has to make the decisions for her.'

In the next episode, 'The Gift', Seven has tried to rejoin the Borg and been stopped. She is now in a cell in the brig, where Janeway shows her pictures of herself as a little human girl and talks to her about her parents (who had been Starfleet scientists). Janeway asks her to remember this litle girl – 'Did she have any siblings? Who were her friends? Where did she go to school? What was her favourite colour?' Seven's response is to insist that she wants only to return to the Borg – and she is scathing of Janeway's hypocrisy in not affording her the freedom that humans supposedly value. She points out (reverting to the Borg plural): 'You have imprisoned us in the name of humanity, yet you will not grant us your most cherished human right – to choose our own fate' – 'you are no different than the Borg'. From Janeway's perspective, anyone wishing to return to the Borg could not possibly have made a full recovery, but Seven's arguments are convincing in terms of Starfleet's own protocols. Much later in this episode, when Janeway has come to visit Seven, she suddenly says the word 'red'. Seven adds: 'The child you spoke of, the girl, her favourite colour was red.' This is a key moment, as Seven is beginning to retrieve her human memory, even if she still refuses to refer to her former self in the first person. Remembering her favourite colour as a child (something of very little obvious value and therefore 'irrelevant' to the Borg) brings her into the fold of humanity.

Seven of Nine

Meanwhile, an internal battle is raging in this poor woman's body. Her human cells are now regenerating but the Borg implants respond by reasserting themselves, while the Doctor reports on – and attempts to manage – this biological war zone. Seven is gradually returning to her human female form ('the sexiest woman in space since Princess Leia wore a gold bikini', according to one magazine). The iconography of this has caused much comment, as the Doctor performs a mixture of necessary and cosmetic operations on her. Under his ministrations her hair is regrown, blond, and at this stage up in a neat french pleat. Her complexion is peaches and cream, her eyes (one prosthetic) matching blue; the remaining sections of Borg implant are refashioned as ornamental body jewellery. Her figure (she wears skin-tight clothes) heavily accentuates the hourglass.

What is happening is – paradoxically – the 'assimilation' of a Borg drone into the human fold. This is accomplished very effectively in the episode 'The Raven', in which Seven has a brutal psychological encounter with the moment of her own assimilation as a child. The human unconscious, as opposed to the Borg collective consciousness, makes a dramatic entrance. Seven is having frightening fantasies, in which she feels theatened by a large bird and has the unusual expe-rience for her (though very familiar to the viewer) of being terrified by Borg assailants who are trying to get her. Meanwhile, her body is being progressively restored to its human functions. She is having her first meal, where she has been learning about chewing and swal-lowing from the restaurateur Neelix. Suddenly a ten-pronged Borg nodule erupts from her hand and she leaves. With many of her Borg capabilities still intact she sails through all the security force-fields and takes off in a shuttle craft, drawn by a Borg homing beacon that her cybernetic implants have detected. *Voyager* sends another shuttle in pursuit, and eventually Tuvok finds out what is happening to her.

As it transpires, the signal is coming not from a Borg ship or outpost as Seven had hoped but from the partially assimilated wreck-age of her parents' dilapidated vessel – a small transport ship called *The Raven*. She and Tuvok go down into the ship and she relives the terror and loss of her childhood experience, as her memory begins to return. The episode brings closure to the ongoing see-saw between human and Borg, as Seven comes to realize that her assimilation was violent and destructive. Although she continues to regard Borg methods as generally superior to those favoured by Starfleet, she also appears to begin to realize the horror of what the Borg did to her. At the end of this episode she is well on her way to developing as a human member of the *Voyager* crew. In the last scene we find Seven with Janeway in her favourite relaxation spot – a holographic recreation of Leonardo da Vinci's studio. Janeway explains that im-agination, creativity and fantasy are an important part of human experience ('because imagination frees the mind, it inspires ideas'). In her Borg mode Seven thought all this a waste of time and 'inefficient', but now she sees the value of it. Later on she even finds interest in reading those records of her human parents.

This dramatic story, dominating the fourth season of *Voyager* and likely to continue as a major theme until the series ends, is about the restoration of human individuality to the most unlikely possible crea-ture – a Borg drone. In the time since Seven has come aboard we have seen her develop in many ways, into a being who is becoming more 'human' all the time. The most obvious difficulty in her 'assimilation' into human society has been in relation to individuality. The Borg think with one (collective) mind and Seven has struggled with the silence of individual thought. 'One' brings this personal crisis to a head when a situation arises requiring Seven to pilot the ship alone for several weeks, something even the most well-adjusted crew-members would find psychologically daunting. We shall return to this episode later when we consider irrationality and madness in recent *Star Trek*, for this experience induces hallucinations and feelings of panic in Seven, as well as crises of confidence in her own individual abilities. Paradoxically, her sense of herself as an individual becomes increasingly defined as she realizes that her function is as a part of a greater community – her final action in this episode is one of altruistic compassion as she diverts her own oxygen supply to power the stasis chambers of her sleeping crewmates.

The relationship here between individuality and collectivity is not a simple one. In 'Hope and Fear' Seven is afraid of what will happen if *Voyager* does return home to earth. As the captain points out, 'It's been hard enough dealing with a crew of 150 individual humans – the prospect of an entire planet must be overwhelming.' Having grown to understand herself as an individual the prospect of so many other individuals in a larger collective is somewhat terrifying. One might be tempted to see this as a final rejection of Borg collectivity; Seven has come to understand what the Borg represent and fears anything that looks remotely similar. Alternatively, it is down to the fact that human communities embrace varying, plural ideas, whereas the Borg 'hive mind' has a uniform mentality. Certainly the idea of an unstable individual mind is something brought about by the pressure of too many conflicting thoughts. The episode 'Infinite Regress'[40] shows us the Borg equivalent of multiple personality disorder when Seven loses control of the various assimilated individuals whose memories she possesses. The representation of this is rather entertaining – the character veers from aggressive Klingon to rational Vulcan to profiteering Ferengi to that most unusual species of all: teenage Californian. The loss of control that this episode depicts, however, is extremely serious; the risk to Seven's mental health comes from the nature of her previous collective existence. At first Seven was keen to return to the Borg collective – she even toys with the idea in 'Hope and Fear' – but by the time of 'Dark Frontier', when the Borg Queen herself puts in an appearance, she has been fully converted and wants nothing to do with her. Ironically, Seven's embracing of human values means that no sooner has she determined to exist as an individual than she feels compelled by altruistic loyalty to offer to return to her previous existence. On this occasion the Borg Queen makes Seven a secret deal: she will spare *Voyager* if her old drone will return to the collective. Seven's responsibility to the ship dictates that she must accept. (Of course, this price is never actually exacted since Captain Janeway sees through the plot in no time, but the decision itself stands as a mark of Seven's development.)

This quality of (essentially human) compassion is another area in which Seven's development has been pronounced, even though she may differ with Janeway on many key humanist issues: 'Your desire to explore space is inefficient, your need for familial connections is a weakness.' The concept of giving oneself up for the good of the many, however, is one that comes easily to her. As we have seen, 'Dark Frontier' allows her to make this choice for the sake of her crewmates; likewise in 'Think Tank' she is willing to leave the ship to join an organization holding *Voyager* to ransom, the ransom in this case being Seven herself. This decision is represented as the logical course of action – 'they are offering us the assistance we require, I am the payment they require' – but it is clearly as much about compassionate humanism as it is about statistics. Perhaps the best example of Seven's emotional development is the episode 'Drone', where she presides over the (extremely rapid) growth of a new super-Borg that is accidentally grown on *Voyager*. (The precedent for this is elaborate, but the new being is essentially several hundreds years' more advanced than anything we have so far encountered.) Seven must teach the new drone – appropriately named 'One' – how to exist within a community, and explain the dangers of the Borg perspective with which it has been hard-wired. 'One' swiftly becomes attached to this strangely maternal figure and follows her around like a baby duckling, unwilling to be left with any other crewmembers. His story is much indebted to *Frankenstein*: though gentle and intelligent his physical appearance is rather horrifying and even *Voyager*'s liberal crew have some difficulties in accepting his presence. 'Do they fear me because I am Borg?' he innocently asks Neelix. Seven, though, becomes increasingly attached to this drone and teaches him everything she can about the society she has come to think of as her own. At the conclusion of the episode, the drone realizes the threat he poses to his new friends – the Borg have become aware of him and will do anything to get hold of his technology – and decides to terminate himself, rather than expose them to further risk. (One cannot help but see a parallel here with the second *Terminator* film, in which the cyborg enacts a similar decision.) He explains: 'I should not exist; I was an accident, a random conversion of technologies . . . I was never meant to be.' The *Star Trek* mandate 'to seek out new life' has failed miserably. Seven herself is deeply upset by this: 'You are unique,' she implores the drone, 'please – you are hurting me.' These words are a repetition of what she said to him earlier on, when his form of (direct mechanical) communication was causing her pain; it is significant that Seven can now feel emotional – rather than just physical – pain, even if she is unable to articulate this. The story echoes that of Data's 'daughter' Lal, who suffered a total system failure in her mechanical brain and died/shut down before she could fully adapt to life on the *Enterprise*. In this case, Data was troubled by his own incapacity to grieve (as an android he was incapable of experiencing emotion); with Seven, this capacity is a marker of her humanizing transition.

Seven's relationship with the drone One is very much consistent with the general trends her character has followed during her time on board *Voyager*. As well as her close (if fraught) relationship with Captain Janeway, Seven has befriended Tuvok (like-mindedly logical) and the Doctor (whose own mechanical status creates a kind of not-human bond between them). The Doctor has taught Seven how to interact with the rest of the crew; his patronizing social skills lessons are a subject of much amusement. Her increasingly polite and courteous behaviour, however, is a testament to his success. Seven has made friends with one other character as well, and one with whom she shares qualities of otherness and naivety. The young child Naomi Wildman was born on *Voyager* and hence knows no other 'home', refers to Seven as 'the Borg lady' and at first is terrified of her; subsequently, however, the two have grown closer together. Seven will play games with Naomi and evidently takes her seriously as a member of the crew. In 'Bliss' the two hold between them the only hope of saving *Voyager* from destruction. If Janeway is her mother and One her son, then Naomi is surely Seven's younger sister in *Voyager*'s 'family'.

We have already explained the Doctor's role in this development and in 'Someone to Watch over Me' he even introduces Seven to the dating game. Previously she was scathingly efficiently minded; in 'Revulsion' she responds to Harry Kim's innocent advances with terrifying hyper-rationality as she senses that he wants to 'redefine the parameters of our relationship': 'Are you in love with me ensign?' she asks. Seeing that he is taken aback by this approach she tries another tack: 'Then you wish to copulate? . . . Take off your clothes. Don't worry, I won't hurt you.' Increasingly, however, it has become possible to show Seven in a more romantic, more feminine regime – she even has a very good singing voice. By the time of 'Someone to Watch over Me' she is ready to try dating her fellow crewmembers, a task she undertakes under the Doctor's careful instruction. Seven's attempts end largely in embarrassing failure – resulting in a form ligament for one man who tries dancing with her – but it is clear that she is not devoid of romantic capacity or attraction. As the episode progresses the Doctor finds himself falling in love with her, despite her evident lack of romantic interest in him. This revelation comes about just at the point in her development where Seven is moving on from cold and insensitive Borg to emotionally literate human. It is worth noting her distress when she realizes the extent of her own failures in this endeavour.

Seven's presentation of self allows a selective use of different genres of femininity. Rather like Captain Janeway, who offers a decidedly 'post-feminist' combination of the macho leader and traditional femininity, Seven has a repertoire of the female self that can – when required – include the vamp. As we might predict, this is most easily expressed in simulations that stage the *Voyager* crew on earth in the twentieth century, such as the holographic recreation of Nazi-occupied France, 'The Killing Game', in which Seven makes an appearance as a nightclub *chanteuse*. *Voyager* has shown us the development of a character who has progressed from what, in the *Star Trek* universe, is the very antithesis of humanity to become a convincing human being herself, if one endowed with some superhuman remnants of her previous life. By the time of the episode 'Relativity', set in a time travel context, this project of rehumanization is complete. Seven has been selected for a commission that requires her to pass as a junior ensign at the launch of *Voyager* some years earlier. For this she appears in Starfleet uniform for the first time and the facial remnant of her Borg implants has been disguised; in appearance at least, she is utterly human at last.

The rehumanization of Seven sums up exactly what *Star Trek* has always been about. The story of her development has been so popular that the episodes focusing on her transformation can now be bought in a special collector's edition boxed set – a privilege not lightly accorded. There is also a special script book devoted solely to these episodes. The questions of what it means to be human and how human individuality can be protected are the themes around which *Star Trek* has revolved from its inception. Seven is a particularly good example of the phenomenon, partly because the character of Janeway had already been established as extremely strongly identified with the 'human' agenda of *Star Trek*. The situation of *Voyager*, driven by her passionate desire to get home, to get back to earth, provides a framework for the emotionally intense validation of human attributes.

Seven is particularly interesting in that, as a human/Borg hybrid, she is the quintessential 'cyborg'. As we shall see next, the comparison of human beings with machine entities has – in a period of the 'postmodern' exploration of cyberculture – become a very important element of *Star Trek*'s attempt to define what is 'human' in a new context.

The human/machine interface

The term 'cyborg' is usually thought of as a contraction of 'cybernetic organism'. Often this means the idea of a hybrid between an organic, flesh-and-blood entity and something mechanical or artificial. The iconic text of cyborg studies, Donna Haraway's immensely influential 'A Manifesto for Cyborgs', takes off from this definition: 'A cyborg is a cybernetic organism, a hybrid of machine and organism, a creature of social reality as well as a creature of fiction.'[41] People speak of medical technologies that involve replacement parts or prostheses in the vocabulary of the cyborg. The image of the cyborg is often that of a human body to which mechanical implants of some kind have been added. A second popular image is the cyborg of the first *Terminator* film: basically a machine, to which human skin, hair and so on have been added for verisimilitude. *Star Trek*'s Data is somewhat like this (despite his unusual skin) – he is an automaton made to resemble a man. According to the definition of a cyborg as a 'hybrid', Data is not really accurately or best described as a cyborg. This definition of a cyborg as a (hu)man/machine hybrid is one based on recent custom and practice. There is nothing wrong with that; words mean what we use them for. But if we are to start making rulings on what is or is not a cyborg – as many writers in the literature do –[42] it might be helpful to go back a step and look at the history of the two terms that have been brought together to make this new word.

Rather surprisingly, the two elements of cyborg do not really generate the popular meaning. 'Cyber' is now officially recognized as meaning anything to do with computers. The dictionary tells us that it is a twentieth-century back formation from 'cybernetics',[43] a term coined by Norbert Wiener in the 1940s, from the Greek *kubernetes* (steersman), as the study of control systems that exhibit similarities to those of human and animal behaviour. Before its restriction to the field of computing, cybernetics was a 'broad based discipline'.[44] The connotations of 'cyber' as non-human, non-organic, as computer-related, and 'virtual', are comparatively recent. And what is an organism? It is certainly not defined by its flesh-and-bloodness; although the 'living animal or plant' is *one* of the definitions, the idea of a system, *or organization of interdependent parts* (which could be mechanical as opposed to alive) is equally important.[45] Organic thus refers to a structure and system; an 'organic' intellectual for Gramsci was not one who was alive but one whose ideas were integrally related to their historical social situation. An organism can be something *like* a living being, without being alive itself.

If we put these two terms together, we arrive at something far more complex than a human being with an artificial joint, or a machine covered in human skin. We could quite plausibly propose a definition of a 'cybernetic organism' thus: a structure that might or might not be alive (organism), to which has been applied an interest in control systems which might apply both to mechanical and living beings (cybernetics). Not very precise! The terms cybernetic and organism do, however, *both* invoke the question of an analogy between living animals and dead systems: put together, the emerging 'cyborg' is a certainly a metaphorical analogy rather than necessarily a literal hybrid. Haraway's view that we are all cyborgs now can clearly be read as an imaginative or even 'performative' statement, rather than a bald description: 'By the late twentieth century, our time, a mythic time, we are all chimeras, theorized and fabricated hybrids of machine and organism; in short, we are cyborgs.'[46] Haraway's ideas have proved contentious, partly because she put forward an optimistic view that stands in sharp contrast to the gloomy, apocalyptic, dystopic vision of most commentators on the future of science and technology. And, importantly, Haraway's view is more optimistic than is found in most science fiction and its commentators.

A word about Frankenstein is in order here. It scarcely needs to be remarked that Frankenstein is the ubiquitous earliest reference-point of the monster who exceeded the expectations of his creator and got out of hand – a trope that has come to dominate science fiction. Frankenstein's creature was made by assembling, or sewing together, parts from dead bodies, infused with a mysterious 'vital' electric spark;[47] the more 'cyborgish' representations of him, involving machinery or metalwork, are a subsequent elaboration. It is perhaps worth dwelling on the fact that in Mary Shelley's novel of 1818, 'Frankenstein' is originally monstrous *only* in his ugly appearance – to which humans react so badly that he retreats from them, slowly being almost forced into the resentful violence that eventually overtakes him. Before he has experienced the extreme hostility that his appearance arouses in people, he starts off very much a 'good guy'. A crucial section of the novel – over forty pages – is devoted to an elaborated narrative of how this new being 'civilized' himself (written in his voice in the first person), in isolation because of his appalling appearance, and taught himself to read, the better to tackle such indexical works of the western humanist canon as Plutarch's *Lives*, Goethe's *The Sorrows of Werther* and Milton's *Paradise Lost*.[48] The monster is so high-minded that he says he 'felt the greatest ardour for virtue rising within me, and abhorrence for vice'.[49] At the end, he tells his creator, Victor Frankenstein, that he has rejected him because 'the human senses are insurmountable barriers to our union', and pleads with him to create a female companion for him, with whom he would retire from human society to the 'vast wilds of South America' where no one lives (!). He concludes: 'The picture I present to you is peaceful and human.'[50]

So the first 'monster' explicitly poses the question of what it means to be human. In some ways 'Frankenstein' embodies a more 'human' set of values than the humans around him. He aspires to a human existence, as do the characters in *Star Trek* who have been 'created' by humans. Figures such as Data, Seven and the EMH are partly alle- gorical. Per Schelde has suggested that such science fiction creatures have taken the place of the trolls and ogres in folklore, beyond the safe boundaries of social life: 'anthropomorphized "embodiments" of the things humans did not understand in wild nature'.[51] Schelde sees the modern equivalent, the androids and other machines in science fiction, as a 'protest' against the mechanization of life, employing (as a number of writers in this field do) a spiritual vocab- ulary counterposing 'science' and 'soul' to consider the issues.[52] Janice Rushing and Thomas Frentz, in their extremely interesting discussion of 'projecting the shadow' of technological menace in film, also take a spiritual route in the longer run.[53] Their account, too, shows them to be rather appalled at what they see as the Frankensteinish victory of a retributive mechanical technology. Rushing and Frentz couch their discussion within the American myth of the frontier hunter. Technology such as the cyborg represents the autonomy of the hunter's tool, which turns against him. (A second theme of the analy- sis follows Robert Bly in calling for the strengthening of atrophied male initiation culture.) '*The Terminator* is a potent wake-up call to face the demonic proportions of the technological shadow we have loosed upon the world.'[54] Brian Winston has argued against what he calls the 'litany' of those who regard technology as a threat. Winston, using the work of Scott Bukatman as an example of the 'best and brightest', argues that 'disabling' technological determinism (which has a post-modern variant) has penetrated deeply – and, in his view, wrongly – into current critical understanding.[55]

Star Trek cannot be accused of following in the footsteps of these bleaker modern Frankensteins. It is more than optimistic in its treatment of its super-folk and superhumans. The debates in *Star Trek* about how Data differs from humans, or what rights an evolved hologram might have, are squarely within a dominant tradition in science fiction. The function of cyborgs, androids and holograms is to counterpoint the specifically human. Peter Fitting summarizes: 'The human/nonhuman dichotomy has always been one of SF's established sources of narrative, where the inhuman machine – as represented by androids and robots – has been read as embodying our contradictory hopes and fears about an increasingly mechanised world.'[56] From Frankenstein onwards, a part of what is feared is that the creature itself does not know what it is; a much discussed element of the very popular film (second in a recent British poll of the 'hundred best films of all time'[57]) *Blade Runner*, where the now standard 'director's cut' foregrounds the question of whether the protagonist Deckard is himself a 'replicant' rather than a human being. As Nigel Wheale points out, the film itself asks the 'anguished' question: 'How can it not know what it is?'[58] It is anguished because the implication is that if it does not know what it is, how do we know who (or what) we are?

Although we may see in *Star Trek*'s treatment of the human/ nonhuman boundary an optimistic version of the future, science fiction generally is more likely to use cyborg or mechanical characters to draw attention to fears rather than hopes about the future. Kevin McCarron makes the same point, with an inflection towards the *inhuman*:

> 'What aspect of humanity makes us human?' The question is a good one. So good, it's been asked a great deal; tacitly, I would argue, any time a writer introduces a cyborg, android, replicant, robot, an Artificial Intelligence Unit. Whenever the textual stress is on prosthetics, on the kind of technology that fuses blood and iron, the debate is really about the human, and its sometimes opposite, the inhuman.[59]

The usual form of the dystopic imagination is to foreground the machine as retributive monster, an image we shall return to shortly. A view that is equally critical and negative, but in an angrier, more political and more immediate register, is that of Ziauddin Sardar, who sees the day within a decade when cyborgs will walk the earth, with holographic man 'not too far off, either', who will be not so much walking as stalking. Sardar questions what 'continues to be human' when humans become extensions of machines.[60] Sardar's argument is interesting for our purposes (although not directly applicable in that his focus is the Internet), in that he uses a model of western colonialism to analyse the 'exploration' of cyberspace. Scathingly citing romantic right-wing parallels that have been drawn between the 'ancient mariners' of early exploration – a 'spirit of invention and discovery' – Sardar asks instead whether we should remember what such exploration did to indigenous peoples and how greed was a less worthy but no less important motivation than adventure.[61] Sardar's view of cyberspace is very bleak: the Internet, a spin-off of the military budget, now runs via commercial carriers that are the modern equivalents of the East India Company (that is, an imperial trading operation). It is completely dominated by western culture; non-western histories may be digitized and stored, but they are in this process being erased. Similarly it is dominated by commercial imperatives, coupled with more local mentalities that involve a lot of offensive graffiti.

Underlying discussions of how the new cyborg-style entities are posing questions about humanity, are complex questions about the body. Foucault's work on the 'technology' of the self and 'biopolitics' has shifted the terms of this debate in social theory;[62] the once-ignored body now even has its own journals, such as *Body and Society*. Philosophically, and popularly, however, the body remains more in its natural condition. In this state of affairs, the monster is not so much a cyborg, but rather, the (maligned) philosopher Descartes, whose separation of mind and body is held to have led us astray for centuries. Mind–body duality has given rise to a denial of the necessary *embodiment* of the human self. Vivian Sobchack, in an assault on Jean Baudrillard's celebration of the 'erotic technophilia' of *Crash*, sees his offensive attitudes as underwritten by a refusal to live in his body rather than think about it. She concludes, 'I wish Baudrillard a little pain – maybe a lot – to bring him to his senses. Pain would remind him that he doesn't just *have* a body, but that he *is* his body, and that it is in this material fact that "affect" and anything that we might call a "moral stance" is grounded.'[63]

Concepts of the human self deployed in science fiction hover around the relationship of body and mind – and the vexed question of spirit or soul gets brought in too at times. Leaving a religious view out of it for a moment, we can draw an opposition between, on the one hand, a popularized Cartesian model, which locates the human in terms of cognition (as in *cogito ergo sum*), and on the other the view that eventually we shall be able to locate every aspect of human emotion or consciousness in a physical form. Samantha Holland, taking Descartes off on a trip to Hollywood, suggests that the 'mind–brain identity theory', which threatens to collapse the human–machine boundary, is a source of anxiety against which the fascination with cyborgs should be understood. Cyborg films, she argues, tend 'to reassert an essentially mental, Cartesian "self" over any materialist conception of selfhood'.[64]

The view that a general category of 'mind' is identical with the physiology of the brain, has made progress in the field of memory. Memory traces (engrams) are known to have a physical existence in the brain, while no comparable evidence exists – as yet, anyway – for vaguer emotional states or aspects of consciousness. Memory is seen by some as the basis of human identity. Gwyneth Jones comments on the vindication of Proust: 'a famous hypothesis from fiction, that *self is memory*, appears to be on a sound experimental footing'.[65] Jones confidently makes a prediction: 'It seems beyond question that the present explosive development of neuroscience will finally dethrone the secret programmer in the human brain, the overseeing mind that is not part of the machine'.[66] It is in the field of memory that science fiction in general, and *Star Trek* in particular, has been exploring the issues of human identity.

Memory as the metaphor for viable identity figures at a key moment in the *Star Trek* motion pictures. *Star Trek II: The Wrath of Khan, III: The Search for Spock* and *IV: The Voyage Home* have as one central story the saga of Spock's death and rebirth in the context of the unique operation of the scientific project 'Genesis'. This tale has many aspects, but what concerns us here is the role of memory in the definition of a life worth living. Before Spock dies, he manages a rapid 'mind-meld' with McCoy and, according to Vulcan culture, McCoy is then carrying Spock's *katra* or eternal soul. Eventually they find Spock's body, regrown where his coffin had been sent, on the regenerated Genesis planet. As Kirk puts it at the beginning of *Star Trek IV*: 'He was alive. His body was regenerated. But his mind was a blank. We took him to Vulcan, where Spock's people attempted a ceremony to restore his memory.' Indeed, in the film, they succeed in transferring the *katra* of Spock from McCoy into Spock's brain-dead body. But the crucial question is whether his memory is functioning; this is the index of whether his continued existence is meaningful.

Human identity, in *Star Trek* as in other forms of science fiction, is often treated through the metaphor of memory. In the film *Blade Runner*, the distinction between the human and the 'replicant' hinges on the question of memory; when human memories are downloaded into a replicant we become uncertain which is which. It is perhaps worth pointing out that ideas of memory are changing rapidly. Not for nothing do we say 'you need to go and get some more memory' – a culture that sells tiny circuit boards as 'memory' is a culture that talks about memory as having a physical existence. (One scene in *Insurrection* has a damaged Data in the Engineering section; 'I appear to be missing several memory engrams,' he opines. Geordi opens his hand to reveal a few chips. The android smiles: 'There they are.')

This is not to dispute that memory leaves physiological traces in the brain, in ways that biologists are now mapping. It is to suggest, however, that the place of individual memories in our understanding of human identity should be a little more nuanced than the idea that memory is something that could be syphoned out, stored and returned. The historians Jay Winter and Emmanuel Sivan, critical of the anthropomorphic concept of 'cultural memory', have sketched out some of these complexities, drawing on a multidisciplinary review of material on memory. Recall is affected by dramatic and emotional intensity; later memories can reshape earlier ones; memories can be distorted before they are encoded; a particular extrinsic context can trigger or enhance recall.[67] Memory traces are overlaid in archaeological strata and are interactive – a situation difficult to reconcile with the simple idea that one can scan a photo album into the brain and thereby create a childhood.

In *Star Trek*, the question of memory has been dealt with in quite complex ways. Among the most interesting figures are the two Daxes in *Deep Space Nine*, who carry the memories of all the previous hosts of their symbiont. Similarly Data is able to make use of the many memory databases with which he has been programmed. Seven, too, has access to the memories of many victims of Borg assimilation – and at one point these other personalities take control. The issue of the relationship between memory and identity is dealt with in a particularly popular episode from *TNG*: 'The Inner Light'. In this curious story, Picard is struck by a probe from a long-dead society on the planet Kataan. Before its destruction over a thousand years before, it had sent a record of its life into space, to be retrieved at some point in the future. That point is Picard, who lives the life of a man on the planet – experiencing more than thirty years in less than half an hour of his own time. As he explains later: 'The *Enterprise* encountered a probe from the planet, before it was destroyed. It scanned me and I lost consciousness. And, in the space of 25 minutes, I lived a lifetime on that planet. I had a wife and children, and a grandchild, and it was absolutely real to me.' Picard had lived the life of an iron-weaver, Kamin. The story emphasizes the importance of his family, offering a contrast between Kamin and the character of Picard, whose childlessness features at various points in the *Star Trek* narrative. Typically, however, Kamin's son was played by the son (Daniel Stewart) of the actor who plays Picard.

The force of Picard's experience is retold in a subsequent episode, 'Lessons', where he falls in love with a new officer on the *Enterprise*: Commander Darren, who has arrived to run the Stellar Cartography department. It is music that brings them together, and particularly, for Picard, the music he learned from living Kamin's life. 'When I awoke,' he tells her, 'all that I had left from that life was the flute that I'd taught myself to play.' The story of 'The Inner Light' has caught the imagination of many people. This is partly because it represents the historic existence of a society not through empirical information but through the lived memories of one individual. The decision of the Kataans to represent their culture in this way is entirely consistent with *Star Trek*'s insistence that individual experience, in this case transmitted through memory, is the essence of human identity.

The 'probe' containing Kamin's memory is a good example of what is now called 'prosthetic memory'. The film *Total Recall*, based – like *Blade Runner* – on a story by Philip K. Dick, is one of the most dramatic representations of this, portraying a man whose identity is rebuilt on a set of memories that he had not experienced. Alison Landsberg questions whether 'realer is necessarily better?', arguing that in the film the 'simulated identity is more responsible, compassionate and productive than the "real" one'.[68] Here we have to differentiate between a cinematic regime of the imagination, in which a spectator identifies with the protagonist, and the technological plausibility of the complex memory transfers that the film rests on. Even with the projected technology of the twenty-third century at their disposal, Data is sceptical about whether his memories (which themselves have been programmed into a database) can be moved and copied. 'I do not believe that you have acquired the expertise necessary to preserve the essence of these experiences. There is an ineffable quality to memory, which I do not believe can survive your procedure.'

Memory is a very significant category in *Star Trek*, more complex than the mind-equals-brain model can allow. Several episodes explore the idea of buried or repressed memories and how they might affect behaviour. Picard has repressed his memories of the Borg Queen. Jadzia Dax has been made to 'forget' that one of the earlier hosts (Joran) of the symbiont actually committed murder. In the book *Mosaic*, written by Jeri Taylor, Kathryn Janeway is only able to confront her demons as a commander when she 'recovers' her memory of a traumatic experience (when, unable to choose which to rescue, her beloved father or her fiancé, she lost them both). An episode of *Voyager* ('Retrospect') rather controversially takes on the topic of 'false recovered memory syndrome', in examining – and eventually rejecting – Seven's claim that she has been 'violated'. The *Voyager* story 'Latent Image' is a treatment of memory that has a wide range of further implications, including questions of sanity, and we discuss it later on.

Picard's experience, in 'The Inner Light' was that of living Kamin's entire lifetime in the space of what was comfortably on the inside of a 45-minute episode of *Star Trek* (he had been unconscious for 25 minutes). In *Deep Space Nine* we are presented with a scenario where four people effectively 'live' *inside* one of Odo's memories. 'Things Past' concerns the guilt Odo feels about three innocent men who were executed under his supervision when he worked as a security chief for the Cardassians. A freak weather condition outside the shuttle that he and his companions are travelling in causes a telepathic bond at the moment that he is contemplating this event. Consequently, the four of them appear to be transported back in time to the scene of the crime – in fact they are simply reliving Odo's memory with him, but in the roles of those men who are about to die. The idea of a memory as fluid yet tangible as this raises serious questions as to the nature of human thought and experience. The relationship of experience, memory and the subjective experience of time is taken up at various points in *Star Trek*. The O'Brien family in *DS9* have had some very unpleasant temporal experiences – but through differing processes. Little Molly O'Brien experiences ten grim, dehumanizing years as an abandoned child; during the very brief period it took her parents to locate and bring her back she had aged physically by a decade. (Fortunately a bit of time travel was able to sort the problem out.) Her father Miles, on the other hand, was on one occasion subjected to a punishment that took the form of an implant causing the mental experience of twenty years in prison, but he emerged the same age as when the sentence began. These devices are used to challenge our assumptions about the linearity and consistency of time.

In this aim, science fiction is not far removed from the efforts of historians. Bill Schwarz, discussing the 'relativization of the conception of historical time', quotes the great historian Fernand Broudel's summation of his life's work: 'My great problem, the only problem I had to resolve, was to show that time moves at different speeds.'[69] From another discipline, anthropology, comes the interesting proposition of 'counter-temporal' worlds that mirror the better-known 'counter-factual' worlds. Alfred Gell defines counter-factual worlds as synchronous, but with differing factual content; counter-temporal worlds are temporal continuations of worlds factually constituted in the same way.[70] This is not the same register of analysis as the observation of a distinction between subjective and objective time – that time goes slowly when you are bored and rapidly when you are enjoying yourself. It points towards the sense of variability in the passing of historical time, as well as the implications, for the experience of time, of post-Einstein astrophysics.

The use of time travel in *Star Trek* is a simple way to explore some of the implications of the idea that one factually constituted world can exist in the same way in another time. It is striking that the mirror universe (a counter-factual world but not temporally removed) shows people who behave very differently in moral terms. Usually, we can conclude, the element of time travel is introduced to underscore and emphasize a proposed or wished-for stability of the human subject across time. *Voyager*'s time travel narratives are particularly focused on the integrity of the human experience. In the episode that solves the mystery of Amelia Earhart's disappearance in 1937, the cryogenically preserved pioneering aviator turns out to be exactly the same type of plucky dame as Janeway ('The '37s'). In 'Future's End', Rain Robinson, an earthling of 1996, is bowled over by Tom Paris in more ways than one – but what she comments on with astonishment is that 'you care about something more than just your own little life.' Tom's altruism, in contrast with the laid-back ethos of Los Angeles, is recognizably a marker of humanity. The period is itself characterized as human – but significantly behind the evolved human nature of the twenty-fourth century as represented by Janeway and her crew. What we will need down there, says Paris, are 'nice clothes, a fast car, and plenty of money' – the last having been dispensed with in *Voyager*'s utopian future. Similarly, the people of the period are described as 'post-industrial barbarians' who fill you with 'primitive pharmaceuticals' when you exhibit signs of stress. In 'Future's End', as in the subsequent time travel episode 'Relativity', the Federation and its human values are central.

The presentation of 'counter-temporal' worlds in *Star Trek* is important in relation to the argument we made in Part I, about the 'expansion' of time and space in a historical period that has been seeing it 'contracting'. Just as distances and communication on our 'shrinking' earth are becoming respectively smaller and quicker, *Star Trek* continues to try and get *Voyager* back within reach of any communications at all. Similarly, just as time is contracting on earth, so it is being imaginatively opened up in space. The possibility of travel in time is theoretically offered by Einstein's General Theory of Relativity, as has been pointed out by none other than Stephen Hawking.[71] The exploration of space required an anti-colonialist measure (the 'Prime Directive' which was designed to stop spacefaring people interfering with the development of other cultures), and we also find that the exploration of time requires such measures. In recent episodes of *Star Trek*, this has been treated in a rather jocular and 'intertextual' manner. In a 1996 *DS9* episode that we shall discuss later, Captain Sisko's activities are investigated by two agents from the 'Bureau of Temporal Investigation' drawn straight from *The X Files*. (The agents are even called 'Dulmer' and 'Lucsly'.) *Voyager* stories have seen the introduction of 'Federation Timeships' *Aeon* and *Relativity* and the statement of the requirements of the 'Temporal Prime Directive'. Time travel technology has been developed to quite an extent, it seems, and 'temporal psychosis' results from doing it too often. Although people are not supposed to do it, in practice there always seems to be a compelling argument as to why it might be necessary to 'clean up the timeline' from previous 'incursions'. Apparently this binds Starfleet personnel who have 'jumped' in time not to discuss it with anyone, and allows the Federation authorities to 'wipe' their memories if necessary. In 'Relativity' Janeway and Seven are told that since they had only jumped backwards to the past, rather than forwards to the future, there would be 'no need to resequence your memory engrams'.

A number of these issues are brought together in the episode of *Voyager* entitled 'Latent Image'. In this story the Doctor (or EMH) discovers that he has a memory blank about an operation he has performed in the past; he finds that Captain Janeway has deleted some files from his program. The issue is whether, now that he has discovered this, he should be wiped and reinstalled (taking him back to a much earlier stage in his development): Janeway proposes to do this, to which the Doctor objects violently as an infringement of his rights. We find that she had already done this on a previous occasion, because he had been driven insane by having to choose which of two staff to save the life of – an unknown 'Ensign Jetal' or Harry Kim. On the instant he had chosen to save Harry, but his program could not cope with this decision – that he had chosen the life of his friend over that of another patient. Hence the Doctor had started to go mad. The issue is whether he should be now 'wiped' again, to save him from his own breakdown.

Janeway has decided to delete and do a clean reinstall; in the case of a hologram this is akin to a forcible brainwashing. Seven objects, arguing that, just as she has been allowed to evolve into an individ-

ual, the Doctor (who has already far exceeded his original programming) should be allowed to as well. Janeway is resolute: he had nearly
destroyed his own program last time round and the ship has to have
a doctor of some kind. Allowing him to wrestle with the issue is just
too much of a risk. More importantly, while Seven is a human being,
'the Doctor is more like that replicator [coffee machine] than he is
like us'. Seven points out that she herself is Borg as well as human:
'part of me is not unlike your replicator, not unlike the Doctor', and
asks whether Janeway will abandon her too. She had always regarded
Janeway as 'a guide to humanity' – but now 'I am not sure'.

This encounter changes Janeway's mind. The next morning she
explains to the Doctor: 'I'd like to think I made my decisions eigh-
teen months ago for all the right reasons. The truth is my own biases
about what you are had just as much to do with it.' She plays him
the tapes showing his 'breakdown', commenting that they showed a
battle inside him between his original programming and 'what he's
become'. What he has *become*, as also 'what you are', is not completely clear. At one point Janeway says to B'Elanna: 'We allowed
him to evolve . . . we gave him a soul . . . do we have the right to take
it away now?' B'Elanna's reply is a wonderful antidote to the senti-
mental Janeway: she says crisply, 'We gave him personality subroutines, I'd hardly call that a soul.'

The attempt to let him fight out his inner conflict is getting
nowhere and Janeway consults Seven, repeating back to her the
words Seven had used to register her problem before: 'I'm having
trouble with the nature of individuality.' What she wants to know is
whether Seven thinks that her own progress towards individuality has
been worth it. Seven says she would not change what happened.
Fuelled by this, Janeway decides to try and see the doctor through
his breakdown – he has become the patient to be nursed. More
quantum nuggets here, as the Doctor struggles to cope with his decision: 'For every action there's an infinite number of reactions – and
in each one of them I *killed* her.' Janeway is sitting with him while
he rants, as she has been for an improbable sixteen hours that day,
despite suffering from flu. She is reading a book which she tells him
is 'relevant to your situation'. The turning point comes when he realizes how tired she is and tells her to go and sleep, that he will be all
right, and wants to cause no more suffering. The Doctor's medical
compassion (arguably his *humanity*) is what ultimately saves his
sanity – not unlike Janeway, whose depression in the earlier episode
'Night' is resolved by the opportunity of doing a good turn. When
the captain leaves he picks up her book and reads: 'In that book,
which is my memory, on the first page of the chapter that is the day

when I first met you, appear the words, here begins a new life.' The sanity of a twenty-fourth-century hologram has been vouchsafed by a lyric poem of 1292, a founding text of Italian culture and the ideas that were later to be known as 'humanism': Dante's *La Vita Nuova*.

This story was predictable, indeed predicted:

> *Star Trek: Voyager* poses the human question around a character who is a hologram – the emergency medical program – another figure whose popularity is growing. His attempts to build human experiences, attributes, senses and feelings into his subroutines are often disastrous, but there is no doubt that his progress in a humanizing direction moves the debate forward. I fully expect an episode reprising 'The Measure of a Man' in which the hologram's claims to sentience, and hence rights, are aired.[72]

An earlier episode, 'Projections' dealt with the question of the Doctor's material identity when a computer problem led him to start believing that he was a human being. In this episode Chakotay and the Doctor's assistant Kes are vehemently supportive of his rights as an automated, but very real, life form: 'Just because you're made of projected light and energy doesn't mean you are any less real than someone made of flesh and blood – it doesn't matter what you're made of; what matters is who you are,' says the commander to a very confused hologram. It is not until 'Latent Image' that we see the Doctor really stand up for himself as an individual – in the face of his treatment by the captain.

The case of Data has been much discussed, and perhaps little needs to be repeated here. A scientist is proposing to dismantle and reassemble Data, so that he can make thousands of replicas of this wonderful machine. Data would prefer to leave Starfleet rather than submit to this, but does he have the right to take this decision or is he – like other machines – Starfleet 'property'? The crucial point in the tribunal was that although Data was ruled to be a 'machine', it was agreed that he was a machine with a right to choose. The case was won on the basis of rejecting 'a race' of disposable people: the model of slavery was rejected.

The cases of Data, of Seven and of the EMH all display a pronounced process of 'humanization'. Critical opinion seems to vary on whether such figures succeed in attracting our sympathies. As far as the viewers are concerned, all the evidence is that these three are some of the most popular characters in *Star Trek*; and polls have even voted Data as the most popular figure in any of the series. Gwyneth Jones, however, has a much stricter view: 'The cyberspace era has room for synthetic humans as comfortingly inept intellectuals, overtly respected and covertly awarded the comic pathos of the Tin Man in *The Wizard of Oz* (Data in *Star Trek*).' Ouch! The phrase 'synthetic humans' is a suggestive one, but the synthetic attribution of humanity is not restricted to individuals like Data. There is a type of 'anthropomorphism' going on here, that is more general. As the fatally wounded *Voyager* is packing up for a final suicide mission at the end of a 'Year of Hell', Janeway insists that Tuvok is quite wrong in describing the ship as merely 'an assemblage of bulkheads, conduits, titanium, nothing more'. The captain, even exceeding naval tradition on this one, sees 'her' as 'much more than that': '*Voyager*'s done too much for us . . . this ship has been our home, it's kept us together, it's been part of our family. . . . It's carried us, Tuvok, even nurtured us, and right now it needs one of us.'

Star Trek's position is far from consistent on such issues, veering from the harshly exclusionist (the cloned crew in 'Course: Oblivion') to absurdly anthropomorphic sentimentalism (the example above must surely fall into this category). A writer in *Star Trek Monthly* magazine put the following question to *Voyager*'s two main executive producers: is the Doctor really alive? From Jeri Taylor he 'received a resounding "Of course," while the same question put to Brannon Braga received a "Definitely not!"'

The idea of a 'synthetic human' leads us to a differentiation between debates about the ontological status of cyborgian hybrids, and the investment of the spectator in dramatic fiction. Data, Seven and the Doctor are highly successful characters because they all function – within the story – as human and more. There is a disjunction between their status, on even the most favourable account of the rights of non-human beings, and the punches they pack as characters whose 'humanity' is assured. This point is worth emphasizing, as it points towards a more general observation concerning the extent to which the boundaries traditionally defending a definition of 'the human' can be said to be withstanding these new arguments. The least plausible boundary is clearly that between human beings and other animals. Ecological, environmental, conservation and animal rights movements have caused us to rethink the privileged status of humanity and instead call humans to account for their responsibilities. All the traditional grounds on which specifically human superiority was based – sole use of language or tool-making, ownership of a soul and so on – have been dramatically eroded.

No such comparable breakdown of the boundary between living human animal and machine is, ultimately, possible – notwithstanding what is said about the increasingly complex ways in which human existence interacts with technology. This point is put in its starkest form by Vivian Sobchack, and her remarks may put her startling desire to inflict pain on Baudrillard in a different light. She does not regard the prosthetic leg she has, the result of major cancer surgery, as a sexy form of cyborg identity or 'some devoutly wished-for trans-formation of my human frailty and mortality'. Confusion between hardware and the body ('meat' in the lexis of cyberpunk) is deadly; the technological status of technology should not be disavowed: 'the new leg is dependent finally upon my last leg. Without my lived-body to live it, the prosthetic exists as part of a body without organs – a techno-body that has no sympathy for human suffering, cannot understand human pleasure and, since it has no conception of death, cannot possibly value life.'[73]

Star Trek is about the human, and endorses a lot of what we might call 'humanist' rhetoric. It frankly favours the human, albeit in an inclusive rather than an exclusive way. It also uses a number of devices to ask questions about how the nature of humanity is to be understood. The series *TNG*, which is about humanity on trial, is interestingly framed in both its first and last episodes by an anomaly in space – in 'Encounter at Farpoint' it is the mysterious creatures made of energy. In 'All Good Things . . .' it is three-way time travel, and a trip to the moment when life on earth began. *Star Trek* uses these types of supernatural phenomena to raise these questions.

The different series, of course, vary in how they relate to the basic question of being human. *DS9* is most sceptical, and it is on *Deep Space Nine* that the utopian side of *Star Trek* is most challenged. DS9 has money! It also has religion – rejected in the secular rational mod-ernist universe of *Star Trek*. It shows more corruption. As we sug-gested earlier, *DS9* shows us more of the case against humanity, in terms of human failure and compromise. It is only in *DS9* that a char-acter (Kira) would accuse herself of having become a despised col-laborator: 'When I was in the resistance I hated people like me.' This series has a fixation with the concept of loyalty, be it national, ideo-logical or religious. Although *Star Trek* in general is about human nature, human morality, and the nature of the human in contrast to other entities or beings, there are significant differences between the various series. We argue that the modern paradigm – so well mapped out in the tropes of exploration used by maritime fiction and reprised in *Star Trek* – is giving way to a characteristically *post-modern* style of representation. It is to this that we now turn.

Part III

The Post-modern Tack

'Far Beyond the Stars', an episode in the sixth season of *Deep Space Nine*, illustrates the extent to which recent *Star Trek* has moved on from the 'modern', 'rationalist' values of its predecessors. Although, as we have seen, *DS9* certainly does share some of the human agenda of *Star Trek* in general, the representational style is completely different. In addition, many of the elements of the secular, rational, modern world-view have completely gone. This episode, and its brief follow-up in 'Shadows and Symbols', condenses these changes in a startlingly imaginative format.

Benjamin Sisko, an African American, is both the commander of the space station from which the series takes its name, and – more problematically for him – has been identified as a religious leader (the 'Emissary') of the people living on the nearby planet Bajor. The episode begins with Sisko being taken ill. He has unusual synaptic patterns; as has happened before, he is having visions. In these experiences the 'prophets' (who live in the Bajoran wormhole connecting the Alpha Quadrant to the Gamma Quadrant) speak to him. In one discourse Sisko is hallucinating, in another his mind is being visited (somewhat against his will) by these supernatural beings. As he becomes unconscious, he falls into a different reality: it is New York in the 1950s, a bleak period at the height of McCarthyite anti-Communism and before the Civil Rights movement of the 1960s challenged racial segregation. Benjamin Sisko has become Benny Russell, a writer. He is retained by a science fiction magazine, *Incredible Tales*, but he has yet to make the big break as a serious writer. At an editorial meeting, a drawing of the DS9 station is proffered and Russell takes it, to write a piece around it. He becomes inspired, writing as if possessed, and writes the story of the station, increasingly feeling that he is himself becoming Sisko. Not having the religious language of the prophets, to which Sisko himself is by now accustomed, his alter ego Russell feels he is 'losing his mind' – he is merely hallucinating, seeing visions, an experience common to followers of the prophets.

The story is recognized as a brilliant piece of writing by the team running the magazine. Dax's *alter ego* character reads gleefully about her symbiotic self ('she's got a worm in her belly – it's disgusting') and comments on Benny's unique genius. But the editor immediately says it cannot be published, which prompts a major row with his more liberal creative team, themselves the cast of *Star Trek: Deep Space Nine*. Many of them are usually heavily made up as non-humans in the show, and the shock value of presenting them in this particular moment, and visual regime, of American cultural history is considerable. The editor of *Incredible Tales*, Mr Douglas Pabst, with slicked-

down hair and glasses, is played by Rene Auberjonois (Odo); Colm
Meaney (Chief O'Brien) plays a rather dim but good-natured fellow
who is the in-house expert on robots. Nana Visitor (Kira Nerys) and
Alexander Siddig (Dr Bashir) appear as a couple, which is an in-joke
as they are married to each other off-screen. Armin Shimerman (the
Ferengi barkeeper Quark) figures as the team member most willing to
stand up to the editor, and to support Benny Russell. Terry Farrell
(Jadzia Dax) puts in an appearance in the office as Mr Pabst's blowsy
secretary. The rest of the cast crop up outside the office. Penny
Johnson (Kassidy Yates, the second Mrs Sisko) plays Benny Russell's
devoted long-time fiancée. Cirroc Lofton (young Jake Sisko) is Jimmy.
Brock Peters (Mr Sisko senior) plays an urban messianic preacher who
speaks to 'Brother Benny' in the language of the prophets – 'walk with
the prophets', 'show us the way', 'write the words', and so on. Cameo
parts are also found for Marc Alaimo (Gul Dukat) and Jeffrey Combs
(Weyoun), who appear as brutally thuggish racist cops, and Aron
Eisenberg (Nog) as a newsboy. Michael Dorn (Worf) gets a very cheery
outing as a stylish and flirtatious baseball star.

A previous scene has already hinted at the problems of a dis-
criminatory society. The editorial team is to be photographed: Mr
Pabst advises 'K. C. Hunter' (who is actually a woman writer) to be
late for work that day, and the same goes for Benny Russell; it cannot
be known that these incredible stories are dreamt up by anyone other
than white men. Benny despairingly lists some black writers: W. B.
DuBois, Langston Hughes, Richard Wright, and so on. Later, he discovers that his own story cannot be published because the hero is
black. Benny Russell is writing the story of Benjamin Sisko, the DS9
station, and the Bajoran religion. Douglas Pabst says a 'negro captain'
is simply not believable and that if he wants it published he must
make the captain white. A compromise appears, which Benny finds
just about acceptable: could it be written as if 'a dream'? Perhaps 'a
shoeshine boy dreaming of a different future'? Meanwhile Jimmy,
who has rejected this dream of racial equality in favour of some petty
crime in the here and now, has been shot dead by the two cops. When
Benny – out with his girl to celebrate the 3-cents-a-word his accepted
story will bring them – intervenes, he is savagely beaten and taken to
hospital.

Weeks later, a still-lame Benny Russell goes to the office to pick up
the new issue of *Incredible Tales* with his story in it. But the propri-
etor has had the issue pulped – even as a dream a 'coloured hero' is
unacceptable to him – and furthermore, Benny is fired. At this
Russell's words, 'I am a human being, dammit', echo numerous *Star
Trek* characters over the years when presented with severe adversity.

He then becomes agitated and hyperventilates, pleading that 'you can pulp a story, but you cannot destroy an idea – it is real,' before he collapses on the floor. We see him taken away by ambulance, stretchered and restrained: he has now 'lost his mind'. In the ambulance the preacher/his father appears; Benny has 'walked in the path of the prophets', he is 'the dreamer and the dream'.

Back on the station, Benjamin Sisko is waking up, restored to health. His father is now able to leave and return to his Louisiana restaurant; he says he has 'fought the good fight . . . kept the faith'. The episode ends with Sisko posing the question as to who is the dreamer and who the dream? What if all of this is the illusion, he asks. What if Benny Russell isn't the dream, but we are? What if we are 'figments of his imagination', rather than vice versa? The story, and this question, are picked up at the beginning of the seventh season, in 'Shadows and Symbols'. Wound into this complex episode is Sisko on a religious mission: he is in the desert searching for the 'Orb of the Emissary', which he must locate and open. Jake and Ezri Dax are with him. The scene cuts from this to the mental hospital where Benny Russell is still being held, against his will. They will not let him go as he is destroying his mind, his sanity, by writing these stories. He is writing them on the white walls of his room, as they have confiscated all paper. The psychiatrist, played by a (human) Damar, wants him to paint over the words – to 'destroy them before they destroy you'. In an extraordinary set of shots, we see Benjamin Sisko with his arm raised (shovel in hand) to strike open the orb, counterposed with the upraised arm of Benny Russell, hesitating as to whether to apply the paint roller to the wall. Russell's narrative has reached the point where Sisko, in the other reality, is dramatically vacillating over whether to open the orb or not. Eventually, Benny has to knock out the two staff restraining him, in order to write 'Opens it' on the wall. Sisko then opens the orb, releasing the trapped prophet, and the Bajoran wormhole miraculously reopens.

This moment is rounded off by an encounter which either reinforces the Christian derivation of Bajoran religion, or emphasizes the non-linear nature of time in a superhuman world. (Q uses the word 'linear' as a term of abuse directed at puny humans.) Sisko is demanding an explanation of what is going on, and a prophet – who, with Sisko's help had been able to cast out the Pah-wraith (false god) and restore the wormhole – comes to talk to him. She comments that 'the Emissary is corporeal, linear', before explaining her hand in his own genesis. She tells him about his ('corporeal') mother, revealing that 'for a time I shared her existence' (offering a parallel with the virgin birth and so on). 'You arranged my birth,' he says accusingly, but accurately. This conclusion is perhaps the least satisfactory element of a complex analogy. Sisko, we are told, has 'fulfilled his destiny', through the actions of Benny Russell, who resisted the psychiatrist, a diversionary ploy by the Pah-wraith itself. It is only as Benny Russell that Sisko could decide to open the orb: in a sense he is quite literally *writing* his own destiny.

This narrative generates many points of interest. In the first place (and the significance of the simple observation should be registered), it is *about* religion and it is *about* insanity. These two are exhaustively excluded from the rational, secular world of *Star Trek* and the development of these themes in the later series (which we explore shortly) constitutes a major change. In the sense that rationality and secularity are modern values, these are unambiguously 'post-modern' themes. If quoting and citation are 'post-modern' characteristics, then we have a rich depository here. The entire story is a mass of quotations. The way in which Benny Russell is beaten up by the cops, for instance, is a visual quotation from the videotapes of the LAPD beating up Rodney King – the event that triggered the Los Angeles riots of 1992. The verbal quotations are so common that they are even a source of comment in the story itself: when Mr Sisko says, 'I have fought the good fight, I have finished my course, I have kept the faith', Benjamin notes with surprise that he is quoting from the Bible.[1] The notion of 'a dream' of racial equality in America in the 1950s is a reference to Martin Luther King's now-legendary 'I have a dream' speech in Washington in 1963. He dreamt of a different future: of the many clauses, let us take: 'I have a dream that my four little children will one day live in a nation where they will not be judged by the colour of their skin but by the content of their character.' At many other places there are lines that are delivered as if they are quotations, or paraphrases, such as 'You are the dreamer and the dream,' and 'You can pulp a story but you cannot destroy an idea.'

The episode makes the characteristic move of being about its own history: bigoted America in the 1950s and a liberal vision of equality; the centrality of racial equality to the vision; the contribution of blacklisted Communists and Jews to the possibility of developing *Star Trek*. The 'K. C. Hunter' character is perhaps a reference to Roddenberry's secretary and leading *Star Trek* writer Dorothy ('D. C.') Fontana. The history of Benny Russell and *Incredible Tales* is the history of *Star Trek* itself. Those who accuse the show of endemic racism should stop and think why the concept was ever put in the future in the first place – to get it past the Mr Pabsts, and the proprietors of the Desilu Studios in 1966. So 'Far Beyond the Stars' is a reflection on the historical moment, and its politics, that *Star Trek* itself comes from.[2] The dream is the dream of science fiction; it is an analogy for *Star Trek* itself.

Relatedly, there is the curious feature that Benny Russell's story starts as a narrative ('Captain Sisko sat at his desk, looking out of the window . . .'), but later shifts into screen directions and the present tense. By the time he is in the mental hospital, Russell is not writing a story; he is telling Sisko what to do. Until he writes the words on the wall, the actions cannot be performed – as is made very clear when Sisko can only open the orb after Russell has written the words 'Opens it'. It seems that the screenwriters of *DS9* are here affording themselves a moment in the spotlight, as Russell's writing is, no doubt, verbatim copy from the script's own stage directions, an acknowledgement of the real authors of Benny Russell's stories. Perhaps the nearest precedent for this type of psychic link between the two realities and Sisko's two identities is the idea of a prefigurative or portentous dream – well known in a range of societies, but not in modern post-Freudian culture. We return to this theme shortly.

Finally, 'Far Beyond the Stars', in casting the Deep Space Nine crew in new roles, poses a very interesting question about the identities of these characters. How far are these figures of the 1950s recognizably the same as the ones from the twenty-fourth century? The continuity and discontinuity is there for us to see. This poses the 'post-modern' question of the self: does the individual have a 'core' identity that is unshifting? Or is the nature of the self better represented by the idea of a character who is actually a shapeshifter? In all these respects, the episode is a highly condensed working of a number of the central themes in 'post-modern' *Star Trek*. In what follows we look at the question of religion, the nature of rationality and the irrational, and then at the implications of some of these ideas for an understanding of identity and the self.

Beyond reason: religion

The arrival of religion in *Star Trek* is extremely significant as a departure from the ideals of the programme's creator, Gene Roddenberry, who was implacably opposed to it – he once said that religion was 'nothing more than a substitute brain'.[3] In the earlier series it is depicted with scepticism or criticism, if not contempt. Roddenberry was, as is well known, a convinced atheist. *The Original Series* has little representation of religion as such, but Greek religious myth sometimes figures. This is notably more amenable to an atheistic treatment than the monotheistic Judeo-Christian tradition. It places emphasis on humans, and their behaviour, as well as focusing on many different gods. The gods behave like humans, with individual personalities. 'The Squire of Gothos' features a powerful entity who plays games with the *Enterprise* crew, in much the same way as Q later does in the subsequent *TNG* series. Q's behaviour is that of one type of Greek god – a childish character who plays with mortals for his own amusement. 'Who Mourns for Adonais?' takes things a step further by representing Apollo as a megalomaniac – a bad god, in other words. This anti-religious stance is taken further, in the disclosure that Apollo was 'really' an alien who visited earth and not a divine being at all.

'The Apple' presents us with the idea of a powerful computer being worshipped by the naïve inhabitants of an idyllic world. The notion that computers are better than humans recurs in *TOS*: computers represent the technological over the emotional. This is generally qualified in a more humanist stance. Here, the computer is god, and god is a fraud – the worshippers are stupid to believe in it. The title is a reference to the biblical Garden of Eden, the inhabitants of the planet having been untouched by knowledge. In this case, the irony is that knowledge entails the discovery that their paradise, and their god, is a fraud. In 'The Paradise Syndrome', Captain Kirk is himself mistaken for a god, by a tribe of people on another idyllic planet. He has amnesia, and so cannot refute this. Quite clearly the worship is misplaced – we know that Kirk is not a god – and the worshippers are therefore foolish. Critics such as Daniel Bernardi view this as evidence of racism (in that it constructs a 'primitive people' who are unable to differentiate between a god and an alien). Certainly the depiction in this episode recycles unpleasant stereotypes, since the people concerned are recognizably caricatures of indigenous American peoples. However, since the two episodes are so similar in plot structure, but the dupes in 'The Apple' are white people, the stance may be (also) driven by a simple hostility to worship.

The Next Generation is adamant in its view that religious belief is a sign of a 'primitive' culture, and that the sooner a society gets beyond it and into science (and space travel), the better. The strategy in *TNG* is to express religious beliefs and practices as if they were cultural differences. They should be respected as such, but no more. This is far from the reverential attitude to religious phenomena that we find later on. Nevertheless, it does not mean that these practices are excluded from *TNG* – simply that they feature as cultural, rather than religious, differences. When *The Next Generation* deals with religion, its judgement is scathing. 'Who Watches the Watchers' is much like *TOS*'s 'The Paradise Syndrome', as in both cases the captain is mistaken for a god. Picard is utterly horrified at this turn of events, and flatly refuses to play along with it.

'Justice' shows a world of worshipping people who fear that their god (actually a machine from another dimension) will punish them for wrongdoing. Unfortunately, young Wesley Crusher is sentenced to execution for a minor misdemeanour. The worshippers see this difficult situation as entirely non-negotiable – they are terrified of disobeying their god. Another *TNG* story, 'The Child', revolves around a story of immaculate conception. It was written during a writers' strike in the eighties and is an old script reworked from the aborted *Star Trek* series *Phase II*. Thus, the story predates not only *TNG* but the *Original Series* films as well and represents a period when Roddenberry's control of the *Star Trek* universe was rather tenuous. This might explain its equivocal religious overtones. 'Devil's Due' presents another flawed belief system. It concerns a planet whose ancestors supposedly signed a Faustian pact with a devil-like entity, giving themselves over to her control at a certain date in the future. This point has now come and she arrives to collect on the agreement. Ultimately it transpires that the woman is a fraud, using technology to appear divine, and Picard uncovers her secret. Once again, religion is proved fraudulent and – in this case – opportunistic.

'The Next Phase' offers a scientific explanation for the phenomenon of ghosts, as Geordi La Forge and Ro Laren are 'phase-shifted' out of reality and become invisible, a strategy entirely consistent with *TNG*'s broader rationalizing mission. Ro (a Bajoran) comments on her lack of faith in religion, a belief system which *DS9* later presents as central to Bajoran identity. In *TNG*, religion is not a defining characteristic of Bajoran culture, whereas in *DS9* a loss of faith is treated as a loss of cultural integrity. 'Rightful Heir' similarly presents a scientific view of religious phenomena. When Worf goes in search of a vision of Kahless, a semi-mythical Klingon hero, he finds a clone of Kahless himself, a very scientific answer to a spiritual quest. Klingon society divides as to whether to accept the clone as genuine, a question of belief versus science.

TNG can here be seen to show the beginning of a transition to the new *Star Trek*, where religion is not simply a misinterpretation of scientific phenomena. In 'Masks', ancient eastern beliefs are touched upon, as a myth about the sun and moon chasing each other holds the key to the *Enterprise*'s survival. Here an old religious belief must be harnessed for our own good – perhaps a sign of new standards falling into place. In 'Journey's End' the superhuman 'Traveller' appears as a Native American mystic – a belief system adopted by many 'new-age' Americans at the time. This very late *TNG* episode, running parallel with the early episodes of *DS9*, shows clearly the effect of this latter series in breaking down the barriers to religion in *Star Trek*. No longer is there a simple difference between 'correct' scientific and 'incorrect' religious perspectives. There is increasingly a duality of interpretation, which can also be seen by looking at the movement in the films, and in the *Voyager* series, towards a less rational, more 'flexible', position on the conflict between rationality and religion. As we shall see, the scientific–rationalist stance is abandoned completely in *DS9*.

The *Star Trek* films, though using the same irreligious crew as the television series, began sending out a message that became decidedly and confusingly different. The first *Star Trek* film, *The Motion Picture*, uses pseudo-religious effects and lighting, and talks of 'creation' and 'new life forms' in an extremely reverential way. This is echoed by the 'Genesis' concept behind the second film, *The Wrath Of Khan*. In *Star Trek III: The Search For Spock*, a mystic Vulcan religion holds the key to Spock's survival. Spock's soul (*katra*) is temporarily housed in Dr McCoy. Sarek, Spock's father, speaks of his soul as being still alive, and still Spock ('How could you leave him there?'), and is furious at Kirk's lack of understanding of Vulcan religion. By this point, Roddenberry's creative role had diminished somewhat.

The Final Frontier was a film about 'God', an alarming departure. The film was widely regarded as tedious, a verdict that time has not overturned. It managed to be both cloyingly and conventionally religious, but also to undermine the general idea of God – presenting it as an externalized projection of an insane consciousness. God in the film is an evil god, who strikes down the crew and fires on ships. He is also a fraudulent old man, rather like *The Wizard of Oz*. Though remembered for its queasily religious storyline, *The Final Frontier* openly degraded religious belief, which was reduced to a quick-fix drug for solving emotional problems. Similarly, in the later film *Generations*, the powerful desire to return to the (heavenly) 'nexus' is represented in the register of drug addiction; Guinan describes it as overpowering and mentally destabilizing: 'If you go, you're not going to care about anything . . . all you'll want is to stay in the nexus.' Picard is able to resist the seductive hold of this 'nexus', when his rational morality defeats personal sentiment. James T. Kirk is less easily persuaded, but ultimately realizes the futility of the eternal utopia offered by the nexus. Bland paradise is not where we humans belong; we are grittier than that. In *The Undiscovered Country*, Spock keeps a print of 'The Expulsion from Paradise' as a reminder that 'all things end'. He tells his young protégé Valeris to 'have faith in the universe', which sounds more like a new-age mantra than traditional religious or rational advice. The film *Insurrection* continues this theme, in presenting an Eden-like planet that modern values and technology are liable to destroy. The inhabitants have infinitely prolonged lives and some fancy time-bending skills; again, their insights (such as 'a single moment in time can be a universe in itself,') are new-agey in tone and feeling.

Star Trek articulates the conflicts between religion and science that continue – perhaps surprisingly after so much time – to recur in modern western thought. Two indexical moments can highlight this: the persecution of Galileo and the controversy about evolution. In both instances the revelations of science were found indigestible by the church. In 1543 Nicolas Copernicus proposed that the earth and other planets revolved in circular orbits around the sun, which was the centre of the universe, a theory that reversed the 2,000 years of orthodoxy of the Ptolemaic and Aristotelian systems, which had held that the earth was the centre. Although the Copernican system was greeted with hostility at the time it was published, it was the fate of the Italian astronomer Galileo Galilei (1564–1642) to carry the brunt of religious persecution for the new ideas. Eventually, he was forced into a formal recantation by the Inquisition, a tribunal for the prosecution of heresy, or the formal denial of doctrine, set up by the (Roman Catholic) church. The trial of Picard and the others for the 'crimes of humanity' in 'Encounter at Farpoint' draws extensively on the iconography of the Inquisition, with Q dressed as the classic inquisitor. The tragedy of Galileo is a symbol of the persecution of scientific rationality by the intolerant institutions of a powerful church. In this, we see both the power of the institutions and hierarchy of the church – its worldly power – and the threat to religious belief that the displacement of the earth was held to pose.

A second key instance arose with the response of the church to Darwin's theory of evolution, first published in 1859 in *The Origin of Species by Means of Natural Selection*, a response which even now in some educational sectors of the USA censors the teaching of evolution. Evolution provided a fundamental challenge to Christian belief about God as the source of creation, explicitly in challenging the account in the book of Genesis, which held that the universe – from heaven and earth to mankind – had been created in six days. Evolutionary ideas were subsequently fleshed out in Darwin's account in 1871 of the descent of humans from the apes, and in the eventual discovery of the laws of genetic inheritance first proposed by Gregor Mendel in 1866. That these ideas offered a challenge to a belief in

God was immediately and controversially apparent. It was the evolutionary biologist T. H. Huxley who first coined the term 'agnostic' in 1869 to describe his position.

Few would now dispute the scientific basis of modern astronomy and an evolutionary perspective, yet both these discoveries were a source of immense controversy and persecution. *Star Trek* has combined elements of both histories in its treatment of the conflict between science and religion, between exploration and dogma. Two episodes in particular explore these issues, the first being 'The Chase', a late *TNG*, first broadcast in 1993. This story, discussed by Roddenberry and the staff in various versions, was intended to deal with the problem that the aliens in *Star Trek* tended – for practical reasons connected with the biology of the human actors, and the limits of make-up and special effects – to take a humanoid form. (Computer graphics underlie the change that we see in much later *Star Trek*; *Voyager*, in particular, has been able to benefit from this.) 'The Chase' addressed the problem by offering an explanation of the humanoid form taken by much life in the galaxy, suggesting that an ancient humanoid 'progenitor' had seeded DNA throughout the galaxy and hence, although the different 'races' had evolved with minor differences, they shared a common genetic inheritance. Picard sets the puzzle in motion when his mentor Professor Galen (the name typically refers to the classical physician) dies leaving some genetic research unfinished. It transpires that the puzzle has clues in four parts, and only when the Federation humans bring about co-operation with the Klingons, Romulans and Cardassians, and pool their knowledge, do they find the answer. The holographic 'progenitor' explains how their now-dead race had seeded the home planets of the four groups assembled. The story is an exploration of the issue of evolution and creationism. It puts forward what might be seen as an alternative 'creation myth' in that the progenitors act here in a god-like role, but a myth that is nevertheless grounded in a scientific framework that accepts evolution as a starting point. The meaning of 'progenitor' is unequivocally derived from the notion of an ancestor rather than a creator, and this endorses the evolutionary over the creationist reading of the story. The progenitor is presented as more of a benign parent than an omnipotent creator.

A far bleaker treatment of issues related to evolution, and focusing on the persecution of scientific truth, is found in the *Voyager* episode 'Distant Origin'. Here a scientist from Voth, in the Delta Quadrant, has stumbled upon the general idea that this lizard-like people are related to a species of warm-blooded mammals in a different part of the galaxy. This is unacceptable to the official 'doctrine' of the Voth, who regard their social and cultural status as being bound up with having a claim to their land as the place of origin of their species. They cannot countenance the notion that they originated elsewhere and are 'immigrants'. Professor Gegen and the *Voyager* database between them prove the somewhat implausible theory that the reptilian Voth evolved from a group of dinosaurs and escaped extinction on earth by setting off in a primitive spacecraft. Although we might be rather impressed by this feat, and Chakotay urges upon them the view that they should admire this new history of their people, the Voth authorities are concerned only to suppress the discovery. An inquisition is conducted, in which Gegen is required to recant his crime of 'heresy against doctrine'. Heresy has here moved from its historic meaning of deviation from the doctrine of the Catholic church, to its subsequent meaning of deviation from any orthodoxy. Gegen refuses, but when the magistrate threatens to incarcerate the entire *Voyager* crew in perpetuity, he does formally recant rather than be responsible for such an unjust punishment. The episode combines a treatment of some issues in contention around evolution with a reference to the harsher history of religious persecution under the rubric of heresy.

Religion in the Delta Quadrant

In *Star Trek: Voyager*, Captain Janeway is a committed rational atheist. (Unlike previous captains, her training is in science, not 'command'.) Yet Janeway does display a consistent and somewhat irrational belief in 'gut feeling' and 'intuition', a typically humanist stance for a *Star Trek* captain. Like Captain Kirk before her, Janeway delights in confounding her Vulcan security chief by following unusual (and often slightly reckless) courses of action – always on the basis of a *feeling* she may have. Generally, if the captain smells a rat there is something going on. One might argue that this is a testament to her abilities as a good judge of character, rather than any kind of spiritual capacity, but it is none the less a rejection of a completely rational outlook.

Voyager's pilot episode ('Caretaker') had an evident religious subtext, with the eponymous grey-haired old man as the traditional image of 'God'. He cares for the Ocampa, keeping them in a state of blissful ignorance of the horrors of the universe and sending them visions on big TV screens. This god dies at the end of the episode; the Ocampa have tasted the proverbial apple and the only one left in

their god's place is the (satanic) Suspiria. She appears in the episode
'Cold Fire' and attempts to lure Kes to become one of her
minions. The title itself is reminiscent of hell: her followers are terrified of her and drawn to her at the same time. They are like a satanic
cult. This is not the only appearance of a Satan figure in *Voyager* –
in 'Coda' one comes in the guise of Janeway's father, in an attempt
to lure her into his 'matrix' (hell), where she will 'nourish' him. He
tries to persuade the captain that she is dead, and existing only as a
ghost, but she refuses to believe this and realizes that he cannot be
her father, finally telling him to 'go back to hell, coward'. Harry Kim
also has an afterlife experience in the episode 'Emanations', when he
discovers a society where preparation for death is elaborate and complicated. The episode leaves us with an open conclusion as the
Voyager crew discover what could be interpreted as the spirits of
these people, existing in a non-corporeal state. Supernatural powers
are given a boost when Kes, on leaving the ship, throws *Voyager*
forward on her journey, as she herself transcends into the ether.

A corrupt belief system is depicted in 'False Profits', where two
Ferengi in the Delta Quadrant have convinced the people of a planet
that they are 'holy sages' and require such things as worship and
money. Their religion is shown to be completely fraudulent, and the
pseudo-church institution not one with any real belief or integrity. In
the *Voyager* episode 'The Omega Directive', a form of (scientific) god
makes an appearance in the form of the Ω molecule, which the Borg
worship as representing true perfection. This molecule is extremely
elaborate in structure but its complex symmetry gives it a beautiful
mystic quality. It is also extremely dangerous if mishandled, hence
the association with the divine. Seven of Nine has a 'spiritual experience' while in contact with this devastatingly powerful substance
before she is forced by Captain Janeway to destroy it. *Star Trek* is
coming to something when even the Borg are not entirely free of
religion.

Two examples from *Voyager* demonstrate the way people's faiths
can change. In 'Sacred Ground', the rational atheist Janeway is forced
to go on a spiritual quest in order to save Kes's life. She is thoroughly
perplexed by the whole experience, and astounded to realize that,
against all scientific reasoning, the quest allows her to do what she
must to rescue her crewmember. Though she does not abandon
science, she comes to appreciate the presence of forces she is unable
to explain. Conversely, in 'Mortal Coil', Neelix suffers a loss of faith
which brings him close to suicide. When he is resuscitated, many
hours after having died, he realizes that his people's beliefs about the
afterlife – where he had believed his dead family to be happily resid-

ing – are completely false: 'I died and there was nothing; there was no one there . . . we just disappear into nothing.' He is unable to cope with this, and the final shred of hope from the tragedy of his life is torn away from him. Ultimately he decides to return to his life, but he does so very much disillusioned with his own faith.

The only character in *Voyager* whose religious beliefs are seriously explored is Chakotay, who, from the start, was established as following in the traditional ways of his people. As in *TNG*, religion is hence presented as a marker of cultural difference, requiring respect, rather than transcendentally 'true'. The first signs of this are in 'The Cloud', when he goes on a 'vision quest' and introduces Janeway to her 'animal guide'. She claims she is willing to use all resources at her disposal (a guide is a handy resource), but it is a sign of her open-mindedness that she is interested in this belief. In 'Cathexis', Chakotay falls into a coma and the Doctor and Torres use traditional Native American medicine in an attempt to save his spirit: this involves the use of a 'medicine wheel'. In 'Tattoo', the commander's tattoo is explained and his relationship to his people and their ways are explored. (Jeri Taylor's novel *Pathways* also has a lot to say on this subject, and in it we finally meet Chakotay's animal spirit guide.) In 'The Fight', Chakotay goes on another vision quest in order to seek guidance, and ends up meeting his senile grandfather. On the purely spiritual front, it is Chakotay who convinces the Doctor that he is a person in 'Projections', and persuades Neelix not to abandon all belief in 'Mortal Coil'. Chakotay, too, is a character invested with an expanded capacity for 'dreaming'; this can take the form of 'waking' or 'lucid' dreaming, and the ability to use dreams as forms of communication.

Crossing the religious rubicon

DS9 is where religion really takes off, and it is useful to look at the account given of this huge change by an executive producer of the series. Ira Steven Behr had worked on *TNG* at the time they were making 'Who Watches the Watchers', an episode that crystallized how appalled Starfleet was by the reversion to primitive religious worship in a culture that had moved forward into rationality. He remembers that, 'according to Gene Roddenberry, there was no religion on earth anymore. God was a concept that had kind of grown out of favour and was replaced by technology and man's basic goodness.'[4] This is perhaps something of an understatement. From the creator himself we get: 'I condemn the effort to take away the power of rational decision, to drain people of their free will . . . all religions which use the notion of God as a weapon against humanity.' Behr argues that *DS9* was conceived with a different structure from that of its predecessors; it is more like a serial than a series of independent episodes, and it is partly this that enables it to develop 'deeper' themes.

According to Behr, the introduction of religion followed once the other great Roddenberry taboo – money – had been lifted. By the twenty-third century of *The Original Series*, money had apparently been rendered unnecessary – but on the new station the gambling in Quark's bar required stakes. They invented a currency for the Ferengi people, and, by extension, the population of Deep Space Nine: bars, strips and slips of (gold pressed) 'latinum'. Odd as it may seem to bracket money and religion, they both represent the collapse of Roddenberry's rational, humanist, utopian vision. Behr comments: 'Once we put money and finances back into the twenty-fourth century, it was just like a line of dominoes.' They found a way to talk about religion that could incorporate the humanists too: they called it 'faith'. Behr argues that 'faith is such a fine concept for both the religious and the secular. Faith in each other. Faith in the system. Faith in ourselves.' The concept of faith, rather than religion, enabled the staff, as well as the key actors, to 'rewire our brains'. In this new universe, religious belief – 'faith' – is not simply a set of cultural practices; it is a 'legitimate and viable subject' in a show which 'has always been about the human experience'.

The link between the introduction of money and of religion can be seen in the parodic and knowing titles of the episodes 'False Profits' (*Voyager*) and 'Prophet Motive' (in *DS9*). An effort is even made to convince us that the Ferengi philosophy is governed by a form of religion (Quark dreams of dying and going to the 'Great Treasury' in 'Body Parts'), but this is somewhat unconvincing as a belief system. Nevertheless, it is typical of *DS9* that even the Ferengi should be shown in a form of idol-worshipping. The departure from the previous *Star Trek* position is pronounced. Even outside the context of actual religion, *DS9* has adopted a religious lexicon. The script of the final episode ends as follows: 'Finally Deep Space Nine becomes just one more bright but distant star in the vast cathedral of space.'

Klingon religion features in *Deep Space Nine*, first when Jadzia Dax takes on an old 'Blood Oath' sworn by her predecessor Curzon Dax (which involves the gruesome eating of hearts), and later when Worf's brother Kurn seeks his assistance in committing ritual suicide (in 'Sons of Mogh'). The marriage of Worf and Jadzia presents us

The Emissary

with more Klingon beliefs – from the trials of Worf's friends on their spiritual quest, to the tales of when the Klingons killed their gods ('You are Cordially Invited . . .'). Finally, after Jadzia's death, the question of her entry to Sto Vo Kor (Klingon heaven) is a subject of great importance, and one which Worf takes extremely seriously. Perhaps more interesting is that all her friends agree to help out – they don't believe in any one true religion, so if Jadzia wanted to go to Sto Vo Kor then that is where they will help her go after death ('Image in the Sand' and 'Shadows and Symbols').

The central religious theme in *DS9* concerns the Bajoran religion and the extraordinary casting of a Federation officer as a major religious figure. From the pilot episode the prophets begin to interfere with Sisko's life and people start treating him as the 'Emissary'. Bajoran religion is based around prophecies, and the concept of Sisko's destiny in this role is crucial. At first he is entirely sceptical, but polite; since the prophets help him to piece his life together, as well as agreeing to open the wormhole to space traffic, he is willing to stay on the right side of the Bajorans by being regarded as the 'Emissary'. Bajoran religion appears to be entirely benign until the death of Kai Opaka (in 'Battlelines') leaves a web of political intrigue and backstabbing, primarily from Vedek (later Kai) Winn. This comes to the fore in 'In the Hands of the Prophets', when Winn accuses Keiko O'Brien of blasphemy for teaching science to Bajoran children, and even destroys her school, in order to arrange an ambush of her political rival Bareil. This is another reference to the idea of persecuting 'heresy against doctrine', and Winn, as the most vocal religious figure, symbolizes all that is historically intolerant about religion. Bareil, on the other hand, is presented as the ideal priest: quiet, sensitive and forgiving. Already *DS9* is defending 'good' religion while indicting 'bad' individual religious practitioners. In 'Life Support', Bareil dies, which helps Winn to pursue her political career; his motives were peaceful while hers are simply aimed at exploitation for her own gain. His altrusitic and heroic death leaves a void in which Winn faces no competition in her goal of becoming Kai (akin to Pope).

Bareil resurfaces later when his mirror counterpart arrives on the station and becomes involved with Major Kira in 'Resurrection'. As an essentially good man from a bad world, he soon becomes intrigued by the promise of 'good' Bajoran religion and its capacity for redemption. Meanwhile, with 'our' Bareil's death, Bajoran religion becomes increasingly political. In 'Shakaar', Winn is only barely stopped from being made First Minister – and hence holding both Bajoran seats of power – and she is revealed as the cruel character we have now come to expect. She still maintains her religious position, however. Winn begins negotiations with the Dominion in 'In the Cards' and helps to prepare the non-aggression pact which Sisko ultimately calls for. They openly disagree, and it is clear that she doubts that he really is the 'Emissary'. These feelings come to a head in 'The Reckoning', when her lack of faith becomes apparent. While Sisko is willing to risk the life of his own son for the will of the prophets, the Kai does not ultimately *believe* that good will triumph over evil.

'The Reckoning' is an episode that allows us to confront just how seriously the religious message is being presented in *DS9*. The forces of good and evil have inhabited two bodies – a prophet is incarnated in Kira and an evil Pah-wraith has taken over Jake (in a classic image of demonic possession, he is given red eyes). Sisko allows the contest to continue, but eventually Kai Winn pulls the plug on it. The obvious reading is connected with faith – the Kai herself does not have faith that the prophet will win in the conflict between good and evil whereas Sisko (the 'Emissary') does have faith that goodness will prevail. On the other hand, Sisko's son is the body inhabited by the evil Pah-wraith, so presumably he is seriously at risk of destruction when the contest is resolved. So strong is this implication that it is difficult not to see the theme of sacrifice: Sisko is willing to sacrifice his own son if this is what is necessary. Kira makes this clear when she confronts Winn about her actions: 'You couldn't stand the fact that a human, an infidel, had a stronger faith than you. The Emissary was willing to sacrifice his own son to serve the Prophets.' The Judeo-Christian resonances of this are apparent. The story of Abraham comes immediately to mind. He obeyed the order to sacrifice his son Isaac, and got as far as tying him up on the altar and raising his knife before God intervened and revealed that this was a test of faith: 'Now I know that thou fearest God, seeing that thou hast not withheld thy son, thine only son from me.'⁵ A convenient ram might be sacrificed instead. The parallel between Sisko and God the Father, in the Christian narrative, is there too – the sacrifice of the Son (in the crucifixion) is necessary for the redemption of humanity. At various points in *DS9*, Sisko is pushed beyond his own desires by the things required of him by the prophets. At the end of the series we are told that he is to abandon his newly pregnant wife Kassidy to take up his training position at the celestial temple. The intimation in 'The Reckoning' is that he is being asked to sacrifice Jake, with whom he has enjoyed an extremely close relationship as a single father with an only child, and that he is ultimately willing to do so.

The sacrificial theme is especially prominent in this father–son dynamic. 'The Visitor' is not an episode about religion, but its exploration of their relationship, and the tragedy of its personal sacrifices, places it very much in the register of this theme. In this episode it is Jake who makes the sacrifice, if somewhat indirectly, when his father is hit by a freak wormhole phenomenon and becomes trapped in 'subspace' (limbo) for eternity. Jake first struggles to get over the loss of his father, but his troubles are then magnified by the discovery that he still exists: Sisko is able to put in a momentary appearance every few years and uses this time to visit his son. The burden of guilt on Jake's shoulders is such that he gives up his successful writing career and devotes all his time to resolving the spatial phenomenon that has imprisoned his father. Sisko is appalled to realize, when he visits his now middle-aged son, that Jake has lost both his wife and his career in his desperate attempts to save him. 'Let go, Jake,' he pleads, 'if not for yourself then for me. You still have time to make a good life for yourself.' Jake eventually discovers that the only way to solve the problem is to kill himself and return his father to the moment of the accident, so that he can avoid the event which sent him into subspace. This he does, despite his father's protestations, and history is set on a more benevolent trajectory. The episode demonstrates the intensity of this father–son relationship, and the sacrifices that it entails on both parts: Sisko would rather live forever in oblivion than see his son throw away his own happiness. These themes are entirely consistent with the representation of family in *Deep Space Nine* and the ways it can conflict with religion. The monastic ideal of giving up one's family is clearly suggested in the conclusion to the series, when Sisko's spiritual development forces him to leave his family behind on the station. The conflict between religion and family, religion and relationships, religion and human love, could not be presented more starkly.

Kai Winn's conversion to the evil Pah-wraiths comes at the hands of the Cardassian Gul Dukat. Feeling unappreciated by the prophets – who will not communicate with her by visions – and saddled with a fundamental lack of faith, she chooses to side with their ancient rivals in a move designed to grant her enormous personal power. Seeing herself as an alternative 'Emissary', she hopes to destroy Sisko and take control of Bajor. Again, Winn's moves are highly political and self-seeking, albeit compounded with muddled belief. Eventually the Pah-wraiths kill her, having chosen Gul Dukat as a preferable vessel. Her final act, however, is one of repentant faith: 'Emissary, the book,' she shouts, helping Sisko to destroy them once and for all.

Aside from Kai Winn's activities, the Bajoran religion gets a very good press. Prophecies generally come true, and the prophets tend to look out for Bajor. In 'Prophet Motive', they turn the Ferengi Grand Nagus into a philanthropist, believing that this is an act of good. However, when Quark pleads with them they are surprisingly reasonable and eventually return him to his natural state. The prophets can generally be persuaded by a good argument, as in 'Favour the Bold', when Sisko convinces them to seal the wormhole, in order to prevent dominion reinforcements from storming Bajor. Twice (in 'Emissary' and 'Far beyond the Stars'), they help to give Sisko a sense of purpose in his life, and they are even thought to be responsible for Dax's ability to bear Worf's child ('Tears of the Prophets'). In 'Rapture', they give Sisko the visions he needs to save Bajor from destruction, endowing him with an almost god-like ability himself. Indeed, as the series draws to a close and 'The Sisko' fulfils his own destiny – the final incarceration of the Pah-wraiths – the prophets adopt him as one of their own, proposing to teach him the ways of being a god. Sisko leaves a son and (pregnant) wife behind him, promising to return ('It could be a year. It could be yesterday,') when he has finished his term in the 'Celestial Temple'. The prophets' orbs, too, are extremely useful. In 'Wrongs Darker than Death or Night', Kira is able to discover the truth about her mother's relationship with Gul Dukat, while in 'Trials and Tribble-ations', a criminal uses an orb to travel back in time. They also provide helpful visions when people are confused about their own path in life.

The evil cousins of the prophets, the Pah-wraiths (who had been thrown out of the wormhole for bad behaviour), first demonically possess Keiko (in 'The Assignment') and then attempt to regain the wormhole in 'The Reckoning' and 'Tears of the Prophets', before making their final bid for control in the conclusion of the series, 'What You Leave Behind'. Their aim appears to be the destruction of the prophets and they have chosen Gul Dukat as their own 'Emissary' figure. His religious practices ('Covenant') are even worse than Winn's, more akin to a suicide cult than a traditional religion. The Pah-wraiths have chosen an insane man as their corporeal messenger.

Aside from the appearances of the actual Bajoran gods (good or bad), religion and spiritual beliefs play an important part in DS9. In 'Destiny', a prophecy comes true before our eyes, much to the chagrin of Sisko and his sceptical scientific crew. In 'Starship Down', Kira reveals her difficulties with her captain being the 'Emissary', and she prays to the prophets for his survival after an accident. In 'Children of Time', she feels ambivalent about following an alternate timeline because she believes the prophets have laid out a 'true' path for her. In various episodes (such as 'The Begotten', and 'Fascination') she presides over or participates in Bajoran religious festivals.

Sisko also has much interaction with Bajoran religion. In 'Accession', he is replaced by another, more traditional, Emissary and finds himself free of the trappings of that post. In 'Image in the Sand' and 'Shadows and Symbols', he goes on a religious quest, to rescue the prophets from the Pah-wraiths. He is frequently seen presiding over religious ceremonies and always willing to put his case to the prophets and garner their support. Indeed, when he ignores their wishes – instead following Starfleet orders – not only is Jadzia killed, but the prophets vanish and their orbs die out as well, leaving Bajor spiritually bereft ('Tears of the Prophets').

The Bajoran prophets are not the only 'gods' to make a regular appearance in Deep Space Nine. The founders of 'the Dominion' are perceived as gods by their servants, by means of genetic programming. In 'The Ship', a female Vorta shows the extent of her devotion in her attempts to rescue a stranded founder. Ultimately a lack of trust between her and Sisko results in its death. The Dominion possess none of the religious pluralism generally shown in *Star Trek* – where one can opt for any faith from Klingon to Bajoran – and Weyoun dismisses the prophets as nonsense while reassuring us that the founders are different: 'They *are* gods,' ('Tears of the Prophets'). While the Vorta and Jem'Hadar are devoted to the founders (the sycophantic Weyoun is a testament to this), Odo is much less keen on his own role as a god. When the Dominion occupy Deep Space Nine, Weyoun is heartbroken at Odo's resistance to joining them, and dismayed that his god does not appear to like him. In 'Treachery, Faith and the Great River', Odo is forced to come to terms with the way the Vorta regard him, ultimately giving his blessing to Weyoun in order to make his death easier. The question of whether Odo is a god is a slightly vexed one, and a parallel with Jesus seems relevant – he is at one point turned into a humanoid, but is essentially a god ('Broken Link').

On the issue of religion, we can see in the later series of *Star Trek* an important historical change from a secular, 'modern' critical position to a more tolerant and pluralist, or 'post-modern', stance. *DS9* and *Voyager* have moved away from the confident faith in science and rationality that characterized *TOS* and *TNG*. *The Next Generation*, in several ways the most 'modern' series of them all in its values, is the most critical of, and sceptical about, religion. As we have already pointed out, *TNG* does not usually offer religion the respect of its own autonomous role, but – in a thoroughly modern spirit – reduces it to a matter of cultural difference: religious practices are similar to manners or cuisine. As good diplomats we respect these cultural protocols, but that is all. In *Deep Space Nine*, however, the rebellion against Roddenberry's secular spirit has triumphed – the series is inexplicable and implausible if you are not prepared to attach even a momentary suspension of disbelief to the action. Of course, it is not entirely clear which religion is being invoked here; the model is a synthetic one, with elements drawn from a variety of sources. Also, we see a differentiation of the corrupt political institutions of 'the church', with its Vedeks and the Kai, and the underlying issues of belief or faith. In *Star Trek: Voyager*, the religious impetus comes mostly from the (somewhat stereotyped) representation of Chakotay's Native American animalist spirituality.[6] *Voyager* has a captain who is a scientist by trade – although she has to accept some manifestations of the supernatural and the scientifically inexplicable as she goes along. The original series of *Star Trek* started out with a more ramshackle, 'Greek gods' view of religion. In these light-hearted borrowings we can find many resonances with classical and secular renaissance culture, rather than with the traditions of Christianity or modernity. Religion in *The Original Series* is more 'pre-modern' than modern in feeling.

Religion is extremely important as it is the most severe antithesis of rationality. Later on, we take up the implications of post-modern ruptures of the boundary between the rational and the irrational. Before doing this it will be useful to mention two groups of phenomena that lie somewhere between the worlds of reason and faith. Both groups figure a great deal in *Star Trek*, and both have a wide set of cross-cultural, as well as western historical reference-points. We have in mind shapeshifting and the interpretation of dreams.

Beyond reason: shapeshifters and dreamers

For some viewers shapeshifters are a little hard on the credulity. Odo is not a spiritual or immaterial phenomenon as such; he is represented as a being that can shift to assume the form of anything he wishes. Most spectacularly, he takes animal, even bird, form, as well as a range of humanoid forms. Donna Haraway, neatly complementing our arguments in Part I, has pointed to the significance of the occasion on which he assumed the form of a rat:

> Beginning with the rats who stowed away on the masted ships of Europe's imperial age of exploration, rodents have gone first into the unexplored regions in the great travel narratives of Western techno-science. Odo, the shape-shifter security chief on the Federation space station Deep Space Nine, in one early episode even morphed himself into the shape of a rat, all the better to get a perspective on the dubious traffic at the entrance to the wormhole, gateway to unexplored regions of space.[7]

Odo is a material being with the capacity for taking lipid or 'solid' form. As one of the 'founders', a community of beings regarded as 'gods' by their people (Vorta and Jem'Hadar), he is able to join his founder colleagues in an experience referred to as 'the link'. Odo is thus a being who can take human form, but need not; who can function as an individual, but can be regarded as one of a collectivity. In these ways, Odo is rather like one of the gods of ancient Greek literature.

We have already drawn a parallel between the long journey home of Janeway and *Voyager* and that of Odysseus. This text also reveals where Odo got his ideas from. The ancient Greeks believed that their gods were always present, usually but not always invisible, constantly playing a part in human affairs.[8] (The Greeks were rather like evangelical Christians who attribute a convenient parking meter to help from 'the Lord'.) D. C. H. Rieu, introducing his revised translation, emphasizes Homer's use of formulaic adjectives. Penelope is always 'wise Penelope' ('even when she is being rather silly'), Telemachus is always 'thoughtful Telemachus', and so on. This is the *Star Trek* style too: pick a trait and blow it up so that a particular group always represents a particular quality. In contrast with the good/evil binary mentality of the Judaeo-Christian tradition, the attributes of the Greek gods are rather similar to those of the proud Romulans, honourable Klingons, and so on. As Rieu comments, this creates an atmosphere of the heroic.[9]

The ubiquitous gods frequently appear as shapeshifters. In the *Odyssey*, the goddess Pallas Athene is protecting young Telemachus as he sets out to look for his father Odysseus. She assumes several different forms – that of Mentor, of a vulture, of a young girl (Nausica's friend Dymas), of a tall and beautiful woman.[10] That this kind of thing goes on is perfectly normal; Noemon says he has seen Mentor 'or some god' looking exactly like him.[11] The gods can also make themselves visible to one person but not another: they do not necessarily grant clear sight. In one very strange incident, the goddess Circe shapeshifts not herself, but Odysseus's sailors, leaving them with their human minds, trapped in the bodies of pigs.[12]

In the Homeric narrative, shapeshifting is intertwined not only with the practical activities of the gods, but with the supernatural, the paranormal, with the ghosts of the dead, and with dreams. It is, indeed, not always clear where the boundaries between these phenomena are being drawn in the text. At one point Athene sends Penelope's sister (who lives a long way away and so cannot go herself) in the form of a visitation in sleep: a shadowy wraith. In short, she plants a dream in the sister's unconscious.[13] Odysseus, meanwhile, is meeting vast numbers of individuals who are dead – he has gone to Hades to look them up. They retain all their mortal personality quirks: one of them (Ajax) is still so angry with him that he refuses to speak to him.[14] Downright paranormal behaviour is exhibited, of which the creepiest is when Hyperion's cows protest at their own slaughter by bellowing from the spits where they are being roasted.[15] A different religious note is sounded in the airing of the concept of 'destiny' in the story. Calypso has seduced Odysseus and is keeping him prisoner on her island. In the end, the messenger of the gods (Hermes) has to go and persuade her to let him go. The tenor of his request is that she must let him go because 'he is not doomed to' stay, 'he is destined' elsewhere.[16]

'Wise Penelope' tells us something that could equally be applied to Benny Russell and Benjamin Sisko, 'the dreamer and the dream'. 'Dreams, my friend,' says the thoughtful Penelope,

> are awkward and confusing things: not all that people see in them comes true. For there are two gates through which these insubstantial visions reach us; one is of horn and the other of ivory. Those that come through the carved ivory gate cheat us with empty promises that never see fulfilment; whereas those that issue from the gate of burnished horn inform the dreamer what will really happen.[17]

It is difficult for the uninitiated modern reader to relate to Penelope's insight, so immersed are we in the contemporary west in the ideas of Freud about the interpretation of dreams. (Indeed when the android Data starts having nightmares, it is to a holographic Freud that he turns for advice.) Dreams tend to be seen in the 'ivory gate' mode of wishful thinking, rather than as announcing what is actually going to happen to us. Foucault notes (in a considerable understatement) that cultural history has dealt with the ethical value of the dream, 'while its premonitional import remains secondary'.[18] The premonitional import of dreams is largely derided in the west, or regarded as mere superstition. In Foucault's discussion of the approach to dreams in the classical author Artemidorus, he offers a far more detailed account of this premonitional side. Specifically, this applied then to the type of dreams that the psychoanalytic model is so easily applied to now: that is, sexual dreams. These were all read as omens of your future fortunes, to be interpreted according to the exact who and how of the sexual positioning.[19]

Dreaming, in different cultures, has a different status. Alfred Gell, to whose concept of the 'counter-temporal' we referred earlier, begins his arguments with an interesting story about dreaming. This case, it may be said in advance, will throw some light on the subject we move on to shortly: the definition of 'reason' in modern societies, and the corresponding approaches to 'unreason' – insanity or madness. Gell tells of a strange incident analysed by the anthropologist Levy-Bruhl in a book with the unappealing title of *Primitive Mentality*. A missionary, whose name is Grubb, working among the Leguna people in Brazil, is visited by an indignant person (not even given a name here) whom he knows; the man accuses Grubb of stealing pumpkins from his garden. Grubb remonstrates that the man lives 150 miles away and Grubb has not been to his village for a long time; in response to this the man agrees that he had indeed not been there. Actually, no pumpkins are missing: this is not relevant. In the end, he explains that he saw this happen (Grubb stealing three pumpkins) in a dream, and that, further, 'If you had been there you would have taken them.'

Missionary Grubb concluded that the man, believing that his dream revealed the 'will' of the person dreamt about, thus accused him of harbouring 'thieving intentions'. Anthropologist Levy-Bruhl is less tolerant than Missionary Grubb. He concludes that because the man thinks both that Grubb stole the pumpkins, and knows that Grubb was not there: 'this is one of the reasons which cause us to regard the the primitive mind as "pre-logical"'.[20] Gell draws a very different conclusion, pointing out that there are parallels in western law, offences such as conspiracy, loitering with intent, attempted murder, and so on, where no 'crime' has been committed. Their *logic* and ours are identical; what differs is the relatively 'contingent' matter of beliefs about dreams. The Leguna believe that dream-experience has a legal status, that people who are dreamt about behave 'in character', and that dreamers tell the truth. Thus Gell concludes there is no difference in logic, simply a difference of opinion about the status of dreams, which are 'representations of counter-factual worlds'. For the Leguna, but not for Mr Grubb or Levy-Bruhl, dreams are closely enough related to the actual worlds for inferences to be drawn.[21]

Another way of approaching cultural variation in the understanding of dreams is to regard them as 'warnings with something less than full evidence'.[22] In some way, this is what Sisko's visions from the prophets often are: they do warn him but without explaining why. Like the witches in Macbeth, or the ghost in Hamlet, they speak outside the rational discourse within which the action mainly takes place. Shakespeare is indeed an important reference to bring in here. As is widely known, of course, Shakespeare's plays abound in what – to readers used to the more recent modern western separation of reason and unreason – is a refreshing play of the rational and the irrational. They act out 'wise Penelope' being foolish once in a while. Shakespeare is full of jesters who say the most insightful things, responsible kings behaving ridiculously, and so on. The plays of Shakespeare represent the high point of pre-modern culture, before the relentless hiving off of 'the fool' to the category of mental illness.

The rationalism of modern western culture is of course oddly restricted by the fact that this is a culture throughout which religion, particularly Christianity, has flourished. It seems that people have learnt to live with this glaring contradiction. Indeed, modern astrophysicists, in their claims to see into 'the mind of God', are carrying on a long tradition of scientists adopting a 'priestly' role, as Margaret Wertheimer has shown.[23] Both Britain and the USA, and many other European countries, are societies where the heads of state are involved in the church in more and less formal ways. Christian doctrine – leaving aside the obvious clash over issues such as evolution versus creationism – contains some highly metaphysical propositions to be signed up to. The idea of a shapeshifter is mundanely plausible in comparison with the idea that the Virgin Mary was herself 'immaculately conceived' as well as conceiving her son by divine intervention, that the Holy Trinity is both divisible and indivisible, that 'the Word' is God. The basic premise of Christian belief, the incarnation of God in a human form, is just the kind of thing that cyborg science fiction is full of: 'Veiled in flesh the Godhead see.' Indeed, perhaps Levy-Bruhl could have included these offences against logic in his disquisition on 'primitive mentality'.

Beyond reason: insanity

Insanity is a particularly important issue when one looks at how *Star Trek* has changed. Viewers of *Deep Space Nine* will have noticed the highly unusual depiction of a mental breakdown in the character of Gul Dukat, a disintegration precipitated by the death of his daughter Ziyal. In 'The Sacrifice of Angels', we see a defeat for Cardassia, which means that all the Cardassians are being evacuated from the (occupied) station. Ziyal is that most unfortunate of hybrids, having a Cardassian father and a Bajoran mother (long since dead), since these two peoples have the bitterest possible history of conflict. Ziyal declares that she will stay on the station, which is where she now belongs, rather than leave with her father. For this decision, she is branded a 'traitor' and shot by Legate Damar, who is trying to persuade Dukat to leave. After her death, Dukat is pictured in a state of utter psychological abjection, curled up on the floor and muttering to himself, and we are told that he is ill for some while.

Dukat's madness stems from a previous experience. As the Cardassian 'Prefect' in charge of Bajor he was responsible for the last days of his people's occupation – a period of concentration camps, death squads, rape, plundering and repression. Unsurprisingly, he is viewed by most Bajorans as the embodiment of that time, and is loathed throughout the galaxy as a war criminal. (In his own words: 'an evil man who sent thousands of Bajorans to their deaths just to satisfy his own sadistic desires'.) As Dukat's psychological state becomes increasingly unstable, we see the devastating effect that this has had on him, and also his inability to deal with the fact that the Bajorans simply disliked him. The death of Ziyal is a turning point, as she symbolizes everything that he cannot come to terms with about his actions in the past. It is not her death that destroys him so much as her siding with the Bajorans – just as the rest of Bajor had previously turned against him. 'I forgive you, Ziyal,' he repeats as he cradles her dying body, unable to accept that her decision was anything other than a mistake. By the time of the episode 'Waltz', he has seemingly recovered from what he terms his 'momentary instability' and is being brought to face trial as a war criminal. When he finds himself stuck alone with Sisko, however, it becomes apparent that his fixation has grown. He now seeks absolution for what he did to the Bajorans and needs to convince the captain that his actions were in fact lenient.

Dukat is presented entirely within the framework of madness: he beats (an already crippled) Sisko when he gets angry; he sabotages their means of escape; he hallucinates friends and enemies who offer different thoughts on his situation. Yet the arguments he gives are surprisingly convincing and it is clear that his position is not entirely irrational. He explains to the captain: 'In my first official act as Prefect, I ordered all labor camp commanders to reduce their output quotas by fifty per cent. . . . Child labor was abolished. Medical care was improved and food rations were increased. In the first month of my administration, the death rate dropped by more than twenty per cent.' We are not in any position to question the facts of these statements and it is clear that Dukat genuinely feels he was as kind as possible. Despite his evident 'madness', he is, in a sense, convincing. 'My name and reputation have been slandered and twisted ever since the end of the Occupation of Bajor,' he tells us. 'I've been vilified by ignorant and small-minded people throughout the quadrant for the past six years'. Dukat simply cannot understand that, however well he treated the people of Bajor, they would still have resented his presence. He is outraged that they continued to sabotage his administration: 'Time and again, I would reach out with the open hand of friendship and time and again, they would slap it away.' Dukat is convinced that his actions were justified and is furious that Sisko will not agree, seeing him as pompous and moralistic: 'Behold Benjamin Sisko – supreme arbiter of right and wrong in the universe. A man of such high moral calibre that he can sit in judgement on the rest of us.' Dukat feels he was merely carrying out his orders – and doing so as compassionately as possible – and yet it is he who has been blamed for the atrocities of the occupation.

The parallels with Nazism should by now be fairly obvious, but Dukat's next justification is a chilling reminder of that connection. Grounded in a rationally held (not inherently 'mad') belief, he explains the principles behind the occupation: 'It was clear that we were the superior race . . . fate handed us our role.' He goes on to explain: 'Militarily, technologically, culturally – we were almost a century ahead of them in every way.' From Dukat's perspective his argument is entirely rational, and he is perplexed by Sisko's refusal to accept it. Ultimately the captain forces out of him the real emotions surrounding his rejection by the Bajoran people: 'I should've killed every last one of them and turned their planet into a graveyard the likes of which the galaxy has never seen.' Dukat has moved seamlessly from a rational defence of his position to the insane rage that his experience has provoked.

This waltz is heavily syncopated: the theme of Dukat's insanity is balanced by the opposing view that he is just downright evil. Is he mad or bad? Having shown us how derangedly mad he is, the episode closes with Sisko's conclusion that Dukat is simply an evil man: 'There are times when life seems so complicated. Nothing is truly good or truly evil. You start to think that everything is shades of gray. Then you spend time with a man like Dukat . . . and you realize there is really such a thing as evil after all.' In later episodes the ambiguity is reintroduced when Dukat becomes converted to the religion of the Pah-wraiths. This is heavily coded with references to satanism and 'black magic'; Dukat is taking up the evil antithesis of (good) Bajoran religion as he leads a group of fifty Bajoran worshippers. At first, it is not completely clear whether this 'conversion' is the result of his insanity, whether it is a ruse or a disguise for some political ambition, or whether he really believes it. It is made clear soon, however, that the last of these interpretations is the correct one. 'The Pah-wraiths have given me an opportunity to redeem myself in the eyes of your people,' he tells the Bajoran colonel Kira. But she is quick to spot the true appeal of this for Dukat. 'How?' she replies; 'By recreating some idealized version of the Occupation? You have your station back, Bajorans to serve your every whim. And the best part is, this time they really do love you.' Dukat's mad fixation with the Bajoran people has led him to embrace the gods of evil and they have granted him everything he ever wanted.

The story of Dukat's madness is one of the most elaborated discussions of insanity in *Star Trek*, but the subject is one that has preoccupied the programme for some time. The ways in which this is represented (and the attitudes behind them) have changed significantly over time, and we shall address this issue shortly. For the moment, however, it is worth noting one area where the various series can be said to be in agreement: the representation of senility and the tragedy of losing one's memory and control. In *TNG* we see the sad decline of Spock's father Sarek (a character who appeared in *The Original Series*) with the debilitating Bendii Syndrome. For a Vulcan this disease is particularly difficult as it involves the loss of control over emotions – a trait these people value over all else. The old man cannot stop himself from crying at a Mozart concert, and his enraged denial of his illness is a wrenching demonstration of his own loss of control. In the episode 'Unification', he eventually dies of the disease, but not before we see him writhing around in his bed, muttering utter nonsense and trying desperately to deal with the emotions he has repressed throughout his entire life. Perhaps not as openly tragic, but equally revealing, is the treatment of Captain Picard himself in the *TNG* finale 'All Good Things . . .', where it is suggested that he may have the twenty-fourth-century equivalent of Alzheimer's Disease: the 'Irumodic Syndrome'. In the future timeline shown in this episode the captain is an old man and though his erstwhile crew go to great lengths to take him seriously, it is clear that they think he has invented everything he tells them. They assist him out of loyalty and gratitude for the man he once was, rather than because they believe the man he has become.

It is in *Deep Space Nine* that we see the harshest treatment of senility, among the Klingon people, who simply cannot cope with this in any traditionally compassionate register. Instead, they prefer to mock the poor old man who cannot remember what is going on. As with Sarek and Picard, the 'Dahar Master' Kor is represented as having been a great man, and when he first comes aboard the Klingon ship the younger crewmembers are awed by his reputation and the tales of his past victories, which they encourage him to relate. It soon becomes clear, however, that the old man's mind is not what it was, and he starts giving reckless orders which the crew follow automatically – and which result in the near destruction of the ship. In the heat of battle, Kor gives orders that make no sense – he has drifted back to a time when the Klingons and Federation were at war and is asking to speak to friends long since dead. Later in the Mess Hall the Klingon crew mercilessly confuse the old man – asking how they should attack the Federation. 'Perhaps he's confused,' offers one officer; the Klingon captain retorts: 'The Dahar Master? Surely not! We must be the ones who are confused!' Kor sits silently, aware of his own confusion and unable to do anything about it. The captain rounds on him: 'Well, say something, old man. Or have you lost your tongue as well as your mind?' The episode is shocking in its presentation of this treatment of the old; far from valuing the old man, the Klingons have nothing but contempt for his weakness. The captain's elderly assistant Darok goes further to show how little respect they hold for their elders. Unrespected by the crew, he is sympathetic to Kor's position: 'They are children,' he tells the old man; 'They are quick to judge and slow to forgive. They still have much to learn.'

The episode is called 'Once More unto the Breach' and the Shakespearean reference is not unusual – the Klingons have been set up (by the film *Star Trek VI*) as very fond of Shakespeare.[24] Despite his evident dementia, Kor is thoughtful and eloquent. As the crew continue their mockery, he exits with classical rhyme: 'Savor the fruit of life, my young friends. / It has a sweet taste when it's fresh from the vine. But don't live too long – the taste turns bitter after a time.' The verse serves to dignify Kor in his mental decline and show up the younger Klingons' cruelty. It seems that they are unable to cope with the notion of mental illness – as a culture obsessed with 'honour' and 'glory', they cannot handle such an ignoble affliction.

Voyager deals with this issue much less harshly but with just as much anxiety, when Chakotay fears he has inherited his grandfather's Alzheimer's-type disease ('The Fight'). An alien species activates the gene responsible for this illness as a means of communication, but the commander's deep-seated *fear* of losing his mind is quite startlingly demonstrated: 'I'm scared! I'm losing my mind! It's too much!' It is worth noting, however, that Chakotay's 'insane' experience is crucial to this communication and, hence, to the crew's survival. The irrational is necessary for *Voyager* to stay in one piece. This is a theme that we shall return to as we examine the representation of madness over time.

The Original Series' 'Whom Gods Destroy' is a delightfully idealistic (one might perhaps say naïve) treatment of the complex issue of insanity. In this story the *Enterprise* has been sent to an asylum for the 'few remaining incorrigible criminally insane of the galaxy . . . a total of fifteen . . . out of billions [of Federation Citizens]'. Perhaps even more impressive than this astonishing figure itself is the actual mission of the well-meaning starship: 'We are bringing a revolutionary new medicine . . . with which the Federation hopes to eliminate mental illness for all time.' A far cry from the gritty portrayal of mental illness in the later series, *TOS* presents us with a future where problems of the mind have all but vanished. As we have already noted, it was in some ways the most utopian of *Star Trek*'s many incarnations. The title can be traced back to an anonymous annotation to Sophocles' *Antigone*, which reads: 'Whenever God prepares evil for a man, He first damages his mind, with which he deliberates.' The rendering of James Duport in the seventeenth century is probably better known: 'Whom God would destroy He first sends mad.'[25] A final point about this curious episode is that the 'incorrigible' Garth, who holds Kirk and Spock captive, is not only insane but also a shapeshifter, and able to assume the appearance of other people, a fact that takes the idea of multiple personalities to new and quite literal extremes.

The Next Generation has no shortage of interest in madness. Thomas Richards, in a thoughtful analysis of *TNG*, argues that the 'ultimate nightmare' in the series is the threat of the 'breakdown of the inner stability of the individual'.[26] Richards makes his point most effectively in his discussion of a two-part episode, 'Chain of Command', in which Picard is captured and tortured by a Cardassian interrogator. Patrick Stewart is known to have prepared for this story by going through material from Amnesty International, and the shocking representation of torture is indebted to his research. As Richards explains, the purpose of this cruelty is to break Picard psychologically so as to extract the information the Cardassians require. Instead of asking what he actually wants to know, the interrogator questions him on a matter of no obvious importance: the number of lights shining directly into Picard's bloodshot eyes. There are four lights, but the Cardassian maintains that there are five – punishing Picard with electric shocks every time he refuses to agree. This sequence is an obvious reference to Orwell's *Nineteen Eighty-Four*, in which the protagonist's will is broken by just such a distinction between four and five fingers:

> O'Brien held up his left hand, its back towards Winston, with the thumb hidden and the four fingers extended.
> 'How many fingers am I holding up, Winston?'
> 'Four.'
> 'And if the party says that it is not four but five – then how many?'
> 'Four.'
> The word ended in a gasp of pain. The needle of the dial had shot up to fifty-five. The sweat had sprung out all over Winston's body. The air tore his lungs and issued again in deep groans which even by clenching his teeth he could not stop. O'Brien watched him, the four fingers still extended. He drew back the lever. This time the pain was only slightly eased.
> 'How many fingers, Winston?'
> 'Four.'

The needle went up to sixty.

'How many fingers, Winston?'

'Four! Four! What else can I say? Four!'

The needle must have risen again, but he did not look at it. The heavy, stern face and the four fingers filled his vision. The fingers stood up before his eyes like pillars, enormous, blurry and seeming to vibrate, but unmistakably four.

'How many fingers, Winston?'

'Five! Five! Five!'

'No, Winston, that is no use. You are lying. You still think there are four. How many fingers, please?'

'Four! Five! Four! Anything you like. Only stop it, stop the pain.'

In Orwell's book the Party succeeds in destroying Winston Smith's autonomy and Winston rapidly acts only in the interests of his own physical preservation – he soon begins to lie that he sees five fingers. Picard, however, realizes the importance of maintaining his free will, even if the point of argument is merely trivial, and refuses to accept what the Cardassian says. Afterwards, though, he tells (ship's counsellor) Deanna Troi how troubled he was that in the end: 'I was beginning to *believe* there were five lights.' What Picard here treats as the ultimate terror, Winston (in his broken form) embraces with open arms: the 'moment . . . of luminous certainty' when he actually sees five fingers. Richards sees Picard as acting to 'retain his very sanity', even in the face of what he actually *sees* before him. Picard's brain has given in and he actually now sees five lights, but consciously the captain continues to resist – fighting for his sanity with reason and rationality, convinced by the memory that before the torture he definitely saw four lights. Picard's defiant position is central to the narrative, but one might have cause to question just how sensible it is. To bring yourself to the point of a functional visual misperception, rather than decide to tell a calculated lie that would be more than justified in the circumstances, is perhaps an odd definition of sanity. Perhaps the good captain has read *Nineteen Eighty-Four*. He knows that he has to tell the Cardassian 'the truth', or his inner integrity is at risk.

Ironically, the Orwellian version is represented as a struggle to *cure* Winston of his own insane beliefs. His mind must be brought back in to line with the policy of the ubiquitous Party. 'You preferred to be a lunatic, a minority of one,' explains his torturer O'Brien. It seems that Picard's objective calculation has little meaning here: 'You believe that reality is something objective, external, existing in its own right. . . . When you delude yourself into thinking that you see something, you assume that everyone else sees the same as you. . . . Reality exists in the human mind, and nowhere else.' Ultimately Winston realizes that in order to function in his society he will have to rewire himself to the beliefs of the Party, to believe, for example, that two plus two is five, regardless of what he knows to be true. (This is the much-quoted notion of *doublethink*.) Winston comes to see that 'sanity was statistical. It was merely a question of learning to think as they thought.' Far from the rational assumptions underlying *TNG*, Orwell presents us with a future where human un-reason has prevailed over that which is manifestly true. Captain Picard, however, is successful in maintaining his own rational standards, even at the expense of his sensory capacity.

In some respects, the story is similar to the Captain Ahab version of Picard in the film *First Contact*. It may not be so much madness that he fears, but the accusation of cowardice, of giving in, and the feeling of fear itself. Picard worries that he will lose control to his fear and pain if he allows the Cardassian to defeat him on this issue. This interpretation might fit in with what happens to Picard in 'Genesis', a strange story in which the *Enterprise* crew 'de-evolve' into earlier life forms. Picard's genetic constitution, we are told, is such that he is starting to become what Data predicts will be a lemur, or a pygmy marmoset. The first signs are psychological: Picard experiences 'intense feelings of fear and panic', which Data explains as primate awareness of larger predators. Captain Picard acting with the body language of extreme fear is a unique sight, and it is this new-found capacity for *fear* that causes him most anxiety, perhaps more than the physical de-evolution.

Another *TNG* episode to focus on insanity is 'Frame of Mind', in which Picard's first officer Riker faces a gruelling existential dilemma. Brannon Braga, then a writer on *TNG* and subsequently an important figure in what we might call the 'post-modernization' of *Star Trek*, charmingly says of this one: 'Riker's a friendly character, he's the one human you can do humour with, you can do action – and here you can jerk him around and drive him crazy.'[27] 'Crazy' is indeed what they make Riker, in a complicated counterposition of his shipboard performance in a play about a mental asylum with the representation of himself as a prisoner held in that same mental asylum, who is told he has delusional fantasies about life on a starship. The strategy of these two realities (neither of which eventually turns out to be the 'reality' in the narrative) enables an exploration of the issue of insanity. Typically, perhaps, Riker 'senses' that none of the options he is being given is the right one, and makes a break out of the nightmare, finding himself on an alien operating table.

These episodes are entirely typical of *TNG* in representing mental instability as the product of outside influence – an alien experiment, or torture by a cruel interrogator. People may suffer brief bouts of insanity, but there is always a cure available and they should be able to return to a perfectly normal life. The presence of a counsellor on the ship as a senior member of staff was viewed as a product of its eighties' inception, but the state of mind of *Enterprise* crewmembers is absolutely vital to their mission. Most of Deanna's work involves relationships, bereavements, child-rearing problems: very few of her patients are actually mad. When a more extreme case occurs she is invariably able to cure it. Take, for example, the young boy who – traumatized by the loss of his parents and unable to cope with his emotions – decided that he was an android, and, as such, incapable of feeling. The touching episode, 'Hero Worship', in which he follows Data around, copying his every action in an attempt to effect this charade, is a testament to the problems that life on a starship can bring. Data's position, however, is resolute. He wishes he had the capacity for emotion, and sees young Timothy's behaviour as a waste: 'I would gladly risk feeling sad at times if it also meant I could taste my dessert.' Only by facing our emotions can we move beyond them and eliminate the mental problems that threaten to overcome us. Note, however, that it is only in relation to a small child faced with terrible experience that *TNG* can really articulate the notion of (reasonably) functional insanity. *The Next Generation* is clearly extremely anxious about issues around madness, where *The Original Series* offered a somewhat cavalier approach. In many ways the former was cast in a mould that is more easygoing than the later *TNG*; in this respect it is somewhat 'pre-modern' in its philosophy. The difference between the two series is analogous to the difference between pre-modern western cultures, such as the classical and renaissance worlds, and the serious, rationalist culture of 'high modernity' in the nineteenth century. We shall now turn towards the post-modern, post-rational, preoccupations of *Deep Space Nine* and *Voyager*.

If *TNG* was just about willing to anxiously engage with madness, the later series have developed a serious interest. All kinds of familiar psychological and mental problems are given an airing: suicide (Quinn) and para-suicidal behaviour (Torres), depression (Janeway), post-traumatic stress syndrome (Marla Gilmore, of the *Equinox*), alcoholism (Damar), addiction and claustrophobia (Garak), psychopathological homicide (Joran Dax), demonic possession (Kes and Keiko O'Brien), dementia (Kor), 'hysterical' pain (Nog), and so on.

Both *TNG*'s Data and *Voyager*'s Seven of Nine have suffered from moments of (exogamous) multiple personality pathologies, though the causes were more technological than psychological. *Voyager* has even developed a serious mental pathology derived from more time travel than is good for you; Captain Braxton has developed the dreaded 'temporal psychosis'! Both Jake Sisko and Harry Kim are shown as obsessively devoting an entire lifetime to a rescue operation (in 'The Visitor' and 'Timeless'). The risks taken by Janeway are on several occasions on the far side of reckless: this is true of 'Scientific Method', 'Year of Hell' and 'Course: Oblivion'. Even the holograms on *Voyager* have psychological problems; the EMH runs through his Byronic paces in 'Darkling', and in 'Revulsion' we are shown an obsession with cleanliness on the part of a fellow 'isomorph'. We have already dealt with the psychological repercussions of the Doctor's experiences in 'Latent Image'.

In the course of five consecutive *Voyager* episodes, three members of the senior staff undergo serious bouts of mental instability. In the episode 'One', Seven of Nine has to cope with the problem of individuality when she is forced to pilot the ship alone through an area of space with properties that threaten the rest of the crew. As a Borg drone she had shared her consciousness with millions of other beings and the 'silence' of *Voyager*'s 100-odd crew had caused her much distress. Faced with only the (holographic) Doctor for company, Janeway is worried that Seven may fall prey to 'cabin fever', a fear which is ultimately justified. Seven becomes increasingly preoccupied with her own individuality and the burden of (individual) responsibility that she bears to the entire crew. Soon she begins hallucinating: other Borg tell her she cannot survive alone, the crew of *Voyager* accuse her of murdering them, an alien captain attempts to rape her. (This theme is a consistent fear of Seven's, and harks back to the violence of her assimilation as a child.) When the ship's systems start to fall apart, Seven has to make a terrible decision: to sacrifice some crew members in order to power the engines. This she does, but the ensuing delusions force her to cut off life support instead, leaving her with neither heat nor oxygen. The selfless gesture is a sign of her inclusion in the community of *Voyager*'s crew. As the episode ends, we see her visiting the mess hall, not with the intention of eating but 'for companionship', a notion she had previously held in contempt. She even offers Paris an explanation for his claustrophobia: 'Perhaps you dislike being alone.'

In the episode 'Night', it is Captain Janeway herself who suffers instability, in the form of depression brought on by a 'void' of starless space. Neelix is diagnosed with 'nihilophobia' ('the fear of nothingness') and cowers on the floor with a blanket, while the captain retreats to her quarters and disengages herself from the crew. 'Rumour has it she never leaves her quarters,' points out Paris at a staff meeting. It turns out that Janeway's problem stems from a decision she made in the past – the act of compassion that stranded *Voyager* in the Delta Quadrant in the first place. 'I made an error of judgement,' she tells Chakotay: 'It was shortsighted and it was selfish.' Janeway remains standing in the darkness and refuses to face the rest of her crew, feeling responsible for their predicament. Like Dukat, she is troubled by actions taken long since; as Tuvok notes, 'guilt has been her constant companion' for the four years that they have been away from home. The presentation of a character (a Starfleet captain, no less) whose daily routine is a constant reminder of her own 'guilt' is very much a feature of recent *Star Trek*. Janeway's single-minded obsession with getting home is crucial to *Voyager*'s success, and is no doubt due largely to her own feelings of responsibility. It is interesting to note that at the very time this episode of *Voyager* was broadcast, Sisko was also facing a crisis of command on Deep Space Nine. These post-modern captains are clearly 'only human', and sometimes they simply crack under the pressure – a far cry from the strict ethos of control on Captain Picard's *Enterprise*.

The third character to suffer such a problem is B'Elanna Torres, who – like Chakotay – was previously a rebel freedom fighter and joined when their ship was destroyed. When *Voyager* first receives messages from earth (in 'Hunters'), news comes that this organization has been crushed: almost all of B'Elanna's friends are now dead. At first she flies into a rage, screaming at Chakotay and generally acting very much in her Klingon mode: 'I'm going to make someone pay, I swear I will. . . . I don't want to be comforted.' Some hours later she tells us: 'I've gone from being so angry that I wanted to kill someone to crying for an hour.' Later on, however, we discover the long-term effects that this has had on her. By the time of 'Extreme Risk', B'Elanna has become increasingly detached. She has lost interest in her work, avoids contact with her boyfriend and takes part in dangerous activities on the holodeck. After one near-fatal incident Janeway visits her in sickbay: 'When the Doctor examined you he found evidence of internal bleeding, fractured vertebrae, contusions, cranial trauma.' B'Elanna refuses to explain these injuries and the captain relieves her of her duties, the Doctor advising that she is clinically depressed. The crew are worried about B'Elanna and resort to snooping around in her holodeck files until Chakotay makes a crucial discovery: 'You created a program to watch our Maquis friends get slaughtered.' He drags B'Elanna down to the holodeck and forces her to explain. Eventually she begins: 'If I sprain my ankle at least I feel something . . .'.

The problem, it seems, is that B'Elanna has lost all emotion: 'I don't *feel* anything – not about my dead friends, not about Tom, you, my job.' 'I'm not trying to kill myself,' she tells Chakotay; 'I'm trying to see if I'm still alive.' The commander offers her his support, maintaining that she has to confront her emotions. It is at this point that we get to the long-term cause of the situation. 'When I was six my father walked out on me; when I was nineteen I got kicked out of Starfleet; a few years later I got separated from the Maquis. And just when I start to feel safe you tell me that all of our friends have been slaughtered. . . . I've lost every family I've ever had.' Like Dukat and Janeway before her, B'Elanna's madness is precipitated by an older problem – her sense of rejection and alienation. What is interesting about this case is that it has gone unnoticed for so long. It is many months since the message that first sparked off this mental crisis. There have been no obvious signs to alert the crew to the problem; while B'Elanna may have lost interest in her work she has carried it out diligently. There has been no effect on her productivity, her ability to reason, her capabilities as an engineer. This depression is something she has lived with, without ever allowing it to surface in front of others. Many months later, Janeway expresses concern about sending B'Elanna on a mission ('Juggernaught'). We have seen nothing of her depression in the intervening period but the captain knows she is still dealing with it in the background. This is not a mental 'disease' that can be identified and removed; rather, it is an integral part of B'Elanna's character and personality. The idea of *living* with this 'madness' is what sets *Voyager* apart from the earlier series.

In *Deep Space Nine* we have a character who also lives with such an affliction: the Cardassian tailor-cum-spy Garak. In 'Afterimage', Garak has been working for Starfleet Intelligence, helping to decode Cardassian/Dominion communications. Garak has a history of claustrophobia – which, we discover in this episode, was started by being locked in a closet as a child whenever he misbehaved. Normally he has no problem in reasonably open areas, but regardless of the physical environment, he now begins to suffer attacks that counselor Ezri Dax attributes to some kind of 'misplaced guilt'. During one such attack Garak tries to open an airlock, and Ezri soon begins a more intensive attempt at therapy. The Cardassian, though, is suddenly defensive. 'Spare me your insipid psychobabble,' he tells her. 'I'm not some quivering neurotic who feels sorry for himself because his daddy wasn't nice to him.' Garak is only interested in work: 'All I want is to free my people from the Dominion. . . . I need someone who can help me get back to work.' It is only when Ezri tells him that his military advice has been acted upon that the true reason for Garak's claustrophobia emerges. 'They'll lose', he tells her, 'because they won't be expecting an attack. They have no idea I broke their code. . . . All those Cardassians are going to die – because of me.' As an exiled but patriotic Cardassian, Garak has been working to end the war that his people are involved in, but only now has the reality of his actions been made clear to him: 'I wanted to believe I was helping my people, liberating them, but all I've done is pave the way for their annihilation. I'm a traitor!' The question of patriotism and loyalty is central to *DS9*'s agenda, and Garak's isolation from his people makes him a pertinent example of these feelings – his opposition to Cardassia's political actions is crucial to his character. It is the conflict between patriotism and morality that has driven him to madness. Like B'Elanna Torres on *Voyager*, though, this is a madness that he must learn to live with.

On Deep Space Nine there is a complex psychological problem suffered by the young Ferengi, Nog. We have already mentioned the circumstances in which he has lost a leg in battle; we shall now turn to the complex question of his recovery.

When Nog returns to the station, he is suffering a form of 'hysterical' pain – he claims that his leg is hurting, despite all contrary medical evidence, and insists on walking with a cane. He is also increasingly unable to have any kind of relationship with his old friends; he won't answer letters, attend his own welcome-home party or cohabit with his roommate. (In fact, he even gets into a fight with him when Jake's girlfriend calls him a hero.) The only solace that Nog can find is in listening to the song that Doctor Bashir had playing during the time of the amputation, and he soon goes to one of the holosuites to request a 'live' performance of this from the holographic Vic Fontaine. He rapidly takes the situation much further when he requests that he be able to live inside the holographic program for the duration of his convalescence, a choice that regulations allow him to make. He lives with Vic in his holographic suite, explaining: 'I don't want to go back to my quarters . . . actually, I don't want to go back to my life.' Though both Vic and the crew are rather sceptical, it is generally agreed that the fantasy is simply a reasonable defence mechanism – 'The kid's had too much reality,' explains Vic to Ezri Dax. Vic tries to take Nog's mind of his real-life problems by giving him the accounts of his casino to take care of and offering him a fancy new (and less sturdy) cane. Soon it is clear that Nog's reliance on the cane is much diminished.

Meanwhile, Vic is making a mental journey of the opposite kind. Normally only running for a few hours at a time, he is experiencing a sense of real life for the first time ever – eating breakfast, sleeping, and so on, are things he has never had to do before. It gradually becomes clear that Nog's recovery is as much of a benefit to Vic as it is to himself, and the hologram becomes reluctant to let him go. When Ezri pays him a visit he is surprised by her assertion that his plans for a new casino are 'just a ploy' ('You're really going to let him live out the rest of his life in a holosuite?' she asks sarcastically). Vic realizes what he has been doing, and forces Nog back into the real world by shutting down the casino program. 'This is just a fantasy,' he tells him, 'it's not real. . . . I'm a hologram, Nog. I'm not a person. In fact, the only thing in this entire program that isn't an illusion is you.' He goes on to explain his position: Nog has shown him 'how much it means to just live . . . Now I'm going to return the favour and give you your life back.' Nog protests, almost in tears, that 'I can't go out there . . . I'm scared'. Finally, he begins to account for his behaviour:

> When the war started I wasn't happy or anything, but I was eager. I wanted to test myself. I wanted to see if I had what it takes to be a soldier. And I saw a lot of combat. I saw a lot of people get hurt. I saw a lot of people die. But I never thought anything was going to happen to me. Then suddenly Doctor Bashir is telling me he has to cut my leg off. I couldn't believe it. I still can't believe it. If I can get shot, if I can lose a leg, anything could happen to me, Vic. I could die tomorrow. I don't know if I can face that. If I stay here, at least I know what the future's going to be like.

Vic's response is a staunch defence of the embracing of exploration that we find throughout *Star Trek*. 'You've got to play the cards life deals you,' he tells him. 'Sometimes you win, sometimes you lose, but at least you're in the game.' In a moment of self-reflective clarity he adds: 'You stay in here . . . you'll become as hollow as I am.' The episode is called 'It's only a Paper Moon', from the song of the same name, the refrain of which is: 'But it wouldn't be make believe/If you believed in me.' Vic realizes that, compared with Nog's, his own capacity for real life is nothing, and he is willing to sacrifice it for his friend's well-being. Fans of Tennessee Williams will note that this is the very song that the deranged Blanche DuBois is constantly singing in *A Streetcar Named Desire*. The most obvious reference, however, is the general Great War ambience that underpins the episode as a whole: Nog's condition is recognizably what we would call shell-shock. The episode's emphasis on Nog's fear of *reality* (and, conversely, the comfort of his madness) makes it stand out from *TNG*, where the opposite is generally the case. It also brings up a parallel with another *DS9* episode ('. . . Nor the Battle to the Strong'), in which Nog's (civilian) friend Jake learns about fear and 'cowardice' on the front lines.

In this episode Jake is helping to retrieve a generator for the evacuation of a field hospital when he becomes terrified by a bombardment of explosions and runs away, leaving Doctor Bashir alone on the battlefield. ('He's lost it, can think of nothing but getting away from the deafening explosions and the danger they represent.') Jake finds his own action extremely difficult to come to terms with. As a civilian living on a military station he is used to bravery and courage as everyday behaviour. 'I keep trying to make sense of it all,' he explains, 'to justify what I did. But when it comes down to it, there's only one explanation. I'm a coward.' Jake's own story is paralleled by that of another wounded officer in the hospital, who, in extreme Great War mode, has shot off his own foot. He explains his actions to Jake in the hospital: 'We were done for, we all knew it. Sully got hit in the leg and the medics pulled him off the line – all I could think was I wish I was him. . . . So I . . . I took my phaser . . . and I. . . . Oh, God . . . what'd I do to myself . . . what'd I do . . . ?' We are told that a court martial is the most likely result of this man's actions, and when Jake suggests counselling as an alternative he is scathing: 'I won't go. . . . Therapy won't change what I did. Nothing can. . . . I just wish I'd aimed that phaser a little higher.' Both Jake and this 'cowardly' ensign have had an experience 'that makes you realize you're not who you thought you were'. In Jake's next attack of fear, the actions he takes allow the patients in the hospital to be rescued and him to be branded a hero. In both cases he describes himself as 'so scared, that all I could think about was doing whatever it took to stay alive. . . . Once that meant running away, and once it meant picking up a phaser.' As Jake himself writes in his account of the story, 'The line between courage and cowardice is a lot thinner than most people believe.' Further credence is lent to this by Sisko, who comments: 'Anyone who's been in battle would recognise himself in this . . . but most of us wouldn't care to admit it.' Jake's temporary unpredictability is not merely understandable, but to be expected.

One final example of mental instability from *DS9* ('Statistical Probabilities') illustrates that mental illness is not only something that is lived with on a day-to-day basis, but can be a side-effect of a gifted personality. A group of genetically engineered humans arrives on Deep Space Nine to be treated by the (similarly enhanced) Doctor for a variety of odd behaviours. One of them is manic, often shouting and threatening others; another is depressed and prone to weep at the slightest provocation; one pathologically attempts to seduce every man who enters her sight; while the fourth is catatonically mute and socially removed. Mental illness is not the only by-product of their engineering; they are also superhumanly intelligent and capable of the most percipient analyses. As Sisko points out: 'They're turning out projections that would take Starfleet Intelligence months to come up with.' Far from being incapacitated by their madness, they soon become an invaluable asset. They quote Shakespeare and dance to classical music. In fact one might say they are a modern version of the Shakespearean fool, the character who – though comic – is often more perceptive than his 'wise' counterparts.

One way of looking at this is to consider Foucault's argument that the balance between reason and *un*-reason – such as we see in the world of Shakespeare, for instance – was one in which both sides were given some mutual respect, at a time when there was a place for the irrational to be valued. Madness was valued for its moral content and for its reminder of the 'animality' of the human. Subsequently, however, this balance was destabilized and the 'reason' side became completely overvalued. Unreason was excluded, with many consequences. As Zygmunt Bauman has pointed out, one consequence is that academic work progressing in the name of 'science' rigorously excludes all ethical considerations.[28] Many historians have rejected Foucault's attempt to suggest a 'landmark' date (1656) for the key moment of the defeat of unreason: *Madness and Civilization: a history of insanity in the age of reason* is a contentious and disputed book.[29] Madness becomes excluded from the centre of society and banished to the margins, rather like in the 'Sanctuary Districts' we saw in *DS9*. The mentally ill are literally housed on the margins in specially built asylums – quite often on the exact location of erstwhile leper colonies. Unreason becomes defined in pathological terms; it becomes a form of illness rather than a different truth. Reason and unreason are no longer in dialogue; the conversation has given way to the monologue of reason.

Foucault's discussion of these issues might make us feel that the paradoxes of quantum multiverses are straightforward. He tells the story of a man who thought he was dead: since dead people obviously do not eat, he was starving to death. In the end a group of people dressed up as corpses and set up a dining table in his room; they persuaded him that dead people do eat and he agreed join in.[30] Thus it was only by acting within the terms of his madness, that the man's friends were able to save his life. The ability to see any 'truth' in illogical behaviour, as we saw in the case of Mr Grubb and Levy-

Bruhl, is one that slips away in the course of this 'separation' and 'exclusion' of madness. It is curious, in the light of the 'nautical metaphor' in *Star Trek*, that Foucault summons up the image of a ship to describe the historical development of the banishment of unreason. Citing the literary trope of the *Narrenschiff*, or ship of fools, Foucault conjures up the maritime traveller who belongs nowhere. 'He has his truth and his homeland only in that fruitless expanse between two countries that cannot belong to him.' The image is not unlike that of the early Anglo-Saxon poem 'The Sea-farer', where we read '. . . how I, weary, / have had to make the ocean paths my home'.[31] He then points to the change from the historical image of a ship setting off with its insane cargo to the later period, where these people would be hospitalized, rather than sent out to travel. 'Madness will no longer proceed from a point within the world to a point beyond, on its strange voyage; it will never again be that fugitive and absolute limit. Behold it moored now, made fast among things and men.'[32]

The prologue of *Star Trek* tells us that the mission is 'to explore strange new worlds'. While this might be taken to refer to exploring space, we have suggested that it can be taken to refer to the explo-ration of human identity. Herman Melville, whose sea fiction has had such an influence on the conception of the *Star Trek* stories, foresaw it all when he wrote:

> But this new world here sought, is stranger far than his, who stretched his vans from Palos. It is the world of mind; wherein the wanderer may gaze round, with more of wonder than Balboa's band roving through the golden Aztec glades.
> But fiery yearnings their own phantom-future make, and deem it present.[33]

One wonders whether the writers of *Star Trek* were familiar with this passage when they wrote the final episode of *TNG*, in which Q sums up the lesson that he has been trying to teach humanity:

> For one fraction of a second [when Picard accepted a paradoxical con-clusion], you were open to options you'd never considered. *That's* the exploration that awaits you . . . not mapping stars and studying nebulae . . . but charting the unknown possibilities of existence.

The strangest world of all, in the literature of the sea, is conjured up by Coleridge's 'Rime of the Ancient Mariner'. Even the preamble (taken from Burnet) refers to a world that is beyond reason and science. 'I can easily believe that there are more invisible creatures in the universe than visible ones. . . . Human wit has always circled around a knowledge of these things without ever attaining it.' The paranormal appears in various ways in the poem, most dramatically when the dead crew are 'inspired'; not unlike Homer's dead cows they begin to groan and move about, eventually even sailing the ship. Coleridge's poem encodes many of the themes still explored two centuries later in *Star Trek*: the voyage itself, inexplicable behaviour, supernatural punishment, dire misfortune, delayed return, and so forth. Throughout, the issue of the sanity or insanity of the Ancient Mariner is put out for inspection.

Modernity and control

Just as secular humanism is a quality of modern culture, so too is bureaucratic control a key feature of modern society. Modern societies require 'populations' of individuals whose behaviour and attitudes are controlled and disciplined. As before, this trend is quite clearly articulated in the *Star Trek* production offices. In *The Next Generation* – the height of modernist representation – the authority of Starfleet is absolute. The Federation is in benevolent control and presides over the galaxy in a benign, if paternalistic, fashion. The crew of the *Enterprise* is loyal to the Federation itself, as much as to the values it represents. It is relatively rare that they have cause to question their orders – which, if flawed, are none the less well intentioned. Captain Picard's authority is rarely questioned. In *First Contact* he points out that 'the crew is accustomed to following my orders' when Lily draws his attention to their uncharacteristic ambivalence towards the commands he has given. The system in *TNG* is one of hierarchical authority and (for the most part) unity within the crew as to the right – usually moral – course of action.

   Voyager presents us with a much less structured system of personal belief. In this series, the value of individual thoughts outweighs the need for consensus and people are encouraged to view things in their own unique ways. 'I dread the day when everyone on this ship agrees with me,' says Janeway. Early on, the series faces the daunting problems of accommodating two completely different crews: one Starfleet, one comprising Maquis terrorists. The arrival of Seven of Nine has led to yet more conflict in this area as her 'efficient' outlook often comes up against Janeway's more idealistic view. As first officer, Chakotay frequently challenges the captain's choice of action, presenting her with alternatives when she slips into the (perhaps necessary) narrow-mindedness of command: 'Your desire to get this crew home is blinding you to other options,' he tells her in one episode.[34] Commander Riker on *TNG* would not dream of such presumption. That this is simply a necessary part of the *Voyager* management structure is evidenced by his remark in 'Year of Hell' ('To be honest I wasn't too fond of the idea myself,') when she rejects his proposal that they abandon ship.

Voyager's insistence on the value of freedom of thought is best exemplified by the episode 'Random Thoughts', which presents us with a society where violent thought has been deemed illegal. (The planet is home only to telepaths, so this is not as implausible as it might otherwise sound.) When B'Elanna Torres's 'violent proclivities' (in Tuvok's words) lead to an incident in the planet's central market-place where another person is overcome by her internalized aggression, she is arrested on the charge of 'aggravated violent thought resulting in grave bodily harm'. The *Voyager* crew is understandably shocked – B'Elanna is to be lobotomized when she has manifestly committed no crime. A culture that forbids freedom of thought is not one with which we should continue to associate. As Tuvok investigates the market-place incident we discover yet more damning evidence against this supposedly peaceful society. By criminalizing aggressive thought, the authorities have simply driven it underground, creating a black market in 'illicit mental imagery'. This violent subculture had deliberately cultivated B'Elanna's thoughts, which had culminated in an accidental murder. The episode is reminiscent not only of Orwell's *Nineteen Eighty-Four* (with its ubiquitous 'thought police') but the dystopic sci-fi film *Strange Days*, in which Ralph Fiennes deals in the illegal sale of human memories – many of which have violent or otherwise reprehensible characteristics. The message of the episode is clear: by criminalizing a natural human quality (such as anger), we will only push it underground. The large majority of 'good' telepaths in the episode have lost their capacity to cope with aggressive emotion and are consequently overcome when exposed to it for the first time. In seeking to control the lives of its citizens, this modern society creates new problems even as it solves old ones.

That *Voyager* embraces different perspectives does not mean that it has no hierarchical control. Janeway's leadership demands obedience and those who disobey (such as Tom Paris in 'Thirty Days') are severely punished. The difference between this system and the version employed in *TNG*, however, is that the loyalty of Janeway's crew to the ideal of 'The Federation', or to any official authority, is far outweighed by their loyalty to each other. Janeway's decisions, often unpopular, are always in the interests of the crew or in support of the beliefs that they are sworn to uphold, rather than some abstract notion of citizenship. As a community, *Voyager* must look out for itself. When the captain overrules her officers, it is for the greater good. Take, for example, 'Nothing Human', when she forces on B'Elanna the (unethical) operation that will save her life, rather than allowing her to make the decision herself. 'Losing you was unacceptable,' she explains coldly. B'Elanna does not accept this argument at all and is furious at the captain's intervention; to the command that she calm down, she responds: 'You can't order someone to get rid of an emotion.' While she may not agree with Janeway, however, she does nothing to question the captain's real authority. While Janeway's authority is absolute, she is not beyond persuasion and a well-placed argument can often secure a change of tack in the captain's decision-making. In 'Latent Image', Seven convinces her to give the Doctor another chance, at the risk of leaving her crew without its most important medical facility. The acknowledgement that different people have different opinions, and the integration of these into a successful management structure, are examples of the post-modern flexibility that *Voyager* embodies.

Deep Space Nine presents us with by far the most complicated (and conflicting) set of loyalties ever seen in a *Star Trek* series, and hence with a major disruption to galactic authority. Crewmembers frequently abscond without warning to fulfil their own personal agendas and, aside from some obligatory tut-tutting, Captain Sisko appears not to mind. It is simply accepted that people have their own problems to deal with and that they must do this individually. Even the normally strict Odo has been known to allow officers to escape from the station in order to do what they feel is necessary: in 'Time's Orphan', he allows O'Brien to steal one of the station's transport vessels to save his daughter from institutionalization. The Federation itself as a significant official body is compromised both by its increasingly dubious morality and its irrelevance to the reality of life on *DS9*. Sisko regularly ignores his orders in the interests of the Bajorans or their religious beliefs.[35] This is perfectly natural; Starfleet, after all, cannot possibly share his capacity to appreciate the nature of a particular local situation. An acknowledgement of differing agendas and loyalties is central to understanding *DS9*, whether they be ties of family, race, politics, culture or religion, the external factors affecting the principal characters have never been so clearly registered.

A development parallel to this dismantling of centralized control is evidenced by the increasing amount of gossip that takes place in what are, after all, military environments. Whereas the bridges of the various starships *Enterprise* were the sites for serious discussions of intergalactic politics, the Operations Centre of Deep Space Nine seems more preoccupied with the romantic activities of the crew. The most inane issues are discussed in minute detail and everyone will chime in with an opinion – even the stoic Mr Worf tends to air his absurdly exaggerated interpretations. In *TNG*, such interaction was only remotely likely when the women were in command: a night shift of Beverly Crusher and Deanna Troi produced a slightly less formal social atmosphere. For the most part the distinction between the (serious) public and the (light-hearted) private existences of the crew was quite sharply drawn. The regular poker games and trips to the bar provided the appropriate occasions for the jocularity of socializing. Geordi and Data might chat privately in Engineering, but to do so on the bridge would be a breach of protocol. On *Voyager*, while not quite reaching the dirt-dishing gossip levels of *DS9*, the crew will frequently be found discussing the minutiae of some trivial event. This destabilization of the gendered private/public dichotomy so evident in modern society is yet another example of the post-modern turn exhibited by the most recent *Star Trek* series. Before considering some stylistic aspects of this development, we want briefly to note a comparable shift in the way in which the self is presented.

Data and Geordi get drinks

The post-modern self

Belief in the values of science and rationality is a central plank of modern 'enlightened' (historically, post-religious) thought; in so far as religious faith is being rehabilitated and the reality of 'unreason' acknowledged, the third and fourth series of *Star Trek* have a substance that is 'post' the characteristic concerns of the thinking described as 'modern'. If science and rationality is one key element, the idea of a stable, centred, self is certainly another. The so-called 'Cartesian ego' could be described as a rational, self-aware individual, able to plan and to act, whose identity was essentially unaltered in the course of his or her life. This model dominated social and political thought, and inflected the 'humanities' generally, for a considerable time, but has now given some ground to different approaches. In practice, the traditional model of the self tended only to render the experience of certain categories of men. It did not really describe situations where individual agency was constrained by circumstances – thus it did not relate well to those on the losing side of class, colonial and gender systems of privilege. In addition, for a variety of reasons, be they technological or resulting from cultural changes, identities are less fixed than they used to be. It is now widely recognized that identities can change a great deal over time, and that our sense of 'who we are' can vary enormously. In this new model the self is radically 'decentred', and opened up to a much more fluid conception of identity.

These changes can readily be seen in the view of identity put across in recent episodes of both *DS9* and *Voyager*. The characters of Data, and subsequently of the holographic Doctor and Seven of Nine, have been bracketed together at various points in our general interpretation. Again, here we find that all three of them encompass a range of personalities that they have either to negotiate or choose between. They exemplify the view that we have 'many selves', rather than one, a view never better put than by Virginia Woolf: '. . . these selves of which we are built up, one on top of another, as plates are piled on a waiter's hand, have attachments elsewhere, sympathies, little constitutions and rights of their own . . . for everybody can multiply from his own experience the different terms which his different selves have made with him . . .'.[36]

The idea of the self as multiple rather than unitary is one that science fiction is able to play with a great deal, on both a literal and metaphorical level. *Star Trek*, with its overriding interest in human nature and human identity, and the 'post-modern' character of the later series, is very well placed to do so. One area that is of particular interest is that of gender and sexuality, where some new developments have occurred in the two later series. Captain Janeway is the first significant woman leader in *Star Trek*; the unfortunate Rachel Garrett, who captained a previous version of the *Enterprise* ('Yesterday's Enterprise'), was destined for a very brief moment of glory. The characterization of Kathryn Janeway is fascinating: she is a classically 'post-feminist' woman. Genevieve Bujold parted company with the show after one day's filming – apparently because she lacked 'authority' – and was replaced by the American actress Kate Mulgrew, a much more confident and decisive character. Many episodes feature Janeway's extraordinary powers of leadership and the loyalty which these engender in the crew, even when her actions are far from orthodox. As Tuvok explains to Seven, 'The captain is always right,' (even when she is wrong). That Janeway's strategies always succeed is attributable to the fact that, as well as being in command of the ship, she is its most distinguished scientist and technical expert. While Picard is grounded in the humanities (consulting Shakespeare as often as Starfleet regulations) and both Sisko and Kirk are clearly strategists at heart, Janeway's real knowledge is in the field of science. (Her switch to the command track was a more recent, if inspired, decision.) This is not to suggest that Janeway is any kind of wimp. She is often portrayed in situations where violence is the only option – and when this is so, the iconography may involve her being stripped down to a singlet with a menacing phaser rifle in hand ('Macrocosm', *inter alia*). Janeway has to take all the difficult decisions on *Voyager*, including the resolution of moral dilemmas as to who shall live and who shall die. In the two-part episode 'Scorpion', she takes enormous risks on very thin moral ice in making an agreement with the Borg, a decision some view as selfish and irresponsible but which is ultimately in *Voyager*'s best interest. In the *Star Trek* universe, Janeway resembles no one so much as the legendary Captain Kirk; like him, she bends the rules constantly, takes enormous risks, and always wins. In comparison, the other two captains on offer are relatively cautious and sensible.

If all this is interesting in terms of gender politics, what is even more surprising is the treatment of Janeway in relation to femininity. It might be thought that the only way this character could function would be as an honorary man – yet her characterization vehemently militates against this. From the first episode, Janeway rejects the Starfleet convention of addressing the captain as 'Sir'. She views *Voyager*'s crew as a 'family' as much as a military team and takes on young Naomi Wildman as her official 'captain's assistant'. She even tries to teach Q about child-rearing, saying that some day she would like to have children herself. Her relationship to Seven is quite evidently maternal, and she shows a belief in the ex-Borg that is by no means common among her crew. The delivery of the part is clearly indebted to a detailed study of Katharine Hepburn: Janeway raises her eyes, sighs, weeps and comforts in the most classic registers of Hollywood femininity. This presentation of Janeway can reasonably be termed 'post-feminist'. The image is that of a woman who has sacrificed not one iota of her femininity in the accomplishment of her job as a military leader. This figure can only be read through an understanding that women's advancement need not be at the expense of compassion, emotional literacy and a very feminine conception of self.

The character of Janeway has an unusual extra-narrative characteristic that privileges her, setting her apart from her crew. It is always Janeway who makes contemporary jokes – she speaks of a 'think tank' and a 'space race', and other late twentieth-century expressions (Tom Paris's allusions tend to venture no further than the fast cars of the sixties). Much is made of her confusion over temporal mechanics, a mystification with which the equally baffled viewer can empathize as her officers rattle on about some implausible science fiction concept. We have even been introduced to one of her relatives from the present, played – appropriately – by the same actress. So it seems that the project is to make Janeway not only a woman of the twenty-fourth century but of our own time as well. This strategy has a strong grounding in literary tradition; Shakespeare, for instance, would pinpoint his real masters of wit by giving them contemporaneous (and hence, to us, often incomprehensible) dialogue. By showing an awareness of our own time, Janeway is depicted as hyper-aware, a fact also well illustrated by her capacities as an author of fantasy. Janeway's exploits on the holodeck are for the most part nothing new to *Star Trek* viewers (her 'Jane Eyre'-style program not so very different from Picard's pulp detective variant). On two occasions, however, the captain has displayed a narrative flair that far surpasses the capacities of her predecessors (and calls to mind once again the complex question of Benny Russell's role as the 'author' of *Deep Space Nine*). In 'Worst Case Scenario' a deadly holoprogram presents grave danger to many of her crew – it transpires that this has been placed, virus-like, by an officer who subsequently jumped ship. With several crew-members trapped inside the holodeck Janeway is forced to keep rewriting the ending of the story, adding new plot elements that keep them from destruction. 'Who says Deus Ex Machina is an outdated literary device?' she confidently proclaims at the end, when

Dixon Hill: *Star Trek*'s pulp fiction

her swiftly scripted alien attack gives them the time they need to escape. In the truly absurd 'Bride of Chaotica' – shot in black and white as part of Tom Paris's fifties sci-fi schlock holoprogram – Janeway carries off the role of 'Queen Arachnia' with great aplomb. As well as a further illustration of her fluid femininity, her performance once again shows her to be a master of fictional story telling. The captain's function is not only within the *Star Trek* narrative, but as a kind of narrator herself. A post-modern approach to textuality is explicitly aired.

The character of Dax in *DS9* is a good one to look at in terms of post-modern identity, since it has maintained a presence on the program in the form of two different people. Dax itself is a symbiont, a large slug-like being that inhabits a humanoid Trill host. For most of *DS9* this host was Jadzia, a young scientist – though for the final, seventh year a new host, Ezri, was brought in. Each host is a very different person, but through the Dax symbiont he or she has access to the memories of all of the previous hosts – so Ezri arrives on DS9 fully primed with Jadzia's six years' worth of experience there. Whether the Dax symbiont itself has any individual identity, however, is rather unclear.

The potential for identity conflicts is ripe, as the Dax hosts carry within them the personalities of many other people. In 'Facets', this is rendered very literally, when Jadzia undergoes a ritual to separate off each individual host from her identity, the better for her to communicate with them. Each host occupies the body of one of her (just about willing) colleagues, whose own personalities are suppressed for the duration. When the Dax host Curzon is joined with Odo, the proceedings get a little more complicated, however, as the changeling physically morphs into the form of this host and their personalities become fused. Odo/Curzon (as he is referred to in the script) is a womanizing and light-hearted version of Odo, combining elements of the two identities, rather like Tuvix in *Voyager*. This provides Jadzia with the opportunity to resolve something that has (understandably) troubled her for a long time. Before Jadzia was joined to the Dax symbiont, Curzon (Dax) had supervised her as a prospective host and kicked her out of the system. It was only when she reapplied some time later that she was accepted for the job and, ironically, given the Dax symbiont itself. Despite having access to Curzon's memories, Jadzia has never been able to comprehend the reasons for his actions, and when she asks Odo/Curzon he avoids the question entirely. Dax suffers a crisis of confidence, concluding that Curzon never had any real faith in her: 'I feel like I don't have your respect. And I'm afraid that when your memories are restored to me, I'm going to feel like I don't respect myself.' Eventually we learn the true reasons for Curzon's decision: he was in love with Jadzia and saw kicking her out as his only escape. He refuses to leave Odo's body, arguing that it is better for them both that they remain as separate identities: 'because I still love you . . . and if we're joined you'll feel [the shame of] it too'. Ultimately, of course, Jadzia persuades him otherwise and the feelings and memories that he experienced are reintegrated into her (joined) personality.

While Curzon (Dax) may be a bit of a rogue, he is not Jadzia's most dangerous predecessor. In 'Equilibrium', she begins to suffer serious mental trauma and is taken home to Trill for treatment, where it is discovered that one of her (unknown) previous hosts is causing the damage. Joran Dax was a poor choice for joining, and had ended up by murdering several people: something the Symbiosis Commission has painstakingly covered up – including the suppression of Dax's memories of this host. The fact that he could be joined in the first place undermines the basis of their selection process (which claims that rejection occurs in over 99 per cent of cases), and they go to great lengths to prevent this secret from getting out – even if this means letting Jadzia die. Sisko ultimately discovers the secret and threatens to reveal it if they refuse to help Jadzia, something they are not willing to risk. They eventually comply and the psychopathic memories are integrated into her own – meaning she must live with the character of a murderer inside her. In 'Field of Fire', this is taken a step further when Ezri Dax decides to use Joran's experience in order to help solve a homicide investigation. Her psychological profiling skills are not up to the job: 'I want to know how [the murderer] thinks,' she explains to Joran in an hallucinatory state. Joran forces Ezri to hold the killer's weapon, aiming it at people and imagining what it would be like to kill them. Initially Ezri is horrified, but she becomes increasingly impressed by Joran's methods and observations, up to the point where she almost kills a suspect, believing him to be the murderer. With Joran's help, however, Ezri is able to track down the assassin and shoot him before he kills her. As the killer lies incapacitated on the floor, Joran urges Ezri to 'finish what you started' and for a moment she considers it; in the end, though, she manages to control this psychotic self and exercise some rational self-restraint. The killer is arrested and Joran is reintegrated into Ezri's memories. 'You know you won't be able to forget me . . . or bury me as deeply as Curzon or Jadzia did,' he tells her. 'I'm a part of you now.' Ezri replies simply: 'I'll have to be careful.'

Clearly not all of Dax's hosts have had such unusual lives as Joran, but the conflicts between past and present host can lead to a variety of questions. Perhaps the most obvious difference is that of gender. Captain Sisko was himself the protégé of Curzon Dax and persists in calling both Jadzia and Ezri 'Old Man', since this is how he thinks of them. Of all the previous Dax hosts it is Curzon whose legacy is most commonly explored; his (typically male) sexual liberty gets Jadzia into trouble very early in the series (in the episode 'Dax'), when one of his indiscretions prevents her from defending herself against a charge of murder. The accusation that there is too much of Curzon in Jadzia is frequently made; her interest in Klingon martial arts stem from Curzon's work as an ambassador to the Klingons. Jadzia is certainly not afraid of sexuality – in fact Worf makes hostile accusations about her in 'Let He Who is without Sin . . .', when they pay a trip to one of Curzon's favourite holiday resorts and Jadzia meets up with a young woman who was particularly enamoured of her predecessor. Worf and Jadzia eventually marry, but after her death he continues to worry about the extent of her fidelity and interrogates Ezri on the matter. 'I don't think there's anyone on the station who wasn't her lover!' replies the new Dax when Worf becomes excessively heavy-handed. There is never any real suggestion that Jadzia's behaviour was unacceptable – Worf is nothing if not paranoid. But the number of old friends who see her simply as a continuation of Curzon means she has a very real male side to her personality. While Jadzia is an attractive young heterosexual woman, her (joined) sexuality is rather more complicated.

'Rejoined' is a controversial episode of *Deep Space Nine* that deals with the complex question of Trill 'reassociation'. When a Trill science team arrives on the station, Jadzia finds herself working with the new host of what was once her wife. Both of them are now in different bodies from when they were married – for one thing, they are both now women – yet there is still a residual attraction between the two characters. Kira immediately suggests they should simply 'pick up where they left off', but this radical suggestion is quite unacceptable in Trill society, which regards reassociation as 'unnatural'. Indeed, such is the strength of this taboo that anyone caught breaking it is exiled for life – with the result that their symbiont must die when they do, rather than being rejoined to a new host. Despite laughing off such an idea at first, the two women soon fall into arguing about their marriage, which was abruptly ended when (Torias) Dax was killed in a reckless shuttle manoeuvre. Doctor Kahn (the ex-wife) starts to become increasingly confused and the complex question of identity is very clearly articulated: 'You were a pilot and it made me nervous – made her nervous. . . . Torias being a pilot made Nilani nervous. . . . I've never had quite this much trouble sorting out my feelings from those of a past host.'

Unsurprisingly, those feelings go beyond anxiety and quarrelling, and the ex-couple become increasingly attached to each other once again as they realize how little has changed: 'I'm looking at a different face, hearing a different voice . . . but somehow, it's still you,' says Kahn. The two fall in love again and soon engage in 'a passionate, loving kiss that they've waited a hundred years for'. Visually this is a shock as it marks the first homosexual kiss in *Star Trek*'s history, an echo of the first interracial kiss on US TV, shown in *The Original Series*. The affair is not to last, however, for while Jadzia is willing to face the consequences of reassociation, Lenara cannot bring herself to 'give up everything I've worked for'. Jadzia pleads unsuccessfully with her to stay on the station. The taboo stands and this intriguing relationship is brought to an end. What is interesting however, is the way the episode is treated in terms of homosexuality (and the associated taboos). Because Jadzia's identity is both male and female she is not constrained by any unisexual biological foundations. The episode stands out as particularly unconstrained about this issue, for as we shall see, *Star Trek* as a whole has some very serious problems with the question of gay representation.

The question of 'reassociation' is here shown as a very serious one, perhaps slightly inconsistent with the broader narrative of *DS9*. Both Jadzia and Ezri have, after all, met up with old friends from previous lives (most notably Captain Sisko himself) and have definitely continued with these (approximately) same relationships. The episode 'Afterimage' (which we have already examined in terms of insanity) introduces Ezri Dax to the crew of Deep Space Nine, who are still mourning the death of her predecessor Jadzia. Ezri is very young and unprepared for the emotional turmoil of her 'joining' (which was performed in an emergency, rather than in normal circumstances). She has not been through the extensive training necessary for aspiring hosts and finds the various memories and ideas of previous Dax hosts rather difficult to control. It is not only Ezri who has problems with her arrival. Worf, in particular, is very uncomfortable around her. He explains his confusion to Chief O'Brien: 'She is not Jadzia, yet she is. How can I honour the memory of the woman I loved when she's not really dead?' When the two meet in the corridor he is extremely rude: 'I do not know you, nor do I wish to.' Ezri is very upset by this as she shares much of Jadzia's affections for the Klingon; she already has a lot to live up to as the 'New Dax', since Jadzia was loved and appreciated by everyone on the station. When she tries to counsel Garak against his wishes he nails her with all her own anxieties: 'You're pathetic. A confused child trying to live up to the legacy left by her predecessors. You're not worthy of the name Dax. I knew Jadzia – she was vital – alive. She owned herself. But you – you don't even know who you are.' Ultimately, of course, Ezri regains her self-confidence and her crewmates grow to accept her as a new (if familiar) member of their group.

While Dax is fascinating in terms of post-modern identity – a multiplicity of selves – it is its specifically post-modern *gender* that provokes the most interesting questions as far as *Star Trek*'s outlook is concerned. To interpret this, it is tempting to refer to Judith Butler's work, which takes a shot at the distinction between sex as a biological category and gender as a social category. In *Gender Trouble*, her first major book, Butler argues that gender is a performance; in the sequel, *Bodies that Matter*, she extends the argument to biological sex difference too.[37] The argument is radically deconstructive of traditional assumptions about biology, in that it claims that men and women as 'biological' categories are not given but the product of a 'heterosexual matrix', in which the supposed bedrock of biological difference is reiterated, performed and constructed. Butler's work draws on aspects of Lacanian psychoanalysis, and on aspects of Foucault's critique of sexual essentialism, and weaves them into a cultural analysis. It is, perhaps, easy to see why it has proved so popular in a context in which 'queer theory' seeks to transcend the fixity of sexual identity and sexual choice. It is a philosophical position from which performance, play, fluidity and choice can take off.

These women characters in *Star Trek* between them raise some interesting issues about gender and sexuality. Janeway is quite explicitly presented as sentimentally romantic, rather than overtly sexualized. (The episode 'Counterpoint', where she becomes involved with an alien defector, seems placed within the romantic register of *Gone with the Wind*, rather than within any more racy modern context.) So far, she has successfully fended off Chakotay's advances, and even the proposition that she mate with Q, and her sexual encounters have been limited in the extreme. Cynics have argued that Seven of Nine was specifically introduced to raise the viewing figures among 18- to 30-year-old males, and this Jeri Ryan has spectacularly accomplished. The 'sexiest woman in space' is also presented with a distinctively 'post-feminist' edge, as we have described it, in that her patience with the etiquette of heterosexual femininity is very limited. She terrifies men who admire or date her, notably injuring one who has the temerity to try dancing with her. In 'The Killing Game', where she figures as a glamorous club singer, she is frustrated at not being able to fight: 'When the Americans arrive and the fighting begins, I don't intend to be standing next to a piano singing "Moonlight Becomes You".'

That Dax has raised the issue of homosexuality, albeit in an extremely oblique way, is very interesting in terms of *Star Trek*'s executive politics, which have frequently been shown as less enlightened than those propounded by the programme itself.[38] *Star Trek*'s refusal to cast an actual gay character has now become so entrenched that paralysis has set in – it is hard to see how anything could live up to the expectations that now surround the issue. Two campaigning groups, the 'Gaylaxians' and the 'Voyager Visibility Project', have not so far achieved their aims in this matter, despite much activity and lobbying. It appears that Gene Roddenberry, who died in 1991, had agreed to the appearance of a gay character (which would indeed have been in line with his general liberal position), but that when his mantle fell on the shoulders of Rick Berman the idea fizzled out. Shortly before his death, Roddenberry went so far as to remark: 'I'm sorry that I have never had a homosexual relationship . . . there must be many joys and pleasures and degrees of closeness in those relationships.' He explained this as the product of 'my time period and background and so on', revealing a belief that everyone is inherently bisexual. With regard to the programme itself he commented: 'I'm in the midst of making a decision about homosexuality, male and female, and how we are going to treat it on *Star Trek*, the lovely ways in which we will treat it, without defying present average conventions.' In a similar twist, Jeri Taylor had enthusiastically agreed to develop a gay character on *Voyager*, but left the show before she was able to do so. In one interview she explained: 'It is something I am absolutely sympathetic with, and I have tried several times to do it. But for various reasons there has always been opposition, and it gradually became clear that this is a fight I could not win.' In recent years Roddenberry's grandson has lent his support to the campaigns for gay 'visibility' on *Star Trek*, as have the actors Leonard Nimoy (Spock), Patrick Stewart (Picard) and Avery Brooks (Sisko). For the moment, however, it seems as though the executive barriers remain firmly in place.

It is rather curious, perhaps, that the issue of homosexuality in *Star Trek* seems of such particular interest to heterosexual fans and commentators. As Constance Penley has made clear, those fans who elaborated an off-screen sexual relationship between Kirk and Spock (the 'slashers' beloved of cultural studies writers on this theme) are mainly heterosexual women. Henry Jenkins, one of the most prominent writers on *Star Trek* fan culture, speaks for the Gaylaxians on the basis of a bisexual identification.[39] The argument is that the construction by fans of a homosexual interpretation of *Star Trek* is a 'resistant reading' that progressively challenges the neo-conservatism of the text itself. This may indeed be true, but it is less clear why there should be so much heterosexual investment in this long-running conflict.

It certainly is odd that *Star Trek* has had so much difficulty with sexuality. Even Robin Roberts, whose book on gender in *Star Trek* (*TNG*) is a welcome antidote to the barrage of righteous indignation addressed to the show, has to concede that 'sexual orientation is the most complicated and resistant social issue'.[40] Of course, there is no actual sex on *Star Trek*, which is a family show on prime time TV, and the heterosexual stories are themselves usually 'teasers'. In *TNG*, Picard and Crusher consider for *seven years* whether to act on their mutual attraction. Similarly Riker and Troi, or Worf and Troi, represent stories where 'high modern' *TNG* seems altogether paralysed on the sexual front. The third and fourth series are more relaxed about all this. By the conclusion of *Deep Space Nine* any number of couples have been paired off, many of them across species boundaries: from the start we have had the O'Briens, a mixed-race couple with two children, one of them carried by a surrogate, Kira Nerys.

Sisko eventually married his freighter-captain girlfriend, Rom and Leeta also tied the knot, as did Worf and Dax. Odo and Kira finally get together and, in the space of the final year, Ezri has a brief fling with Worf before launching herself towards Julian. Gul Dukat and Kai Winn even end up together, in a bitterly ironic twist of fate. In *Voyager*, we have B'Elanna and Tom as a couple, and even a baby in the shape of fast-growing Naomi Wildman. These two later series (and the film *Insurrection*) are less terrified of sexuality, procreation, physicality and long-term relationships than either the 'boys' camp' of *TOS* or the high-minded staff of *TNG*.

The idea of a 'symbiont' that can inhabit the body of either sex does (as we saw in the case of Jadzia Dax in the episode 'Rejoined') allow the visual presentation of a same-sex passion: ostensibly it is two women who are involved, even if we also 'know' that the Dax who first fell in love with Kahn was a man. This device had been used in *TNG*, in one of the two (much discussed) episodes in that series that were 'about' homosexuality. In 'The Host', Beverly Crusher falls for a Trill man, not knowing he is joined to a gender-neutral symbiont; he dies, and the symbiont is momentarily parked in Riker, to whom Crusher transfers her desire. When, however, the symbiont is given a permanent host who is a woman, Beverley backs out very rapidly. It seems the *Enterprise* is just not bold enough for the strange new world of queer theory. The other treatment of this issue is metaphorical. In 'The Outcast', Riker falls in love with a woman from an androgynous culture that does not allow heterosexual practice. It is a mirror reversal of heterosexist discrimination against gay people. All does not end well, and Riker fails to protect her from the punitive reprogramming of her illicit desire for him that J'naii justice determines.

Deep Space Nine has run a more recent variant of the 'Rejoined' story by using another device – not this time a symbiont derived bisexuality, but an 'alternate' sexuality that is part of the 'alternate' reality of the 'mirror universe'. This is not without its negative overtones; in 'The Emperor's New Cloak', Kira (as the sadistic intendant) and a leathered version of Ezri Dax play up some lesbian innuendo in a visual regime that has mildly pornographic connotations. Apart from anything else, this activity takes place in an 'alternate' (and in general, a morally inferior) universe – perhaps not the liberal breakthrough we might have hoped for. Some of the peripheral materials of *Star Trek* have taken on complex questions around both gender and sexuality. By far the most outlandish is the bisexual hermaphrodite who features in Peter David's sequence of novels in the *New*

Frontier series. As another device to 'loosen up' on sex, this is fairly dramatic. Burgoyne 172 is biologically a 'Hermat', whose sexual orientation is not restricted to persons of one sex or another. These novels are published by Pocket Books, and copyrighted by Paramount, the same outfit who cannot seem to cope with a gay character on mainstream *Star Trek*. New pronouns have had to be invented. As well as the obvious application of 's/he', people have to respond to orders with yes, 'shir'. Burgoyne leaving with a smile is rendered as: 'And s/he flashed hish sharp canines and walked out.'[41] Dream on, queer theorists! Burgoyne is outrageous, explicitly and predatorially sexual in 'hish' style of relating to people of both sexes; the series describes an unusual *ménage à trois* in which Burgoyne has both a man and woman as sexual partners. One book concludes with the news that s/he is about to become both a mother and a father by these respective characters.

In comparison with this transgressive character, a gay figure is positively unchallenging. Jeri Taylor, whose status as co-creator and long-time producer of *Voyager* gives her a particular authority, has actually shown this. *Pathways* is a sequel to Taylor's book on Janeway's history; it is the 'back story' of the other main characters. Here we discover that while Harry Kim was at the Starfleet Academy, his best friend (George) fell in love with him, assuming (erroneously) that Kim was gay. In passing, set in the present story, we hear that 'Brad Harrison and his partner, Noah Mannick, asked to stay together, a request Chakotay was happy to accommodate. They had only recently become a couple and were still in the early flush of romantic intensity.'[42] Taylor's presentation of the issue of homosexuality is very matter of fact, and it highlights the extraordinary narrative 'devices' that *Star Trek* has used to air this topic on television.

The recognition that sexuality is more fluid and changeable than people used to think has been an important element of the way in which a more decentred, flexible and 'post-modern' view of the self has emerged. In *Star Trek* this has been a complicated issue, since the show has traditionally been quite wary of addressing sexual activity in any direct form, despite Kirk's constant flirtations with exotic alien women. When the film *First Contact* (which showed the Borg Queen in a sexual light in relation to both Picard and Data) came out, there was much comment on the fact that *Star Trek* was being sexualized – and the role specifically of writer Brannon Braga in this. The issue of sexual preference is one that *Star Trek* still seems to have a surprisingly serious problem with; since this appears to bother older

The Captain and his Queen

people far more than younger ones, it is probably out of touch with its audience on this one.

Jadzia and Ezri Dax are true hybrids, prime examples of the new identities that can increasingly be found in *Star Trek*. We have suggested that these new identities represent a move beyond the 'stable' and 'centred' self that was characteristic of the high point of modern, rational culture. We have introduced the 'post-modern' self as a complement to the others aspects of the decline of modern thought and culture that we have already discussed. We have looked at the rise of religion and the irrational in later *Star Trek*, key examples of the loss of faith in science and rationality. We have suggested neither that this is a good nor a bad thing, simply that *Star Trek* is moving in a direction beyond the characteristic assumptions of what is called 'modern' culture. In this sense, *Star Trek* is becoming 'post-modern'. But it is important to register that it is post-modern in terms of its *substance*. All too often post-modernism is reduced to the question of *style*, and for this reason we wanted to emphasize the ways in which the post-modernization of *Star Trek* is to be found in its rejection of some of the key *ideas* of western modernity. In addition, there are of course ways in which the *style* of *Star Trek* is itself becoming post-modern, and it to this question that we turn to make our final point.

Post-modern style

We have already seen many examples of the post-modernization of the style of *Star Trek*. The earlier analysis of 'Far beyond the Stars' emphasized the ways in which that particular episode was self-referential in that it told of *Star Trek*'s own history as it related that of Benny Russell and Benjamin Sisko. Self-referencing like this is one of the forms that can be taken by the more general development of 'coding' – double coding and multiple coding – that we find in post-modernism. Charles Jencks has argued that this kind of 'coding', typically an ironic reference to pre-modern forms, is the defining characteristic of post-modernism.[43] This type of self-knowing coding is often referred to as 'intertextuality'. *Star Trek* has always been inclined towards in-jokes, as well as more serious references to episodes of the previous series. One particularly striking example of this was an episode of *DS9* that was made to celebrate the thirtieth anniversary of *Star Trek*. Entitled 'Trials and Tribble-ations', it was a commentary on an episode from *TOS*, 'The Trouble with Tribbles'. Without going into the very silly story, we can comment on the way in which it was done. Some members of the Deep Space Nine crew go back to the original *Enterprise*. This is done by very cleverly cutting in footage of the original episode with new material, which thus enables Jadzia and Sisko to see Kirk and Spock in the corridor; there is even a scene where Kirk is interrogating a line of suspects, including Miles O'Brien. A fight scene is re-choreographed, to include some different people. And finally, Sisko takes the place of a young officer getting Kirk to sign off a duty roster – he has thereby got himself an autograph from his hero.

The idea behind the episode is to play with the relation between the original *Star Trek* and present-day *DS9*. Simply to have them change their uniforms for those of the sixties gets this off to a good start. In this instance, the technology now available is a considerable help, and this leads to another point. *Star Trek* is changing fast, and partly because it has new technology that enables it to do different things. For example, the restriction to humanoid appearance is stretching further and further. It was less that Gene Roddenberry preferred the humanoid look, than that it was simply too expensive to do anything else. Now, computer simulation makes all kinds of things possible. The morphing of Odo can only be done in this way. Species 8472, for example, who appeared in *Voyager*, were done by computer animation – a technique simply not available to earlier series. It seems likely that the special effects will increasingly make use of these new film technologies.

Star Trek's holodeck is a technological development that has enormous significance for the exploration of virtual reality. Janet Murray's *Hamlet on the Holodeck* gives an extensive and interesting treatment both of the holodeck itself and of the interactive approach to narrative that it has facilitated.[44] To see where this is all going, we might look at a very entertaining moment in the *Voyager* thirtieth anniversary tribute, 'Future's End'. Orbiting above California in 1996, Neelix and Kes have the task of monitoring the broadcast medium to find out whether their presence has been noticed by this primitive pre-warp culture. The two of them are completely riveted by soap opera. They stand there watching a wall of video screens picking up different channels. Harry asks how anyone can watch an entertainment in which they cannot participate, but Kes observes that there could be some charms in just sitting back and 'letting the narrative sweep over you'. As the scene concludes, Neelix is tantalized by American popular culture – 'I can't wait to find out whether . . .'.

The Next Generation is the most 'modern' of the successive versions of *Star Trek* and its high-minded project is the easiest to mock. *Treks not Taken*, a collection of literary parodies of *TNG* created by Steven Boyett, endorses our emphasis on Melville and Conrad as significant progenitors of the *Star Trek* universe. Boyett's tribute to *Moby Dick* ('abridged') features Worf-Worf as Queequeg, as well as the characters Piker, Email and Captain Piquod. The opening lines are irresistible: Ishmael's post-modern counterpart declares that he is enlisting on a Federation starship, 'for just as some men hold the briny Sea in their hearts, I have empty Space in my head'. Doubly self-referential, this elaborate spoof rephrases the quotations made by *Star Trek* from Melville in another key: 'I'll chase her 'round the Coal Sack and the Crab Nebula 'afore I give her up! That's what ye've signed on for, men! – We're bucking for an Emmy this mission!' Requoting Khan's quoting of Ahab at the end of *The Wrath of Khan*, this 'not Melville' offers railing words to the ex-Shakespearian actor Patrick Stewart: 'To the last fade-out I grapple with thee; from hyperbole's heart I act at thee; for King Lear's sake I vent my spleen at thee. . . . *Thus* I give up my career!'[45] 'Trek of Darkness' ('not by Joseph Conrad') presents itself for a close reading by Daniel Bernardi. Space is very black: 'the mournful gloom of dark black space lay brooding darkly and blackly'; 'we stared placidly at the vast expanse of black that was like death'. Via the Coppola Nebula (a glance towards the director of *Apocalypse Now*) they reach an outpost staffed by 'indigenous aliens who were black-skinned and wore black clothing and write only in black ink'. Mr Kurtz is revealed as Mr

Kirk, suffering 'the horror' of decades of enforced guest appearances as Captain Kirk.

Treks not Taken offers an encapsulation of the themes of modern rationalism we have identified in *Star Trek: The Next Generation*. In the voice of 'not Kurt Vonnegut', we hear that 'Godard [Picard] belonged to a religion called Vulcanonism, which preaches that religion is humbug and preaching is useless. Vulcanonists have no credo of faith, because they have a superstitious belief in the powers of science and logic. Vulcanonists vehemently despise strong emotions and have a dread fear of cowardice.'[46] Pastiche and parody are much-cited elements of 'post-modern style' and the 'post-modernization' of *Star Trek* brings them entertainingly to the fore. But this accompanies rather than substitutes for the emphasis we have made on a 'post-modern' content. *Star Trek* is now a show that concerns ideas that are historically later than (and critical of) the classic themes of 'modern' society.

We can close by looking at a typical example of late *Deep Space Nine*, an episode called 'Take Me out to the Holosuite'. Humanity is being challenged to a baseball game by Vulcans. The popular fifties song 'Take Me out to the Ballgame' should come to your mind. This game takes place in holographic reality, but Sisko's team are all too real in their terrible standard of play – notwithstanding the fact that they have tried to practise. The match is a return fixture for a previous occasion and Sisko's honour is at stake. The story is interesting in that there is no level playing-field: Vulcans are endowed with a massive physical superiority over the motley bunch that make up Sisko's team. Nevertheless, the home team (having been trounced in the game) decide to celebrate their feeble score in the bar afterwards. They refuse to accept that they should be miserable – mainly to annoy the Vulcans, which it certainly does. The moral is that human idiosyncrasy has won out, together with pluckiness in the face of impossible odds. In this, as in much else treated more seriously on *Star Trek*, the style may well be 'post-modern' but the content is most definitely not 'post-human'.

Conclusion:
Exhuming the Human

Earth is more than just a pretty picture. The *Earthrise* photographs provided an iconic image for the education of 'primitive' people in *Star Trek*: primitive being defined as people constrained by the inability to travel faster than the speed of light. The representation of earth itself (as distinct from any other planet) is increasingly a point of more contention. The planet Earth in *Star Trek* has symbolized not merely human beings, but *humanity* in a generic sense: it signifies the *Star Trek* values of rationalism, compassion, and so on, which can be exhibited by any species. 'Course: Oblivion' shows us a crew that we know are not human, but who have decidedly *humanist, humane, humanitarian* values. At one point the captain refuses to follow an immoral course of action for the sake of her crew on the grounds that 'we're Starfleet officers – we can't forget that' (despite the fact that they are none of them *really* members of Starfleet at all). 'Our humanity is intact,' she tells them, and it is this that drives her to return to earth, instead of following a biological attachment to their more 'real' demon-class home.

Recently, *Star Trek* and the earth have been diverging. The new post-modern *Star Trek* presents us with a conflicted view: the earth is both central to our understanding of human beings, and obsolete to human identity in an age that has moved beyond it. Contrast two observations on the subject from the very latest *Star Trek* outputs: in the 1998 film *Insurrection*, Captain Picard described his own 'Earthrise' experience as one of the defining moments of his life ('when time seemed to stop and you could almost live in that moment'). In

Voyager, however, where the drive towards earth ('home') is more pronounced than ever, we are seeing a distinct shift away from the earth-bound human that Heidegger had insisted upon. Seven of Nine and young Naomi Wildman (who was born on the ship and has never been to earth) are unable to see the attraction. They stare blankly at an *Earthrise*-style picture, entirely unmoved by the experience: 'it is unremarkable'. In fact, in the episode 'Bliss' it is precisely this detachment that enables them to save the ship – the rest of the crew is lulled into an illusion that is based around their own return to earth, while Seven and Naomi maintain their rational faculties. In 'Hope and Fear', Seven even has the temerity to point out to Janeway that 'your infatuation with this planet is irrational'.

Star Trek, then, is juggling with a certain amount of dualism in its representation of the earth; it appears to have a post-modernly split personality on the matter. If we trace the development of this representation through the various series, we shall perhaps be better able to appreciate the problem. It is crucial to accredit the role of the planet Earth as an *originating agent* – it represents the beginning of all human life and hence the majority of Starfleet's membership. In 'All Good Things', Q takes Picard to the moment when the first protein was assembled from the earth's primordial soup, the moment of 'life's' inception. The possibility of this not happening (hence the loss of all human life in the galaxy) is treated with much pathos, and Picard holds his head in his hands at the thought that he might play a part in such a catastrophe. Earth, though, is not just the place of origin of human beings; in 'Distant Origin', we meet an alien society distantly descended from earth – in fact, somewhat incredibly, from the dinosaurs of our pre-history. While the prevalent doctrine prevents social acceptance of this fact, the scientist who discovers it treats earth in the same romantic way as the rest of us – up to the final touching scene where Chakotay gives him the gift of a sculpted globe. It is not just humans who can appreciate the significance of earth.

Both these examples, though, rely on a concept of earth in the past – the landscape upon which life was to be formed – a planet, in fact, devoid of humanity but with the potential for a propitious future. The earth itself is an agent in galactic affairs, much as the sea is treated as a form of entity in much of the nautical literature we have looked at, or as Janeway personifies her own ship in *Voyager*. When we bring earth forward into the present, however, we discover a slightly less optimistic view. The earth is suddenly, and unfortunately, populated with humans.

Star Trek finds much to criticize about our own world's societies, and perhaps the most obvious examples of this are the occasions when its characters are displaced into our own time, which is invariably less tolerant, enlightened and civilized than theirs. In *The Original Series*, it was our dabbling in nuclear weapons ('Assignment: Earth') and our foolish destruction of our own wildlife (*Star Trek IV: The Voyage Home*); in *Voyager*, our obsession with money and power ('Future's End'), our selfish and conflicted positions ('11:59'). *Star Trek* does not pull its punches in showing us just what a mess we have made of our planet. By extension of this, it shows us the earth of our near future (*Star Trek*'s past, of course) in the more traditionally dystopic mood of science fiction. This is a world where our own shortcomings have taken over, as in 'Past Tense', where mental illness is left untreated and the poor are ghettoized in appallingly deprived and overcrowded 'Sanctuary Districts'. It is a world where a nuclear holocaust has left humans involved in bitter conflict and surviving in isolated areas (*Star Trek: First Contact*); where errors of genetics have created evil supermen (as in 'Space Seed' and *The Wrath of Khan*); where poor diplomacy has led to decades of conflict ('First Contact'). In our own past we have been racist ('Far beyond the Stars'), violent ('Encounter at Farpoint') and, in numerous examples, fascist and inhumane (the examples of the Holocaust have already been discussed). Earth in *Star Trek* is not only the home of the benevolent Federation: it is the source of a deep and violent history.

But even in *Star Trek*'s own time, of the projected twenty-third and twenty-fourth centuries, the earth is far from perfect. While it is presented as a pleasant location, its function often serves to undermine, rather than enforce, the *Star Trek* narrative. Earth is a nice place and one much favoured for holidays and convalescence – but is life there really just a bit too easy? When Picard is assimilated by the Borg, he returns to earth afterwards to recover and even considers taking up a job there: working on a rather boring scientific project, rather than exploring the galaxy. There is a great temptation for him to stay on earth for ever, instead of facing what we might term 'the real world'; earth is a refuge for those who are afraid to explore. Sisko also returns to his home planet in a state of depression and despair when his old friend Dax has been killed, and the prophets of Bajoran religion have vanished, leaving Bajor (and Deep Space Nine) abandoned. The suggestion that he might not return to duty is a horrifying one – his participation is crucial to the Federation's war effort – and it is the planet Earth that represents his soft alternative.

Not only is the earth the site of protracted convalescence, it is generally the preferred location for a lonely and obscure retirement. Captain Kirk comes to realize his own mistake in turning in his command for a gentle time in the country, and later implores Picard not to 'let them do anything that takes you off the bridge of that ship'. Retired life is, for him, a miserable alternative to space travel. In *Deep Space Nine* another lonely old man, Jake Sisko, in the counter-factual events of 'The Visitor', is living out his last days in an isolated cottage on earth; Sisko's own father, too, though happily running his Creole restaurant in Louisiana, seems entirely alone in his earth-bound old age. Earth is clearly somewhere for people who are in some sense 'past it'; the ubiquitous Starfleet Academy, with its faculty of crotchety, grey old admirals calls to mind the old adage: 'If you can't act, teach.' In 'All Good Things . . .', we see the rather unsatisfying later years of our favourite characters from *TNG*: Picard and Crusher are lonely in their divorced state; Worf has been reduced to a faceless bureaucrat, Riker to an imitation of his much-despised father, and Data to a tedious and cynical Lucasian Professor at Cambridge. Only Geordi displays any sign of happiness in this timeline through his successful cultivation of a family, an area in which both Kirk and Picard lament their own failings. For those who give their lives to Starfleet, old age is a decidedly depressing affair, and is usually enacted back on earth – away from the excitement of their earlier lives in space.

In *Deep Space Nine*, earth was for a time referred to as 'paradise' (see, for example, 'The Maquis'), a reputation that was perhaps bound to be undermined. In the appropriately titled 'Paradise Lost', the question of how to police this idyllic planet is addressed when it becomes clear that there are enemy agents working, on earth, to destabilize the United Federation of Planets. 'Paradise' soon finds itself under martial law with McCarthy-style witch-hunts pursuing the changeling infiltrators. Earth is not all that it had seemed to be – a common theme of *DS9*, where the idealism of the previous series is challenged as characters realize the limitations of their optimistic Starfleet philosophy. (In 'Hard Time', Chief O'Brien comments on his own behaviour: 'they used to tell us that humanity had evolved . . . but when it came down to it . . . I repaid kindness with blood'.) The question of corruption on earth is one that has been around in *Star Trek* for some time, however. The distance from Starfleet HQ to the ships and stations of the Federation means that significant political events can take place surreptitiously on earth, often requiring our crews to sort them out. While *Star Trek* has never quite reached the extremes of *Babylon 5*, where the central story arc was for some time the righteous war against the fascist earth regime, the Federation Council has been seriously corrupted on a number of occasions. In *Star Trek VI: The Undiscovered Country*, it contains elements pushing for the continuation of war; in *Insurrection*, it issues orders for the forced relocation of a minority ethnic group to suit its own military ends – in defiance of Starfleet's own Prime Directive. High-ranking Starfleet officers have been involved in all kinds of dubious shenanigans – from assisting the amoral Section 31 ('Extreme Measures') to subverting their own peace treaties with other governments ('The Pegasus') and covering up crucial information ('Paradise Lost'). Commonly this kind of behaviour takes place on – or is orchestrated from – earth, making it hard for our own characters to get to grips with the problem. Earth can be a source of constant consternation to the well-meaning space-dwelling officer and is far from the impeccable base it is thought to be. It is not the home of moral and just decision-making; the real issues are debated out in space. Its significance to humanity, in *Star Trek*, has become quite limited. Compare the horror of the possibility of a Borg attack on earth in *TNG* ('The Best of Both Worlds') with the Dominion's destruction of San Francisco in *DS9*. While this latter event is presented as a shocking tragedy, it has little real effect on the war. It seems that human beings can get by quite well enough without their little blue planet.

We have already commented that *Voyager*'s stance on the planet Earth is perhaps the most reverential, as it seems to use the word almost synonymously with the more generic term 'home' – a concept that is bandied about quite a lot in *Star Trek*. One's home is a defining feature of one's identity: it represents an idealized *location* in space and time, a point of maximum happiness. While Janeway talks personally of returning to 'earth', she actually orders her helmsman to 'set a course for home'. But *is* earth the only viable 'home' for characters in *Star Trek*? We have already seen that Seven of Nine and Naomi Wildman do not think of it as such (in fact, Seven is very much afraid of returning to the planet, as is shown in the episode 'Hope and Fear'). When questioned by Lily Sloane in *First Contact*, Picard confesses that he does not think of earth as his home – that privilege being reserved for the *Enterprise* itself; in *DS9* we are told that Sisko, though (at least largely) human, is 'of Bajor', and he talks of building a house there. Many in the *Voyager* crew are originally from planets other than earth: Chakotay is from Trebus, Torres from Nessik, Tuvok from Vulcan and Neelix from Talax in the Delta Quadrant. Tom Paris *is* from earth but the only memories he has of it are harsh ones: 'What I have on *Voyager* is so much better than anything I had back there.' Like Seven, he feels ambivalent about returning to the place.

That 'home' is not always synonymous with 'earth' is clearly illustrated in the *DS9* finale. 'What You Leave Behind' wraps up the series pretty comprehensively by sending the vast majority of characters back 'home'. Yet while Chief O'Brien and family take up a posting on earth, the majority of the crew diverge all over the galaxy: Worf returns to the Klingon Homeworld as an ambassador; Garak lays the foundations for a new life on Cardassia; Rom goes back home to Ferenginar to take up the role of Grand Nagus; Odo returns to the home of his people in the Gamma Quadrant; Deep Space Nine is returned to its legitimate Bajoran leadership under Colonel Kira; and Sisko himself goes off to live with the immortal prophets, finally taking up his rightful place as a god. Very few characters in this series have any real allegiance to earth itself and the series' position is perhaps best summed up by Quark's remark that 'earth's nothing more than a rotating ball of boredom'. The real adventures take place out in space.

We have seen that in *Voyager*, too, the crew's objective to reach earth is somewhat unconvincing. What most of these characters do share, however, is a desire to return to the *Alpha Quadrant*, a much broader concept of 'home' that allows us to define it as distinct from a very *other* location – in *Voyager* the Delta Quadrant, in *DS9* the Gamma Quadrant. Increasingly in *Star Trek* these quadrants are used to show us where we belong, rather than limiting ourselves to an individual planet. *DS9*'s Dominion War was being fought for control of the entire Alpha Quadrant – which equates roughly with the extent of mapped and divided space in *Star Trek*. (Once this war is over, the crew disband towards their more specific homes.) The Alpha Quadrant is the system we understand: a territory of Humans, Vulcans, Klingons, Romulans, and so on. In essence it is the home of *Star Trek*. It is perhaps this that the Federation is fighting for, and this that Janeway's crew is seeking to return to – the *Star Trek* world that they understand and feel comfortable in. If, in the projected twenty-fourth century, humans are not limited to earth itself, they at least remain fixed in the larger 'home' of our own *Star Trek* portion of the galaxy. In this, although planet Earth is now displaced and decentred, the project of *humanity* is still very much centre-stage.

Earth and moon from space

Notes

Introduction: Earthrise

1 Contact Wimberly Allison Tong and Goo (WAT&G) Inc.
2 SETI (Search for Extraterrestrial Intelligence) runs an enormously popular program for home computer users to contribute to its work (www.SETIathome.com).
3 Quoted in Keith Tester, *The Inhuman Condition*, pp. 1–2. See also Richard Wolin (ed.), *The Heidegger Controversy: a critical reader.*
4 Stuart Hall, 'The West and the Rest', in Stuart Hall and Bram Gieben (eds), *Formations of Modernity.*

Part I   The Starry Sea

1 David Gerrold, *The World of Star Trek: the inside story of TV's most popular series*, p. 3.
2 Taylor Harrison et al. (eds), *Enterprise Zones: critical positions on Star Trek*, p. 7.
3 Yvonne Fern, *Gene Roddenberry: the last conversation*, p. 66.
4 C. W. T. Layton, *Dictionary of Nautical Words and Terms.*
5 Michael and Denise Okuda, *Star Trek Chronology: the history of the future.*
6 The details of warp physics are elaborated in Rick Sternbach and Michael Okuda, *Star Trek: The Next Generation technical manual*, esp. ch. 5: 'Warp Propulsion Systems'.
7 Peter Padfield, *Maritime Supremacy and the Opening of the Western Mind: naval campaigns that shaped the modern world, 1588–1782.*
8 Ibid., p. 287.

9   Ibid., p. 288.
10 Michael Adas, *Machines as the measure of men: science, technology, and ideologies of Western dominance*, p. 2.
11 Ibid., pp. 212–13.
12 Wess Roberts and Bill Ross.
13 Herman Melville, *White-Jacket*, p. 24.
14 Ibid., p. 23.
15 C. S. Forester, *The Happy Return*, in *Captain Hornblower R.N.*
16 Gerrold, *The World of Star Trek*, p. 9.
17 Melville, *White-Jacket*, p. 369.
18 Michel Foucault, *Discipline and Punish*.
19 C. S. Forester, *Hornblower in the West Indies*, in *Admiral Hornblower*, p. 713.
20 Melville, *White-Jacket*, p. 281.
21 Tony Tanner, Introduction to *White-Jacket*, p. xviii. Tanner also writes that 'Melville is clear enough that it is entirely abhorrent that white men should be flogged like black slaves. He is not quite so clear that it is equally abhorrent for blacks to be whipped – or to be slaves either for that matter' (p. xviii).
22 *Voyager*: 'Thirty Days'.
23 *Voyager*: 'Scientific Method'.
24 Paul Gilroy, *The Black Atlantic*, p. 4.
25 Herman Melville, *Moby Dick*, p. 188.
26 Ibid., p. 190.
27 Ibid., p. 189.
28 There are echoes, here, of the analysis of the Holocaust as the solution to a 'problem' that is wholly in the spirit of modern technological rationalism. See Zygmunt Bauman, *Modernity and the Holocaust*.
29 *Voyager*: 'Hope and Fear'.
30 Curiously, the misquoted passage is weaker in Picard's version than in what is attributed to Ahab in *Moby Dick* itself. A metaphorical description of something that did happen to Ahab is reduced to a hypothetical. Picard says: 'And he piled upon the whale's white hump the sum of all the rage and hate felt by his whole race . . . and if his chest had been a cannon, he would have shot his heart upon it.' Melville reads: '. . . all evil, to crazy Ahab, were visibly personified, and made practically assailable in Moby Dick. He piled upon the whale's white hump the sum of all the general rage and hate felt by his whole race from Adam down; and then, as if his chest had been a mortar, he burst his hot heart's shell upon it' (p. 187; editions vary in the use of mortar and cannon in this passage).
31 Jules Verne, *Twenty Thousand Leagues Under the Sea*, p. 253.
32 Ibid., p. 258.
33 Ibid., p. 262.
34 Ibid., p. 72.
35 Ibid., pp. 80–2.
36 Ibid., p. 92.

37   Ibid., p. 244.
38   Tony Tanner, Introduction to *Moby Dick*.
39   C. L. R. James, *Mariners, Renegades and Castaways*.
40   Melville, *Moby Dick*, p. 190.
41   Ibid., p. 192.
42   *Star Trek Voyager Year 3 Writers'-Directors' Guide*, or 'Bible', refers to his 'Maya ancestry'.
43   S. E. Poe, *A Vision of The Future: Star Trek Voyager*.
44   *DS9*: 'Children of Time'.
45   Joseph Conrad, *The Nigger of the 'Narcissus'*, p. 19.
46   Ibid., p. xli.
47   Ibid., p. 18.
48   Ibid., p. 151.
49   Berthoud, Introduction to *The Nigger of the 'Narcissus'*, p. xiii.
50   Ibid., p. xiv.
51   Lord Byron, 'Childe Harold's Pilgrimage', Canto CLXXIX.
52   Conrad, *The Nigger of the 'Narcissus'*, p. 161.
53   Ibid., p. 160.
54   Conrad, Introduction to Medallion Collected Edition (Gresham, 1925).
55   Joseph Conrad, *Heart of Darkness*, p. 240.
56   See the fascinating collection of images and other records in Norman Sherry *Conrad*.
57   Conrad, *Heart of Darkness*, Introduction, p. xxi.
58   Ibid., p. 186.
59   Achebe's paper is based on a lecture at the University of Massachusetts in 1975, in which he described Conrad as a 'bloody' racist.
60   See Nicholas Tredell (ed.), *Icon Critical Guide to 'Heart of Darkness'*, pp. 80–2.
61   Sherry, *Conrad*, p. 93.
62   Tredell, *Icon Critical Guide*, p. 81.
63   Berthoud, Introduction to *The Nigger of the 'Narcissus'*, p. xvii.
64   Lawrence M. Krauss, *The Physics of Star Trek*, pp. 36–8.
65   Melville, *Moby Dick*, pp. 184–5.
66   Tamas L. Gombosi, *Physics of the Space Environment*.
67   Ahab says: 'I'll chase him round Good Hope, and round the Horn, and round the Norway Maelstrom, and round perdition's flames before I give him up' (*Moby Dick*, p. 166).
68   Ibid., p. 580.
69   Some of these phenomena are explicated in Andre Bormanis, *Star Trek: Science Logs*.
70   Ibid., pp. 17–18.
71   Ibid., pp. 149–51.
72   Captain of the *Bounty*, famous for the mutiny of the crew.
73   Captain Phillipa Louvois, who turns up to judge the tribunal on Data's status in 'The Measure of a Man'.
74   These novels were begun in the 1930s and terminated in 1967 with Forester's death. They are set during the Napoleonic wars. Forester's

fictional hero has been reconstructed with great verisimilitude in a spoof biography of the legendary sailor: Northcote Parkinson's elaborate embroidery of *The Life and Times of Horatio Hornblower* was first published in 1970. Positively post-modernist in its rejection of a distinction between biography and fiction, it has now been reissued at what the publisher's call 'a timely moment', coinciding with a revival of the novels as drama on British television.

75 C. S. Forester, *A Ship of the Line*.
76 C. S. Forester, *Flying Colours*, p. 145.
77 Fern, *Gene Roddenberry*, p. 78.
78 C. S. Forester, *Hornblower and the Atropos*, p. 118.
79 Ibid., pp. 9–14.
80 Forester, *Flying Colours*, p. 94.
81 See the title of *Star Trek VI: The Undiscovered Country*. (The film includes a play on the meaning of Hamlet's 'undiscovered country from whose bourne no traveller returns'. When a Klingon toast is raised, with the intention that this refers to the future, the Federation diners are alarmed, as they register it in terms of death. This atmosphere of anxious cultural confusion exemplifies the feel of the film in general.
82 C. S. Forester, *Hornblower in the West Indies*, p. 628.
83 Patrick O'Brian, *The Wine-Dark Sea* (a reference to Homer's *Odyssey*).
84 Diane Carey, *First Strike*.
85 Layton, *Dictionary of Nautical Words and Terms*.
86 Diane Carey, *Fire Ship*.
87 Patrick O'Brian, *Master and Commander*, pp. 94–102, followed by more on the below-decks set-up and useful statistics (pp. 103–7).
88 Diane Carey, *Ancient Blood*, p. 62.
89 Jonathan Raban (ed.), *The Oxford Book of the Sea*.
90 Ibid., pp. 3–7.
91 The Austen reference is from *Sanditon*. See Raban, *Book of the Sea*, pp. 8–9, 174–5.
92 *Voyager*: 'Night'.
93 Berthoud, Introduction to Conrad's *The Nigger of the 'Narcissus'*, pp. ix–x.
94 Gilroy, *The Black Atlantic*, p. 13.
95 Berthoud, Introduction, pp. x–xi.

Part II   Humanity on Trial

1 Zvi Dor-Ner, *Columbus and the Age of Discovery*, pp. 149–50.
2 These arguments are examined critically in Michèle Barrett, 'Human Nature', in *Imagination in Theory: essays on writing and culture*, pp. 170–85.
3 *TNG*: 'Who Watches the Watchers'.
4 Ludwig Feuerbach, *The Essence of Christianity*.
5 Karl Marx, *Economic and Philosophical Manuscripts*.
6 Karl Marx, *Critique of the Gotha Programme* (and *Communist Manifesto*).

7   Vintage 1992, title page.
8   Collins *Etymological Dictionary* (n.d.).
9   The definition given in David Crystal (ed.), *The Cambridge Encyclopaedia*.
10 Tony Davies, *Humanism*, pp. 125–6. Tony Davies has kindly explicated this etymological trail in personal correspondence. 'The humanus derivation goes roughly as follows: (Indo-European *ham*) → Sanscrit *ham/hum* → Greek *chamai* (on/from the ground) → Latin *homo/humilis* (low, at ground level) / *humanus* (of/from/made of earth) – to say nothing of Old Middle German *gomo*, Gothic *guma*, Old English *goom* etc.'. See Lewis and Short, *Latin Dictionary* (*homo*); Ernout and Meillet, *Dictionnaire etymologique de la langue Latine* (Paris, 1939).
11 *DS9*: 'Past Tense'.
12 The title is taken from the proverbial 'dance with the Devil in the pale moonlight'.
13 This connection is brought out explicitly in Diane Carey's *Voyager* novel *Fire Ship*, p. 223, where this slogan is given a page to itself before chapter 20.
14 *Star Trek Monthly*, 39 (May 1998), p. 15.
15 Episodes concerned are *TNG*, 'The Sins of the Father', 'Reunion', 'Redemption' and 'Birthright'.
16 For criticism of the anti-humanism in social theory see Michèle Barrett, *The Politics of Truth: from Marx to Foucault* and *Imagination in Theory*.
17 See the material in Henry Jenkins, *Textual Poachers: television fans and participatory culture* and Daniel Bernardi, *Star Trek and History: racing toward a white future*.
18 *Star Trek Monthly*, 15 (May 1996), p. 17.
19 *Hamlet*, Act 2, scene 2: 'What a piece of work is a man! How noble in reason, how infinite in faculty, in form and moving how express and admirable, in action how like an angel, in apprehension how like a god – the beauty of the world, the paragon of animals!' (Norton Shakespeare, p. 1697).
20 Michael and Denise Okuda, 'Life-forms (known)', in *The Star Trek Encyclopaedia*, pp. 266–73.
21 A. M. Farrer, 'On dispensing with Q', originally published in D. E. Nineham (ed.), *Studies in the Gospels* (Blackwell, 1955). Web version by Mark Goodacre cited here: www.bham.ac.uk/theology/q/.
22 Derived from the Latin participle meaning 'having spoken', the name 'Locutus' is intended to refer to the idea of a representative spokesman, a human 'counterpart'.
23 'Man is the measure of all things' (the view of Protagoras, according to Plato), quoted in Davies, *Humanism*, p. 122.
24 See the films *Predator* (John McTiernan, 1987) and *Predator II*, (Stephen Hopkins, 1990).
25 Bernardi, *Star Trek and History*, p. 127.

26   Wagner and Lundeen are criticizing a paper by Leah R. Vande Berg, 'Worf as metonymic signifier of racial, cultural, and national differences', in Harrison et al. (eds), *Enterprise Zones*. This collection is devoted to an exposition of the neoconservative politics of *Star Trek*, as seen by academics who also describe themelves as 'fans'.

27   'In these films the question of sexual difference . . . is displaced onto the more remarkable difference between the human and the other.' Constance Penley, 'Time travel, primal scene and the critical dystopia', in A. Kuhn, *Alien Zone: cultural theory and contemporary science fiction cinema*, p. 123.

28   As in the 'perfectly white and subtly rounded starship' described by Bernardi, in *Star Trek and History*, p. 70.

29   Richard Dyer, *White*.

30   Ibid., p. 57.

31   In a note to Conrad, *Heart of Darkness*, Cedric Watts explains that Lucifer was a name given to Venus, the 'morning star' when it appears before sunrise. It was subsequently applied to Satan, who fell from heaven through pride and came to rule in hell (p. 263).

32   Collins *Etymological and Reference Dictionary*, London and Glasgow, Collins (n.d.); David Crystal (ed.), *The Cambridge Encyclopaedia*.

33   'Dream, imagination and existence', in Michel Foucault and Ludwig Binswanger, *Dream and Existence*, pp. 30–78. Foucault's essay was first published in 1954. Passages quoted can be found on pp. 47, 48, 49, 53, 61 and 63–5.

34   Sternbach and Okuda, *Star Trek: The Next Generation*, pp. 102–9.

35   Krauss, *The Physics of Star Trek*, pp. 65–74.

36   Roger Penrose, unpublished Radio 4 discussion. See also his 'Minds, machines and mathematics', in Colin Blakemore and Susan Greenfield (eds), *Mindwaves* (Blackwell, 1987).

37   Danah Zohar, *The Quantum Self*, p. 80.

38   Stephen Horigan, *Nature and Culture in Western Discourses*.

39   Curiously, there is an *Intendant* – the 'Intendant of Livonia' – in one of the *Hornblower* stories, and *the Intended* appears as Kurtz's fiancée in *Heart of Darkness*.

40   The Latinate title is no surprise. We have already mentioned Picard's transformation into 'Locutus'. The relationship between the Borg and the (world-conquering) Romans is consistently evoked.

41   Donna Haraway 'A Manifesto for Cyborgs: science, technology and socialist feminism in the 1980s', *Socialist Review*, 80 (1985). Reprinted in Linda J. Nicholson (ed.), *Feminism/Postmodernism*, p. 191.

42   Rushing and Frentz rule that the between the two *Terminator* films the cyborg in the first is joined by a 'simulation' in the second: the T-1000 played by Robert Patrick 'can no longer be called a cyborg'. The T-1000, they note, is more ordinarily human in his speech and appearance, and less like a machine in that his polymer shapeshifting capacities are superhuman. See Janice Hocker Rushing and Thomas S.

Frentz, *Projecting the Shadow: the cyborg hero in American film*, pp. 185–6.

43 Collins *Millennium Dictionary*, p. 391.

44 *Cambridge Encyclopaedia*, p. 328.

45 *OED* definition.

46 Haraway, 'Manifesto for Cyborgs', p. 191.

47 Mary Shelley, *Frankenstein*, p. 56.

48 Ibid., pp. 99–140.

49 Ibid., p. 125.

50 Ibid., p. 141.

51 Per Schelde, *Androids, Humanoids, and Other Science Fiction Monsters: science and soul in science fiction films*, p. 4.

52 Schelde's attempt to define the 'soul' in his subtitle is very disappointing in that the language of 'God', 'salvation' and 'heaven' (all very Christian despite his disclaimer) moves effortlessly into that of a 'Supreme Being' and then breathtakingly announces that, 'put another way', the soul refers to 'individuality', 'self' and '*free will*' (p. 20).

53 Rushing and Frentz, *Projecting the Shadow*.

54 Ibid., p. 178.

55 Brian Winston, 'Tyrell's owl: the limits of the technological imagination in an epoch of hyperbolic discourse', in Barbara Adam and Stuart Allan (eds), *Theorizing Culture: an interdisciplinary critique after postmodernism*, p. 232.

56 Peter Fitting, 'The lessons of cyberpunk', in Constance Penley and Andrew Ross (eds), *Technoculture*, p. 301.

57 *Guardian*, 8 December 1999, p. 6 (BBC poll). The popularity or otherwise of this film is much disputed.

58 Nigel Wheale, 'Recognizing a "human-thing": cyborgs, robots and replicants in Philip K. Dick, *Do Androids Dream of Electric Sheep?* See also Ridley Scott's *'Blade Runner'*, in Nigel Wheale (ed.), *The Postmodern Arts: an introductory reader*, p. 113.

59 Kevin McCarron, 'The body and cyberpunk', in Mike Featherstone and Roger Burrows (eds), *Cyberspace/Cyberbodies/Cyberpunk: cultures of technological embodiment*, p. 264.

60 Ziauddin Sardar, 'alt.civilisations.faq: cyberspace as the darker side of the West', in Ziauddin Sardar and Jerome R. Ravetz (eds), *Cyberfutures: culture and politics on the information superhighway*, p. 37.

61 Ibid., p. 17.

62 See Michel Foucault, *The Care of the Self: technologies of the self*, ed. Martin et al.; see also the section on bio-power in *The Foucault Reader*, ed. Rabinow.

63 Vivian Sobchack, 'Beating the meat/surviving the text, or how to get out of this century alive', in Featherstone and Burrows (eds), *Cyberspace*, p. 213.

64 Samantha Holland, 'Descartes goes to Hollywood: mind, body and gender in contemporary cyborg cinema', in Featherstone and Burrows (eds), *Cyberspace*, p. 170.

65   Gwyneth Jones, 'The neuroscience of cyberspace: new metaphors for the self and its boundaries', in Brian D. Loader (ed.), *The Governance of Cyberspace*, p. 62.
66   Ibid., p. 53.
67   Jay Winter and Emmanuel Sivan, *War and Remembrance in the Twentieth Century*, pp. 11–15.
68   Alison Landsberg, 'Prosthetic memory', in Featherstone and Burrows (eds), *Cyberspace*, pp. 182–3.
69   Bill Schwarz, 'Memory and historical time' a paper read at the 'Cultural memory' conference in London in 1999; for Braudel's remark, see Peter Burke (ed.), *The French Historical Revolution: the Annales School, 1929–89*, p. 39.
70   Alfred Gell, *The Anthropology of Time*. See p. 259, for definitions.
71   Foreword to Krauss, *The Physics of Star Trek*, p. xiii.
72   Michèle Barrett, 'Human nature', in Barrett, *Imagination in Theory*, p. 180.
73   Vivian Sobchack, 'Beating the meat', in Featherstone and Burrows (eds), *Cyberspace*, p. 213.

Part III   The Post-modern Tack

1   II Timothy 4: 7.
2   Histories of *Star Trek* at the beginning include Herbert E. Solow and Robert H. Justman, *Inside Star Trek: the real story*.
3   Fern, *Gene Roddenberry*.
4   *Star Trek Monthly*, 41 (July 98).
5   Genesis 22: 12.
6   See Jennifer E. Porter and Darcee L. McLaren (eds), *Star Trek and Sacred Ground: explorations of Star Trek, religion, and American culture*, for an exploration of this theme.
7   'Cyborgs and symbionts: living together in the new world order', in Chris Hables Gray (ed.), *The Cyborg Handbook*, pp. xv–xvi.
8   D. C. H. Rieu, Preface to rev. edn of E. V. Rieu's trans. of *The Odyssey*, p. ix.
9   Ibid., p. ix.
10   Ibid., pp. 25, 41, 85, 244.
11   Ibid., p. 63.
12   Ibid., pp. 149–53.
13   Ibid., p. 68.
14   Ibid., pp. 160–76.
15   Ibid., p. 190.
16   Ibid., p. 73.
17   Ibid., pp. 301–2.
18   Foucault, 'Dream, imagination and existence', pp. 52–3.
19   Foucault, *The Care of the Self*, Part I.
20   Gell, *The Anthropology of Time*, pp. 56–7.

21 Ibid., p. 58.
22 Foucault, 'Dream, imagination and existence', p. 46.
23 Margaret Wertheimer, *Pythagoras' Trousers: God, physics and the gender wars*.
24 It has even been suggested that the dramatist was himself a Klingon. The (restored) *Klingon Hamlet* explains: 'During the years when the Empire and the Federation were at war . . . certain individuals resorted to crude forgeries of Shex'pir, claiming him as a conveniently remote mediaeval Terran, a certain Willem Shekispeore, and hoping by this falsification of history to discredit the achievements of Klingon culture . . . these forgeries were as thorough as they were meticulous: gigabytes of allegedly Industrial Age back-dated so-called Shekispeorian Criticism were fabricated, and the works disseminated as part of a well-organised campaign.' For more information, consult the Klingon Language Institute, the organization behind the restoration of Shakespeare's plays to the 'original Klingon': www.kli.org.
25 *The Oxford Dictionary of Quotations* (1992 edn).
26 Thomas Richards, *The Meaning of Star Trek* (in fact it is restricted to *TNG*), p. 32.
27 Larry Nemecek, *The Star Trek: The Next Generation Companion*, p. 244.
28 Bauman, *Modernity and the Holocaust*.
29 Michel Foucault, *Madness and Civilisation*, p. 39.
30 Ibid., p. 190.
31 Raban (ed.), *Oxford Book of the Sea*, p. 37.
32 This argument is discussed in more detail in 'Virginia Woolf meets Michel Foucault', in Barrett, *Imagination in Theory*.
33 Herman Melville, *Mardi and a Voyage Thither*, p. 557.
34 'Scorpion' (*Voyager*).
35 See 'The Rapture' for a good example of this.
36 Virginia Woolf, *Orlando*, pp. 217–8.
37 Judith Butler, *Gender Trouble: feminism and the subversion of identity*; see also her *Bodies that Matter: on the discursive limits of 'sex'*.
38 For more information see the Online Freedom Federation campaign (http://www.off-hq.org/index.html), which supports the rights of *Star Trek* fans against the authority of the monolithic Viacom corporation that now owns the programme.
39 Constance Penley, *NASA/Trek: popular science and sex in America*; Jenkins, *Textual Poachers*; John Tulloch and Henry Jenkins, *Science Fiction Audiences: watching Dr Who and Star Trek*; see also the interview with Henry Jenkins in Harrison et al., *Enterprise Zones*.
40 Robin Roberts, *Sexual Generations: 'Star Trek The Next Generation' and gender*, p. 124.
41 Peter David, *Into the Void*, p. 101.
42 Jeri Taylor, *Pathways*, p. 176.

43 Charles Jencks, *What is Postmodernism?*
44 Janet H. Murray, *Hamlet on the Holodeck: the future of narrative in cyberspace.*
45 Steven R. Boyett, *Treks not Taken: a parody,* p. 133.
46 Ibid., p. 158.

Bibliography

Achebe, Chinua, 'An image of Africa', *Massachusetts Review*, 18: 4 (winter 1977), pp. 782–94; extracts, with commentary, in Nicolas Tredell (ed.) *Icon Critical Guide to 'Heart of Darkness'*, Cambridge, Icon Books, 1998.

Adam, Barbara and Allen, Stuart (eds), *Theorizing Culture: an interdisciplinary critique after postmodernism*, London, UCL Press, 1995.

Adas, Michael, *Machines as the measure of men: science, technology, and ideologies of Western dominance*, Ithaca and London, Cornell University Press, 1989.

Barrett, Michèle, *The Politics of Truth: from Marx to Foucault*, Cambridge, Polity Press, 1991.

Barrett, Michèle, *Imagination in Theory: essays on writing and culture*, Cambridge, Polity Press, 1999.

Barrow, John, *Theories of Everything: the quest for ultimate explanation*, London, Vintage, 1992.

Baumann, Zygmunt, *Modernity and the Holocaust*, Cambridge, Polity, 1989.

Bernardi, Daniel Leonard, *Star Trek and History: race-ing toward a white future*, New Jersey, Rutgers University Press, 1998.

Bormanis, Andre, *Star Trek: Science Logs*, New York, Pocket Books, 1998.

Boyett, Steven R., *Treks not Taken: a parody*, New York, HarperCollins, 1998.

Burke, Peter (ed.), *The French Historical Revolution: the Annales School 1929–89*, Polity, 1990.

Butler, Judith, *Gender Trouble: feminism and the subversion of identity*, London, Routledge, 1990.

Butler, Judith, *Bodies that Matter: on the discursive limits of 'sex'*, London, Routledge, 1993.

Carey, Diane, *First Strike* (vol. 1 of the *Star Trek: Invasion* series), New York, Pocket Books, 1996.

Carey, Diane, *Ancient Blood* (vol. 1 of the *Day of Honour* series), New York, Pocket Books, 1997.

Carey, Diane, *Fire Ship* (vol. 4 of the *Captain's Table* series), New York, Pocket Books, 1998.

Conrad, Joseph, *The Nigger of the 'Narcissus'*, World's Classics edn, introduced by Jacques Berthoud, Oxford, Oxford University Press, 1995.

Conrad, Joseph, *Heart of Darkness*, World's Classics edn, introduced by Cedric Watts, Oxford, Oxford University Press, 1998.

Crystal, David (ed.), *The Cambridge Encyclopaedia*, Cambridge, Cambridge University Press, 1990.

David, Peter, *Into the Void* (vol. 2 of *New Frontier* series), New York, Pocket Books, 1997.

Davies, Tony, *Humanism*, London Routledge, 1997.

Dor-Ner, Zvi, *Columbus and the Age of Discovery*, London, HarperCollins, 1991.

Dyer, Richard, *White*, London, Routledge, 1997.

Featherstone, Mike and Burrows, Roger (eds), *Cyberspace/Cyberbodies/Cyberpunk: cultures of technological embodiment*, London, Sage, 1995.

Feuerbach, Ludwig, *The Essence of Christianity*, New York, Prometheus Books, 1989.

Fern, Yvonne, *Gene Roddenberry: the last conversation*, Berkeley and Los Angeles, California University Press, 1994.

Fitting, Peter, 'The lessons of cyberpunk', in Constance Penley and Andrew Ross (eds), *Technoculture*, Minneapolis, Minnesota University Press, 1991, p. 301.

Foucault, Michel, *Discipline and Punish*, London, Penguin, 1979.

Foucault, Michel, *The Foucault Reader*, ed. Paul Rabinow, Harmondsworth, Penguin, 1984.

Foucault, Michel, *The Care of the Self* vol. 3 of *The History of Sexuality*, New York, Vintage, 1988.

Foucault, Michel, *Technologies of the Self: a seminar with Michel Foucault*, ed. Luther H. Martin et al., London, Tavistock, 1988.

Foucault, Michel, *Madness and Civilisation*, London and New York, Routledge, 1989.

Foucault, Michel, Dream, imagination and existence, in Foucault and Binswanger, *Dream and Existence*, New Jersey, Humanities Press, 1993.

Foucault, Michel and Binswanger, Ludwig, *Dream and Existence*, New Jersey, Humanities Press, 1993.

Forester, C. S., *Captain Hornblower R.N.* (contains *Hornblower and The Atropus*, *The Happy Return* and *A Ship of the Line*), London, Penguin, 1987.

Forester, C. S., *Admiral Hornblower* (contains *Flying Colours* and *Hornblower in the West Indies*), London, Penguin, 1996.

Gell, Alfred, *The Anthropology of Time*, Oxford, Berg, 1996.

Gerrold, David, *The World of Star Trek: the inside story of TV's most popular series*, London, Virgin Books, 1996.

Gilroy, Paul, *The Black Atlantic*, London, Verso, 1993.

Goodacre, Mark, 'On dispensing with Q' by A. M. Farrer (originally published in D. E. Nineham (ed.), *Studies in the Gospels*, Oxford, Blackwell, 1955). Web version by Mark Goodacre cited here: www.bham.ac.uk/theology/q/.

Gombosi, Tamas L., *Physics of the Space Environment*, Cambridge, Cambridge University Press, 1999.

Hall, Stuart, 'The West and the Rest', in Stuart Hall and Bram Gieben (eds), *Formations of Modernity*, Cambridge, Polity, 1992.

Haraway, Donna, 'A Manifesto for Cyborgs: science, technology and socialist feminism in the 1980s', *Socialist Review*, 80 (1985). Repr. in Linda J. Nicholson (ed.), *Feminism/Postmodernism*, New York and London, Routledge, 1990.

Haraway, Donna, 'Cyborgs and symbionts: living together in the new world order', in Chris Hables Gray (ed.), *The Cyborg Handbook*, New York and London, Routledge, 1995.

Harrison, Taylor et al. (eds), *Enterprise Zones: critical positions on Star Trek*, Boulder, Colorado and Oxford, England, Westview Press, 1996.

Homer, *The Odyssey* (rev. edn of E. V. Rieu's trans.), London, Penguin, 1991.

Horigan, Stephen, *Nature and Culture in Western Discourse*, London, Routledge, 1988.

James, C. L. R., *Mariners, Renegades and Castaways*, London, Allison and Busby, 1985.

Jencks, Charles, *What is Postmodernism?* London, Academy Editions; New York, St Martin's Press, 1986.

Jenkins, Henry, *Textual Poachers: television fans and participatory culture*, London, Routledge, 1992.

Jones, Gwyneth, 'The neuroscience of cyberspace: new metaphors for the self and its boundaries', in Brian Loader (ed.), *The Governance of Cyberspace*, London, Routledge, 1997.

Krauss, Lawrence M., *The Physics of Star Trek* (foreword by Stephen Hawking), London, HarperCollins Flamingo, 1997.

Kuhn, Annette (ed.), *Alien Zone: cultural theory and contemporary science fiction cinema*, London, Verso, 1990.

Landsberg, Alison, Prosthetic Memory, in Mike Featherstone and Roger Burows (eds), *Cyberspace/Cyberbodies/Cyberpunk: cultures of technological embodiment*, London, Sage, 1995.

Layton, C. W. T., *Dictionary of Nautical Words and Terms*, Glasgow, Brown, Son & Ferguson (1st edn, 1955; 4th edn rev. A. G. W. Miller, 1998).

Loader, Brian D. (ed.), *The Governance of Cyberspace*, London, Routledge, 1997.

Mackinnon, Neil, 'Suddenly human', *Cult Times*, 4 (Jan 1996).

Melville, Herman, *White-Jacket*, World's Classics edn, Oxford, Oxford University Press, 1996.

Melville, Herman, *Mardi and a Voyage Thither*, Evanston, IL, Northwestern University Press, 1998.

Melville, Herman, *Moby Dick*, World's Classics edn (Introduction by Tony Tanner), Oxford, Oxford University Press, 1998.

Murray, Janet H., *Hamlet on the Holodeck: the future of narrative in cyberspace*, Cambridge, MA, MIT Press, 1997.

Nemecek, Larry, *The Star Trek: The Next Generation Companion*, New York, Pocket Books, 1995.

Nicholson, Lee Ann (ed.), *Radio Times Official Collector's Edition: Star Trek, 30 years*, Ontario, Paramount Pictures Corporation, 1996 (distributed in the UK under licence by *Radio Times*, BBC Worldwide Publishing Ltd, London, 1996).

Nineham, D. E. (ed.), *Studies in the Gospels*, Oxford, Blackwell, 1955.

O'Brian, Patrick, *Master and Commander*, London, HarperCollins, 1996.

O'Brian, Patrick, *The Wine-Dark Sea*, London, HarperCollins, 1997.

Okuda, Michael and Okuda, Denise, *Star Trek Chronology: the history of the future*, New York, Pocket Books, 1993.

Okuda, Michael and Okuda, Denise, *The Star Trek Encyclopaedia: a reference guide to the future*, New York, Pocket Books, 1997.

Orwell, George, *Nineteen Eighty-Four*, London, Penguin, 1990.

Padfield, Peter, *Maritime Supremacy and the Opening of the Western Mind: naval campaigns that shaped the modern world, 1588–1782*, London, John Murray, 1999.

Parkinson, Northcote, *The Life and Times of Horatio Hornblower*, Stroud, Sutton Publishing, 1999.

Penley, Constance and Ross, Andrew (eds), *Technoculture*, Minneapolis, Minnesota University Press, 1991.

Penley, Constance, *NASA/Trek: popular science and sex in America*, London, Verso, 1997.

Penrose, Roger, 'Minds, machines and mathematics', in Colin Blakemore and Susan Greenfield (eds), *Mindwaves*, Oxford, Blackwell, 1987.

Penrose, Roger, *Shadows of the Mind: a search for the missing science of consciousness*, London, Vintage, 1995.

Poe, Stephen Edward, *A Vision of the Future: Star Trek Voyager*, New York, Pocket Books, 1998.

Porter, Jennifer E. and McLaren, Darcee L. (eds), *Star Trek and Sacred Ground: explorations of Star Trek, religion, and American culture*, New York, SUNY Press, 1999.

Raban, Jonathan (ed.), *The Oxford Book of the Sea*, Oxford, Oxford University Press, 1992.

Richards, Thomas, *The Meaning of Star Trek* (published in Britain as *Star Trek in Myth and Legend*), New York, Doubleday, 1997.

Roberts, Robin, *Sexual Generations: 'Star Trek The Next Generation' and gender*, Urbana and Chicago, Illinois University Press, 1999.

Roberts, Wess and Ross, Bill, *Make It So*, New York, Pocket Books, 1995.

Rushing, Janice Hocker and Frentz, Thomas S., *Projecting the Shadow: the cyborg hero in American film*, Chicago, Chicago University Press, 1995.

Sardar, Ziauddin, 'alt.civilisations.faq: cyberspace as the darker side of the West', in Sardar and Ravetz (eds), *Cyberfutures: culture and politics on the information superhighway*, London, Pluto Press, 1996.

Schelde, Per, *Androids, Humanoids, and Other Science Fiction Monsters: science and soul in science fiction films*, New York and London, New York University Press, 1993.

Shakespeare, William, *The Klingon Hamlet* (Klingon Language Institute), New York, Pocket Books, 2000.

Shelley, Mary, *Frankenstein*, London, Penguin, 1992.

Sherry, Norman, *Conrad* (in *Literary Lives* series), London, Thames and Hudson, 1988.

Solow, Herbert E. and Justman, Robert H., *Inside Star Trek: the real story*, New York, Pocket Books, 1996.

Star Trek Voyager Year 3 Writers'–Directors' Guide, 1996–1997 Season.

Sternbach, Rick and Okuda, Michael, *Star Trek: The Next Generation technical manual*, New York, Pocket Books; London, Boxtree, 1991.

Taylor, Jeri, *Mosaic*, New York, Pocket Books, 1996.

Taylor, Jeri, *Pathways*, New York, Pocket Books, 1998.

Tester, Keith, *The Inhuman Condition*, London, Routledge, 1995.

Tredell, Nicholas (ed.), *Icon Critical Guide to 'Heart of Darkness'*, Cambridge, Icon Books, 1998.

Tulloch, John and Jenkins, Henry, *Science Fiction Audiences: watching Dr Who and Star Trek*, London, Routledge, 1995.

Verne, Jules, *Twenty Thousand Leagues Under the Sea*, abr. Robin Waterfield, London, Penguin Books (Puffin), 1986.

Wagner, Jon and Lundeen, Jan, *Deep Space and Sacred Time: Star Trek in the American mythos*, Westport, CT, and London, Prager, 1998.

Wertheimer, Margaret, *Pythagoras' Trousers: God, physics and the gender wars*, London, Fourth Estate, 1997.

Wheale, Nigel, 'Recognizing a "human-thing": cyborgs, robots and replicants', in Wheale (ed.) *The Postmodern Arts: an introductory reader*, London, Routledge, 1985.

Wheale, Nigel (ed.), *The Postmodern Arts: an introductory reader*, London, Routledge, 1985.

Winston, Brian, 'Tyrell's owl: the limits of the technological imagination in an epoch of hyperbolic discourse', in Barbara Adam and Stuart Allan (eds), *Theorizing Culture: an interdisciplinary critique after postmodernism*, London, UCL Press, 1995.

Winter, Jay and Sivan, Emmanuel (eds), *War and Remembrance in the Twentieth Century*, Cambridge, Cambridge University Press, 1999.

Wolin, Richard (ed.), *The Heidegger Controversy: a critical reader*, Cambridge, MA, MIT Press, 1993.

Woolf, Virginia, *Orlando*, Harmondsworth, Penguin, 1972.

Zohar, Danah, *The Quantum Self*, London, HarperCollins Flamingo, 1991.

General Index

Index of Episodes